Belo Horizonte

Around the World in 80 Years

To Shavand David Sorenson

⚓

Richard B. Abbott

Richard B. Abbott

Lost Coast Press

Fort Bragg, California

Belo Horizonte
Copyright © 1995 by Richard B. Abbott

Lost Coast Press
155 Cypress Street
Fort Bragg, CA 95437
(707) 964-9520

Publisher's Cataloging in Publication Data

Abbott, Richard B.
  Belo horizonte / Richard B. Abbott.
  P. cm.
  ISBN 1-882897-01-3
  Library of Congress Catalog Card Number: 94-79311

  1. Abbott, Richard B.   2. Voyages and travels—Biography.
3. Sailing—Biography.   I. Title.

G530.A23 1995   910.92
                                                    QBI94-2117

Book production by Cypress House, Fort Bragg, CA
Manufactured in the U.S.A.
First edition

I dedicate this book to my wife, Sandra, who interrupted her teaching career to go with me for a seven year cruise on a 38' sailboat.

Belo Horizonte

Introduction

B elo Horizonte, which means beautiful horizon in Portuguese, is the story of my life from 1911, when I was born, until 1995. From pan-handling on the streets of San Francisco to becoming president and owner of a profitable shipping company, from working as an ordinary seaman on a rusty old cargo vessel to a seven year cruise on my sailing yacht, Belo Horizonte, this book describes my efforts to obtain an adequate education while attending a native Argentine grammar school in a suburb of Buenos Aires to working my way through three years of prep school at Andover Academy in Massachusetts. It describes how I obtained a law degree by attending night school for two years before World War II in Oklahoma City and for two years in Los Angeles after the war.

To a seaman, the horizon is an important part of life. He spends a long time at sea and looks for a landfall. As the time approaches, he scans the horizon at every opportunity. Finally, land appears and then, on the horizon, a town takes shape. After having been at sea so long, he imagines the town has marble buildings and the streets are paved with gold. This amazing city is inhabited by beautiful, approachable maidens who are eagerly looking forward to becoming acquainted with a sailor who has traveled the world.

I have named this book *Belo Horizonte* because I have been that sailor and because the ship, Belo Horizonte, was a very lucky ship for me. Her first voyage under my management was laden with army cargo for Vietnam and was more profitable than any of the ships I handled during the twenty years I was engaged in the shipping business.

During World War II, I served in the Merchant Marine in various capacifies, starting out as an "able bodied seaman" in August of 1942 and finishing as chief mate on a C-2 cargo vessel in 1946. The Eagle Wing, my last ship, loaded nuclear cargo at Port Chicago on Suisun Bay, near San Francisco. While we were discharging our cargo at Tinian Island in the Marianas, the cruiser Indianapolis docked near us to deliver the warhead for the first bomb. The Indianapolis was torpedoed and sunk while on its return trip, but the B-29 bombers were able to drop the atomic bombs on Japan to end the war.

I have been discouraged on many occasions when, in spite of my efforts, a project appeared likely not to materialize the way I'd envisioned. If a view of the ocean was available, I would watch the sun set below the beautiful horizon and usually, the next morning, my problem would be solved.

Richard B. Abbott

Chapter One

My First Voyage

In 1918 my father resigned his job as city editor with the Houston Chronicle to become publicity director for the Southwest Bell Telephone Company. He must've been pretty good at it, because Lt. Governor Will Hobby tapped him to manage his gubernatorial campaign. After a rough and tumble campaign, Hobby was elected Governor of Texas by the largest majority ever received, and my father was not only out of a job but Hobby told him to leave the country until things settled down. After arranging employment for my father as manager of the International Correspondence Schools for the Buenos Aires branch of an American bank, Hobby went on to become the most decent governor since San Houston. While my father was establishing himself in Argentina, the rest of my family went to Lincoln, Nebraska to live with my grandparents.

I was eight years old, and I already bore a few scars. A few years earlier I'd been hit by a Ford touring car traveling at twenty miles an hour. I couldn't get out of the way, so I rolled between the wheels. Fortunately, cars were built higher then. My older brother, Charles, saw me stretched out cold in the middle of the road, my head and face covered with blood, so he ran home to tell Mother I was dead. She started toward the door, then fainted.

A neighbor who'd witnessed the accident called her husband, who was a doctor, and after checking for broken bones, he picked me up and carried me inside. Aside from a concussion and a few cuts, I was all right, but when I regained consciousness I had a terrible headache.

Another time, I slipped and fell down a manhole, landing on my head. Blood was running down the side of my head as Charles helped me walk home. He told me that I was bleeding from my temple, which meant I would soon die. Mother was hysterical, but grandmother summoned the doctor downstairs who patched me up and sent me home. Classmates told my teacher what had happened and said I'd be back soon if I didn't die first.

The only thing I can remember about Lincoln was a fight I got into when I tried to stop a big kid from beating up a little kid. I ended up on the ground with a black eye, two broken front teeth and a cut on my cheek. I still have the two broken teeth in spite of the attempts of several dentists since then to repair them. So much for heroism.

The trip on an old British passenger ship from New York to join Father in Argentina changed my life. We were originally scheduled to travel on the Vestris, but it burned and sank in the West Indies, and so we sailed on the Vauban, a slow ship that took about a month to sail from New York to Buenos Aires by way of Rio de Janeiro, Santos, and Montevideo. From then on, I loved the beautiful, powerful, magical sea.

My first sea voyage was not without its discomforts. My mother, brother, sister and I shared one small cabin with twin upper and lower bunks. In those days, fresh water on ships at sea was scarce, so in order to take a bath we had to schedule it in advance. The steward meted out a small ration of fresh water, then removed the handle from the faucet to prevent us from adding more water to the tub. But mundane irritations like this did not stop me from enjoying that month at sea.

Our first house in Argentina was in Olivos, a suburb of Buenos Aires. Father sublet it from a couple who were spending the year in England. The house came with a cook and maid, who were husband and wife, and a gardener. My father was the only one in the family who could speak Spanish, and during the day he worked in downtown Buenos Aires. My mother had trouble telling the cook and the maid what she wanted for dinner, and how she wanted the house cleaned. My sister, Betty, astonished us when she began saying whole sentences in Spanish, having picked them up from listening to the servants. She quickly became mother's official interpreter.

Charles and I weren't so eager to catch on, and since we attended an English school for the children of expatriates, it didn't look like we were going to learn Spanish. At least not quickly enough for our father. He became impatient with us and hired a young Englishman who had lived in Argentina for quite some time to teach us the language. After instructing us in basic grammar and conversational Spanish, he took us on trips and told us the Spanish words for what we saw. But boys being boys, we made the man's life miserable by mimicking his stilted manner of speech. We got his English accent down quite well, but we didn't learn Spanish.

When father found out about it, he took us out of the English school and enrolled us in a native school where no one spoke any English. We felt left out by our inability to communicate, and desperately wanted to know what was going on around us. Fortunately, the teachers and students were eager to help us learn their language. Our classmates never made fun of our grammar or teased us about our faltering attempts to speak Spanish. They wanted us to learn their language so they could learn more about America. During recess, classmates would point to objects and identify them. Within three weeks we were communicating in class and on the playground. After two months, we were able to express ourselves just as well in Spanish as in English.

At the end of our first year, Father rented a house in San Fernando, a suburb of Buenos Aires on the Rio de la Plata. The house was on the Baranca with a wonderful view of the river. This house, too, came with a cook, a maid and a gardener. The cook and the maid spoke Spanish, but the gardener was Portuguese. My sister quickly learned Portuguese and again became the interpreter for our mother. By the end of our second year, Mother decided she didn't want to raise us in a foreign country, so we headed back to the United States.

I was excited about another trip at sea. We were booked on the Pan American, a new American flag line, and my excitement increased as the sailing date approached. When the day arrived, I was beside myself with anticipation. The ship was luxurious compared to the Vauban. We had two outside cabins: one for my mother and Betty, one for Charles and me. Both cabins were equipped with private bathrooms, and the fresh water wasn't rationed. The Pan American had desalination equipment to convert salt water to fresh. There was even a large swimming pool on the ship, and my brother and I learned how to swim.

When we arrived in New York, we spent the night at the then-luxurious Pennsylvania Hotel. The next day we took a train to Houston, where my father's parents lived. My brother and I went to public school there, and our English accents attracted the attention of our peers. After a few weeks of constant teasing, we were drawling like native Texans. Then we moved again. Mom went to Brookline, Massachusetts with Betty, while Charles and I stayed in Houston to finish out the school year. Then we joined them there.

Father, meanwhile, was still in Argentina. A couple of years later, a Texas company hired him to negotiate an oil drilling concession from the Colombian government. His predecessor had been killed in an airplane crash while flying between Bogota and Baranquilla. Because of the accident, my father was not allowed to fly. He made the trip by river boat up the Magdalena River. The boat had no refrigeration, so in order to have meat for the passenger's meals, live cattle were carried on deck. The cattle were butchered as the need for meat arose. In 1930, he was able to secure the concession from the Colombian government. Unfortunately, the Texas company was near financial ruin. They sold out to a large oil company, and my father was once again out of a job. The "Great Depression" had arrived.

At the time, Charles was attending Phillips Andover Academy, and the year following I received a scholarship there through the efforts of a wealthy alumnus. My first year at Andover went smoothly. I went out for soccer, having learned the game at the English school in Argentina. At the end of the first year, the coach selected me for the varsity squad.

During my second year Father couldn't help out much, so Mom took a job as housemother at a girls' school. My mother was a beautiful lady. In her younger days, when she walked into a room, every man and many ladies would turn to look. Her instincts about clothes were perfect, but in other matters she was not very practical. When my father lost everything, she advertised her apartment furnishings for sale. The grand piano attracted the attention of Miss Cook, who owned three girls' schools. Miss Cook bought all the furniture in my mother's apartment, and offered her a job as house mother at Dana Hall, a girls' school in Wellesley, Massachusetts. When they later became better acquainted, Miss Cook asked my mother to design the new uniforms. My mother contracted for the manufacture of the uniforms and maintained a fitting room where the uniforms could be altered when necessary.

Charles was now attending the University of Nebraska and living with a relative in Lincoln. I did well in school until spring, when I started feeling bad. I knew there was something wrong, but I continued to attend classes. At track, while I was running the low hurdles, the coach gave me a funny look and called me over. He put his hand on my forehead, then sent me to see Dr. Page. the campus doctor. After examining me and taking my temperature, the doctor put me in the infirmary. I had pneumonia.

For three days I was unconscious. When I came to, Dr. Page was by my bed. Since my family couldn't afford to send me to the hospital, he let me recuperate in the infirmary. I was so sick, I didn't get out of bed for a month. When I was feeling a little better, Dr. Page let me take a walk down the hill to town. I bought a magazine, then started back up the hill to school. After walking a block I became exhausted and had to sit on the curb to rest. Fortunately, a street car came by and I climbed aboard. I barely made it back to the infirmary. As soon as I got into bed I proceeded to get rid of everything I had eaten in the past twenty-four hours. This didn't make me very popular with the nurses who had to clean up the mess.

Eventually I returned to classes, but I was too weak to resume my job in the dining hall waiting tables. I was supposed to carry food up a steep flight of stairs to the dining hall, then carry the dirty dishes back down to the pantry. The job was too much for me but I needed to make a living. When I told my soccer coach about my problem, he gave me a job waiting tables at the Grill, a small restaurant he managed for the school. The Grill was open all day. When the students missed a meal at the Beanery, which is what the dining hall was called, they could get something to eat at the Grill. Working there wasn't as difficult as working at the Beanery, since there were no stairs to climb.

Because of my illness, I had little time to catch up with my studies and prepare for final exams. That's when the trouble started. My Latin professor summoned me to his office. "Mr. Abbott," he said, "did you pass your second year college board Latin exam?"

"Yes, Mr. Jacobs," I said.

"What grade were you given on that exam?" he asked.

"An 86," I said.

"I am not satisfied with the narrow margin by which you passed my exam. If you intend to take third year Latin, you'll have to get a higher grade on the second year final," he said.

"You mean I have to take the final again?" I asked.

"Yes, if you want to take third year Latin. And remember," he said as I was getting up to leave, "you'll have to earn a higher grade."

I took another second year final and passed it, but Mr. Jacobs still wasn't satisfied. He insisted that I take the exam again before I returned to school in the fall. It wasn't the best way to start summer vacation.

I had a summer job on a farm in northern New York state, and after pitching hay in the sun all day, I didn't feel like studying Latin half the night. When I returned to school in the fall, I told Mr. Jacobs that I hadn't been able to study during the summer, but that I would study with a tutor and take the final again when I felt better prepared.

Latin wasn't a third year requirement, and I could have gone quietly to work on my third year courses instead of forcing the issue with Mr. Jacobs. But I didn't like being pushed around.

None of the Latin professors were available to tutor me except for the head of the Latin department, George Hinman. I'd heard he was tough. If his students didn't quickly answer his questions in class, he would put a pencil in his mouth and start breathing hard. If the student still couldn't answer, he would get so mad, he'd bite the pencil in two. Hinman only turned out the best Latin scholars, and didn't allow anyone to tarnish his record. The other Latin professors gave in to all his demands; his suggestions were orders, his word was law.

I called him as a last resort, and he agreed to tutor me at night in his classroom. When I walked in, he was waiting for me. In order to find out how much I knew about Latin, he had prepared a list of questions to ask me. My responses were supposed to reveal my aptitude. I was able to answer the first several questions, but when I hesitated at conjugating a verb, he put his pencil in his mouth and waited for me to reply. I couldn't, and he started breathing hard. I winced in anticipation of the pencil splintering and was relieved, if somewhat disappointed, when he took the unbroken pencil from his mouth and announced that I knew nothing about Latin.

"Did you take the second year Latin college board exam?" he asked.

"Yes," I said. "I passed with an 86."

"There must be some mistake. You know nothing about Latin," he shouted. "Get out!" he said, pointing at the door.

Two weeks later I was called to the registrar's office. The faculty had voted to expel me from school, and I had twenty- four hours to vacate my room in the dormitory. I asked the registrar how my marks compared with those of other students in my class. He looked at his records and said that twenty-seven students, approximately one-third of the class, had lower marks. My grades were not the reason I was being expelled. I appealed, asking my professors why they had voted to expel me. With only twenty-four hours left to live in the dormitory, and two weeks to wait for the appeal to go through, I had to find a place to live. Dr. Page came to my rescue by giving me room and board at the campus infirmary. I didn't like being reminded of my illness, but any bed was better than none.

I spoke with most of my professors the day after I moved into the infirmary, and they all said the same thing. They knew I had lost some time because of my illness the previous year but thought I was catching up quickly, considering the circumstances. They all denied that they had voted for my expulsion. Believing that my professors were behind me, I thought everything would be okay. Someone had made a mistake, and I was surely on my way back to school. Unfortunately, when I went to the registrar's office to tell him the good news, he gave me some bad news. "You cannot move back into the dormitory until after the faculty meeting next week."

While I was waiting for the faculty decision, a lecturer visited Andover. His name was Count Von Luckner and he made a great impression on me. He had written a book about his exploits during World War I. Although his family was well to do, he left home and went to sea on a German merchant ship. By the time the war started, he was captain of a merchant ship and was chosen to command the Seeadler, a raider disguised as a Norwegian merchant ship. The ship looked like a square rigger, but she had a large diesel engine and concealed guns all around the deck. The crew even went so far as to dress up one of their own men as the captain's wife, because in those days it was customary for the captain of a Norwegian sailing ship to have his wife with him. Count Von Luckner broke through the blockade of the North Sea, capturing crew members before sinking many of the Allies' merchant ships. He ended up on a South Pacific atoll.

Count Von Luckner told fascinating tales of his adventures at sea. As an ordinary seaman, he'd fallen overboard and saved himself by grabbing the feet of an albatross, which had swooped down to investigate what had come off the ship. When the bird started to complain, the crew heard the racket and rescued Von Luckner. At the end of his lecture, the count asked for a phone book, then tore it in two with his bare hands. I was impressed. I bought his book, and because I didn't have to go to classes, I read it cover to cover in two days.

The morning after the faculty meeting, confident that I was back in school, I stood at the registrar's counter but was ignored. When the registrar walked by, I asked what had happened at the faculty meeting. "Nothing," he mumbled, and walked away.

I went back to the infirmary where I told my story to Dr. Page. He advised me to keep quiet while he investigated the matter. When I saw him the next day, he told me that the only professor who voted to have me expelled was George Hinman. "Stay around the infirmary," he said. "You'll be hearing from the registrar by tomorrow at the latest." George Hinman wasn't the only person on campus with clout, as Dr. Page soon proved.

Sure enough, the next day the registrar called to tell me I could go back to my room in the dormitory. When I asked if I could also resume my classes, he said he couldn't authorize me to do so. I moved back into my room and hung around, wondering if I should stay in school after all.

My mother was having a hard time keeping my sister and brother in school on her salary as housemother. Charles had received a scholarship to attend Yale. If I went to work, I thought, I could help my family. Although I knew the value of a good education, the way I'd been treated at Andover had stifled my desire to continue. I talked to George, a friend who had a relative working for the Munson Steamship Lines. Munson operated the Pan American, the ship on which we'd returned from Argentina. I asked George if he could get me a job on a ship. He seemed confident that he could and called his relative. When he hung up, he told me to report to the personnel department in New York City. I had a job in the steward's department on the next sailing. I was exhilarated and relieved, but I had yet to decide whether to leave school and catch the night bus to New York City.

That evening I wrote a letter to my mother, telling her I was leaving school, had a job on a ship, and not to worry. I also wrote a letter to Dr. Page, thanking him for all he had done for me. Because of his help, I now concluded that my future didn't depend on my staying in school.

The last time I had been in New York was in 1925, when we arrived from Buenos Aires on the Pan American. No expensive hotel for me this time. I went to the YMCA and the next day went to join the Western World, a sister ship of the Pan American.

Everything went according to schedule at the offices of the Munson Steamship Company. I was given a slip of paper in an envelope addressed to Mr. Fenty, the chief steward of the Western World. When I arrived at the ship, Mr. Fenty was busy, so I was turned over to the second steward who sent me to the head waiter of the first class dining room. He looked me over and decided I was too small to carry large trays of food and dishes in a rough sea. Mr. Fenty came by and told us I looked smart enough to be a bell boy. They sent me to the tailor shop where I was fitted for a white jacket and a pair of dark pants.

The fo'c'sle had 14 bunks in it with one porthole. It was in no way luxurious. There was little ventilation and a prevailing bad odor, probably from the putrid head across the passageway. But I had asked for the job, so I couldn't complain. The next day another Andover student joined the ship as a bell boy. He said he had heard about me. Already I was setting an example.

The Western World had good weather as she departed New York and headed for the east coast of South America. The first class passenger quarters were almost full, but the small second class section had only a few occupied cabins. As soon as we got beyond the three mile limit the bar was opened. I was one of three bell boys, and we could hardly keep up with the demand for drinks. Most of the room bells rang constantly. This was during prohibition, so passengers had an unquenchable thirst for spirits. Our first stop was Rio de Janeiro which boasts one of the most beautiful harbors in the world. Our next stop was Santos, Brazil.

After a short stop in Montevideo we went across the mouth of the Rio de la Plata to Buenos Aires. The passengers disembarked, but we were kept busy cleaning and painting the first class public areas. I did get ashore on a couple of occasions, and had time to walk around the fancy shopping area along Calle Florida.

When I returned to New York City, I went to see an admiralty attorney, a friend of my family who represented the Port of New York as well as several steamship lines operating out of New York. "Can you get me a job as an ordinary seaman on a freighter?" I asked him.

"I can, and I will, if you promise to return to Andover next year," he said.

"Okay, I'll go back to Andover, but only if I earn enough money to pay my tuition for the whole year," I said.

He picked up the phone and in two minutes I had a job on the S.S. Martinique, operated by the Colombian Steamship Line.

The Martinique was a small freighter of a type known as a Laker since the class was built on the Great Lakes at the end of World War I. When I went aboard I reported to the chief mate. He complained that I was too small to do the work my position called for.

"Wouldn't you like to work as a mess boy instead?" he asked.

"I'll only take an ordinary seaman's job," I insisted.

I was taking quite a chance because there were more than twenty unemployed seamen on the dock waiting for a job. I must have been convincing, though, because the chief mate made me a quartermaster and I learned to steer the ship, which didn't require much strength.

Our first port was Cape Haitian, and I will never forget approaching in the middle of the night while the third mate told me the history of the island as I steered the ship. Christophe, a native black leader with no formal education, took control of the Haitian army, then drove out the French settlers and their army and proclaimed himself emperor. He then designed and built a castle to live in, erected a citadel out of stone at the top of a mountain overlooking the town and harbor, and armed it with cannons to prevent the French from returning. There is no road leading up to the Citadel and it can be visited only by horseback, but somehow Emperor Christophe had the huge pieces of stone and cannons moved to the site.

In 1930, when I was there, so too were the U.S. Marines, but I was more thankful for a small book the third mate handed me as my watch at the wheel was relieved by the next quartermaster. Entitled "The Seaman's Handbook for Shore Leave," it warned that syphilis and malaria were prevalent in Haiti. I was cautious.

The food in the crew's messroom on the Martinique was terrible. Apparently the chief steward had gotten a good price on some liver that was about to spoil. I guess he thought he could get rid of it quickly. No such luck. When our mess boy brought us liver for lunch for the second time, we told him if he ever showed up with the stinking liver again, we would throw him overboard. On the third day, instead of placing the liver on the table, he threw the container in the door and ran. We opened the container and sure enough, there was more of the stinking liver. I couldn't take it any more.

"If you follow me, I'll take the liver up to the captain and stick it in his face," I told the crew.

Everyone stood up and said, "Let's go."

First we went to the officers' mess room. The table was set with food in serving dishes, but none of the officers were present yet. We opened the dishes and saw that instead of rotten liver there was lean roast beef. We were furious as we made our way to the navigation bridge. The mate on watch stopped us. We told him we were looking for the captain. As the mate said, "He's not here," the captain walked out of the chart room.

When he saw us he said, "What's going on here?"

"Captain," I said, "we want some decent food."

"You receive the same food as the officers," he said.

"Captain, we were just in the officers' mess room. We didn't see any stinking liver, just lean roast beef." With that I put the plate of liver under his nose.

"What is that?" he yelled. "Take it away."

"This is what we're supposed to eat for lunch." I said.

"I don't want any trouble with you. Go back to your mess room and I will have the steward send something else down to you," he said.

We did as we were told, and soon had a tasty lunch of lean roast beef.

We unloaded our cargo at Cape Haitian, then went on to Port Au Prince, Haiti. While we were there, I got a taste of the kind of work the rest of the crew did while I was steering. They suspended me over the offshore side of the ship, chipping rust, wire brushing and red leading the hull. The temperature was well over one hundred degrees, and the particles of rust stuck to my sweaty face and hands. The bo'sun in charge of the maintenance work kept a close eye on me. The minute I stopped chipping he would look over the rail to see if I was resting, and yell at me to get back to work.

One night, some of us went ashore to a bar in Port Au Prince. We got into a fight with the crew of a German ship. Schotts, an able seaman from the Martinique, flattened one of the Germans while I pushed one out the window. He grabbed the sleeve of my jacket as he went, tearing it off. I went outside and fetched the sleeve from the spot where the German had landed. I took it back to New York where I had it sewn back on by a tailor.

Our next stop was Port Antonio, Jamaica, where we loaded a full cargo of bananas. On the way back to New York, when we felt a need to change our diet, we took a stalk of bananas out of the hold and hung it up in the engine room. The heat quickly ripened the bananas. When they were ripe enough for our taste, we took them back to the fo'c'sle to eat at our leisure.

On our last day in Port Antonio, I went ashore in the afternoon to get something before we sailed. Upon my return to the ship an hour later, I noticed a large Jamaican man at the door to the fo'c'sle. When I started to open the door to my living quarters, he said, "No! No!" I wasn't about to let him tell me I couldn't go in. I pushed him aside and opened the door. It was dark inside, and it took a few seconds for my eyes to adjust before I could see anything. As I gradually made out the figures in the lower bunks, it dawned on me. The man who guarded the door had brought some native girls on board for the sailors. As I turned around to leave I could see a girl on each lower bunk, each with one of the seamen. I made a quick retreat.

When we arrived in New York City, most of the crew was undecided about making another trip on the Martinique. Since I had played a part in the stinking liver episode, I wasn't sure they would even give me a choice. Seaman Schotts told me he was going home to Youngstown, Ohio. "If you come with me," he said, "I can get you registered with the Lake Carriers Association in Conneaut. If you get on a Great Lakes ship, you can earn $85. a month instead of $25."

The prospect of making more money sold me. As soon as we got paid we headed for Ohio by hopping freight trains. Hopping trains reminded me of my childhood in Buenos Aires. When we lived in San Fernando my long trips to school involved riding first an electric train, then a steam train, with a lot of walking and waiting in between. While waiting for the steam train I sometimes went all the way to one end of the platform, hopped on a freight train and rode it to the other end of the platform. The skill I learned when I was a bored child in Buenos Aires came in handy on the way from New York to Ohio.

The Lake Carriers Association was created to prevent the saltwater seaman's unions from getting started on the Lakes.

At Conneaut, Schotts introduced me to the office manager of the Lake Carriers Association. Schotts told him I had worked on the Martinique with him, and I was an experienced seaman. I was instantly accepted.

In Ashtabula, Ohio, we parted company. Schotts went to Youngstown, and I talked to some of the unemployed seamen in Ashtabula Harbor. I learned that I could get a bunk in the basement of the Salvation Army for twenty-five cents a night. There was a small restaurant across the street from the shipping hall where I could get a cup of coffee and a doughnut for a dime. When I was really down and out, I bought a bowl of rice for a nickel.

I counted my money and discovered that what I had earned on the Martinique was just about gone. If I didn't get a job soon, I would be panhandling on the corner in order to stay alive. The shipping hall was full of unemployed seamen looking for jobs. Most of them hung around a small restaurant across from the shipping hall. My first break came when I got a job washing dishes there. The pay for washing dishes was only my meals, but it was an improvement over the coffee, doughnuts and rice I was surviving on. Every day I washed the dishes until there were no more to be washed, then spent an hour across the street at the shipping hall, waiting for a job to be called.

One night after the shipping hall was closed, I took a walk back to the restaurant. I said hello to Don, one of the unemployed seamen who spent his evenings standing out on the curb in front of the restaurant. He told me the chief steward from an ore ship was in the restaurant looking for a second cook. The ship was sailing early in the morning before the shipping hall opened, and the chief steward needed someone right away.

"I'd have taken the job myself if I knew anything about cooking," Don said.

"I'll take anything from captain to chief engineer if it's offered to me." I said, and went into the restaurant.

The owner of the restaurant was keeping the chief steward's coffee cup full, waiting for me to return. I told the chief steward that I would take the second cook job. "All I have to do is pick up my clothes. I can be on the ship in half an hour." I showed him my seaman's papers and the deal was made.

When I boarded the John A. Donaldson, Jim, the deck watch, told me that the chief cook had his girl friend with him in our cabin, so I had to sleep somewhere else. Jim took me below the bridge to a passenger cabin, which was considerably better than the second cook's bunk located next to the galley over the engine room. I had the cabin all to myself, except when we had a pilot on board, then I shared the cabin with the pilot and slept in the upper bunk.

Called at 4 a.m., I had to be in the galley at 4:30, ready to work. Since the ship was sailing at 3 a.m. for Duluth Minnesota, I turned in knowing that I would at least have a good breakfast. When I arrived at the galley ready for work at 4:30 the next morning, I found myself alone except for the dishwasher who was cleaning up from the night lunch. I didn't know where to start. I put on an apron and asked the dishwasher what the second cook was supposed to do. He told me to bring the dirty dishes from the night lunch to the sink, then make some oatmeal and start a pot of coffee. Pretty soon the 6 a.m. watch officers began giving me their orders. Then the chief cook came in and soon I was flipping hotcakes and filling breakfast orders. The cook watched me work and told me what to do. I finished off the morning waiting on the officers in their mess room. Several times during the next two months the ship carried complimentary passengers between two ports, and I became their waiter during mealtime.

We made two trips from Ashtabula to Duluth, and one trip to Milwaukee. A bulk carrier, she spent little time in port, and it wasn't unusual for us to sail without a crew member who wanted to see the end of a movie or have one last drink at the bar. One time when the ship was in Duluth and I had finished my work in the galley, I decided to go ashore. The stevedore superintendent told me I had three hours before they completed discharging. I thought it was plenty of time to see a movie, but when I returned to the dock they were hoisting up the gangway. If someone hadn't thrown a rope ladder over the side for me, I would have spent the night in Duluth.

One day we were notified that the ship was going to be laid up in Conneaut. I asked Pat, the porter, what he planned to do. He had some relatives in Sacramento he wanted to visit, and I had always wanted to see San Francisco, so we decided to travel together. He told me that freight trains were the only kind of transportation he could afford, and I told him about my childhood train trips in Buenos Aires and my subsequent journey from New York to Ohio via freight trains. Pat had been riding freight trains for twenty years, so I thought I could learn something from him.

My first lesson from Pat was to travel light. We packed our suitcases, then lugged them to the American Express office, and shipped them to San Francisco. The San Francisco office would hold them until we arrived, if we arrived.

We had no difficulty getting to Chicago, but we hopped the wrong train out of Chicago and wound up in small town in Wisconsin. It was getting dark and it looked like we were at the end of the line for the night. We wrapped ourselves in newspapers and tried to catch some sleep in a box car, but we nearly froze to death. The next morning we made it back to Chicago and hopped a train to Council Bluffs, Iowa. The last two days we rode on a gondola car loaded with sand. The weather was getting colder all the time.

Halfway between Cheyenne and Laramie, Wyoming, we were standing in a gondola car leaning against the top rail that ran around the car when I felt something in my back pocket move. I turned just in time to see my Lake Carriers Association discharge book with two loose discharges drop over the side of the car. I quickly realized I would never get a job on a ship unless I could show those discharges. Fortunately, the train was moving slowly through a network of switches. I told Pat what had happened, and jumped off the train. I fell down but wasn't hurt, and as I brushed myself off I saw Pat jumping off the train down the track a ways.

I found my Lake Carriers' book first and kept an eye out for the loose discharges. I knew they couldn't be far from the book. Pat joined in the search, and we walked up and down the track for what seemed like hours looking for those discharges. We found the last one just before dark.

We started walking down the track towards Laramie after realizing that we might have to wait all night for a slow moving train, and then be unable to get aboard. We walked and walked and walked. In the middle of the night, a freight train came down the track, but it was going too fast and we didn't have a chance to get on it. A couple of hours later we saw a light ahead. We hoped that it was a town, but it turned out to be a solitary cabin at the entrance to a ravine some ways from the tracks.

We were getting pretty tired, but if we didn't keep moving we'd freeze to death. As dawn approached, we saw a couple of buildings ahead of us near the tracks. They were empty and no one was around, so we kept going. Before long we came to some more buildings and a dirt road that ran alongside the tracks. Finally, we arrived in Laramie, where we hopped a train that took us the rest of the way to Council Bluffs. Then we walked across the bridge to Omaha, Nebraska. We got something to eat, a cot in a dormitory, and slept for twenty-four hours. After showers, clean shirts and breakfast, we were again on our way to San Francisco .

When we arrived in Oakland, Pat took a bus to Sacramento and I took a ferry to San Francisco . I found an old, run-down hotel where I could get a cot for fifty cents a night if I came back before the place filled up. I had to leave my suitcase at the desk for safekeeping and to insure payment of rent. Now that I had a place to sleep, I walked up Market Street from the Embarcadero, enjoying the sights of the city. I celebrated my arrival by taking in a Loretta Young movie.

As bad as the hotel was, it was better than sleeping in a boxcar, but I was running out of money and had to find a job soon or starve to death. The shipping hall was crowded with out-of-work seamen. When a job was called, the men closest to the window would throw their discharges in, hoping that they would be picked up. It was not an easy way to get a job.

Told that the Dollar Line was hiring seamen who could prove they had worked for Dollar before, I tried to buy some Dollar Line discharges. A couple of days later, a seaman offered to sell me his Dollar Line discharges for $2. They looked all right, but the man was twenty-two years old. I was just eighteen and looked fifteen. I had to try something, though, so I bought the discharges.

I went back to the hotel and had a good night's sleep. The next morning, fortified with a hearty breakfast, I walked into the Dollar Line shipping office. The man at the desk asked if he could help me. "Yes, I'm looking for a job on a ship," I said.

"Have you sailed on Dollar Line ships?" he asked.

I handed him the discharges. He looked at the first few, then looked at me. "Sorry, I can't help you."

Having lost money I couldn't afford to lose, I was down to some change in my pocket, nothing to eat and nowhere to sleep. Then things got worse. I walked the streets at night, and when I got tired I ducked into a run-down hotel lobby for a nap. After being kicked out a couple of times, the desk clerks were on the lookout for me, and I couldn't even close my eyes before I was seen and kicked out.

Back then, the wholesale fruit and vegetable markets were situated where the Golden Gateway Apartments are now located. Tracks ran adjacent to the warehouses and various types of freight cars sat on the tracks to be loaded or unloaded. A couple of times I spent part of a night in one of these rail cars. Some of the old cattle cars were used to carry crates of grapes, and it was possible to reach through the slats and get a hold of a bunch of grapes. I used to steal the grapes from the crates, then walk down to the docks, sit on the edge of the Bay and enjoy a relaxed meal. At 2 a.m. one night, a cop showed up. He asked me what I was doing there. I told him I was trying to find something to eat and somewhere to sleep.

"My orders are to pick up people like you and lock them up for the night. But if you start getting picked up and staying in jail at night, associating with the other prisoners, you'll spend the rest of your life in and out of jail. I don't want to be responsible for that happening to anyone. I'll put you in a boxcar if you'll promise to stay inside until daylight. "

"Thank you," I said. "If there are some newspapers inside the box car, I can use them to keep warm. I promise I'll stay inside until the sun comes up."

He helped me find a car with some packing paper inside. I climbed in and stayed there until daylight. Then I sat in the sun on a dock eating grapes for breakfast. Afterwards, I went to the shipping hall and cleaned up. I asked some of the other unemployed seamen how they got along without money. They told me they stayed at flop houses, where a person could get a canvas cot in a plywood partition for twenty-five cents a night. The flop-houses also provided wash basins and toilets. When I asked where they got the money to pay for it, they told me they panhandled in front of the Ferry Building in the morning when people were going to work.

Ferry Building contributions came in regularly, as long as I didn't get discouraged. With experience I could predict which people would give me money and which would ignore me.

Another unemployed seaman told me he had a different method of getting money and food. He went to the apartment district in the afternoon and knocked on back doors. Most of the occupants slammed the door in his face, but when he kept at it he eventually got food or change from someone. The first few times I tried this, I got the door slammed in my face. At another building I noticed that the refrigerators were on the landings next to the back doors. One of them had a note attached that read, "If whoever has been stealing food from this refrigerator will knock on the back door, I will gladly give him something to eat."

"I'm not going to bed hungry tonight," I said to myself.

When I knocked on the door, I asked the man who answered if there was any work I could do for something to eat.

"Come in and sit down," he said. "What would you like to eat?"

"Whatever's handy will be fine," I said.

"How about ham and eggs?"

"Yes, please."

He cooked and I ate. Before I left I asked again if he had any work I could do for my meal, but he said no. I thanked him for his kindness and left. I hadn't felt so good for a longtime. I was stuffed.

I was walking down Geary Street on my way back to the dock area, when I realized I didn't have enough money for a cot that night. I saw a kindly looking man walking toward me, and when he got near I asked, "Could you give me a dime for a cup of coffee?"

First he shook his head, then suddenly he turned and called to me. "Are you really hungry?" he asked.

"Yes," I replied.

He took me to a restaurant, sat me down, and handed me a menu. He told me to order anything I wanted. I was caught. When the waiter came to take my order I thought maybe if I took my time, my would-be benefactor would leave. But no. He stayed and ordered me a full dinner from soup to nuts. He watched me eat everything. I was having a tough time stuffing anything more down, but he ordered apple pie and ice cream for desert. When he finally left, I thanked him, and properly acted like he saved me from starvation.

A few days later I was walking down the street in shoes whose soles had almost completely separated from their uppers. One sole flapped every time I took a step. As I flapped by the city fire station, a fireman said, "You look like you need a new pair of shoes."

"You got that right," I said.

"Come here," he said. I followed him behind the station to a pile of old shoes the firemen had thrown away. "Take your pick," he said. With a good pair of shoes the gloomy day suddenly became bright and cheerful. I went to the new union shipping hall and they called an ordinary seaman job just as I entered. I threw my discharges onto the counter and was hired on the San Felipe bound for Portland, Oregon.

I went aboard the San Felipe without foul weather gear. During the voyage up the coast into Puget Sound I was on lookout at night for long periods during which it rained constantly. Without protection, I got soaked from the icy cold rain. I vowed that as soon as I received my first pay I would buy foul weather gear.

We had a great Thanksgiving dinner along the way, which made up for the many meals I missed while ashore in San Francisco. After calling at several ports in Puget Sound, we arrived at Portland. Now that I had some money, I immediately went to a clothing store and bought foul weather gear. When I returned to the ship, the bo'sun told me I was fired. The captain had promised my job to his nephew when the ship arrived in Portland. I packed my suitcase and went ashore. After getting a room at a waterfront hotel, I returned my new foul weather gear, but they only gave me half what I paid for it. I took what I could get.

I checked in at the shipping hall in Portland and spent most of the next few days waiting for a job to be called. As soon as the office closed I went to a hamburger joint to get something to eat. After I ate, I went to the public library to read until I felt sleepy, then returned to my room. I paid for a week's rent with the last of my money and got credit at the hamburger joint. When they cut off my credit I stopped at several bakery shops on my way to the library to ask if they had any stale bakery goods I might have. Along with the occasional nickel or dime I managed to bum on the street, I stayed alive. When I got behind on my rent, I returned to my hotel room late at night in the hope that I wouldn't run into the hotel manager.

One night as I headed for the bakery, two policemen walked towards me. I quickly stepped behind a telephone pole to avoid confronting them, but they saw me and came right to where I was standing. They said I looked like someone who'd stolen a car. I told them it wasn't me and where I had been all day, but they took me to jail anyway.

I sat in a jail cell until midnight, then was escorted to a room where a stool in the center of the room was surrounded by a circle of chairs. A bright light shone on the stool. I was directed to sit on the stool and the policemen who surrounded me asked where I was going when they'd picked me up.

"To the library," I said. They laughed as if it was a big joke.

"You've been living at the Waterfront Hotel, room eight. Is that correct?" one of them asked.

"No," I said, "I live in room seven of the Waterfront Hotel."

They asked me the same questions over and over. This went on for hours, until I was so tired and sleepy I almost said yes just to get out of there and get some sleep. Finally, after several more questions, they asked me what my father did for a living. When I answered honestly, the officer reached over and hit me alongside the head, knocking me off the stool. I staggered back to the stool, sat back down again, and answered more humbly. Half an hour later they told me to get out, which I gladly did. It was dawn and the sky was just beginning to light up. I made up my mind that I would go to the shipping hall and stay there until noon. If I didn't have a job by that time, I would get my suitcase and catch a freight train.

I washed up at a public rest room and bummed a cup of coffee. By the time I'd finished drinking it, the shipping hall was open and I joined several others who were waiting for a job to be called. I happened to be near the window when the dispatcher called out, "One ordinary seaman."

I threw my papers in the window. He picked them up and said, "Okay, you got it." The ship was located at a lumber mill on the Columbia River, twenty-five miles from Portland. I asked the dispatcher if they were going to pay my way from Portland to the ship. He said no, but if I couldn't get down there, he was sure some of the other men in the hall who were looking for a job could. I quickly said I would find a way to get there.

Now I had the unpleasant task of facing the hotel manager. My suitcase with all my worldly possessions could be held hostage for my unpaid rent. When I met up with the manager I had my suitcase in my hand. She took the suitcase away from me and called out to her husband. She said she would go through the suitcase and take anything of value she could find. I pleaded with her to leave my work clothes because I needed them for work. She checked the size I wore and said her husband couldn't use them anyway since they were too small. I had three dress shirts which he tried on and took. They couldn't find anything else they could use so they let me go. I promised to send them money as soon as I had some to send.

It was raining and I had a twenty-five mile walk ahead of me. I'd walked about five miles in the rain when a truck came along and picked me up. When he let me out I was still several miles from the ship. I was worried that the ship would sail before I got there so I walked as fast as I could. I made it to the sawmill's private dock before the ship had arrived. I was dead tired, hungry and soaking wet. I sought shelter under the end of a pile of lumber, and sat on my suitcase, shivering and worrying.

At midnight the Coya arrived. No one was on the dock to take their lines, so I took the heaving line and managed to get the ship's head line on the dock. The pilot swung the stern in and two crew members came ashore to help me tie up the ship. Then I went on board and attacked the night lunch. When two men from the engine room crew came in looking for food, they grumbled about how little I'd left for them. They wanted to know who I was. They'd never seen me on the ship before, and it was obvious that I was responsible for the shortage of good food. I told them I was an ordinary seaman who had just joined the ship, and that I hadn't had anything to eat all day. They said they wouldn't leave the ship in Portland if getting another job was as difficult as I described.

The Coya was operated by the Grace Line and ran regularly between the west coast of the U.S. and the west coast of South America. Built by the Shipping Board at the end of World War I, the Coya had three sister ships in the same trade that were operated by the Grace Line. They were the Cuzco, Casique and Charcas. From the Columbia River, we went up to Puget Sound and stopped at a number of lumber company docks loading general cargo below deck and lumber on deck. We also carried a few tons of dynamite for the nitrate mines on the coast of Chile. The last port of loading was James Island off the coast of Vancouver Island. Christmas came and went while we were loading around Puget Sound. With three meals a day, I was feeling great and gaining some weight.

Our first port going south was Callao, the port for Lima, Peru. Of principal interest to us when we arrived in port after a long time at sea was liquor and women. After we had been in port for awhile we did a little sight seeing, but our limited finances and the lack of sights worth seeing in the little towns along the coast kept such activities to a minimum. More often, we found a good

The deck crew of the S.S. Coya, 1931. Abbott is in the second row, middle.

bar and got acquainted with the people who ran it. The regular customers were waterfront workers, and occasionally they invited us to their homes. Time ashore was limited because in 1931 most American merchant ships had a two-watch system. Day work started at 6 a.m. and finished at 6 p.m., with an hour off for lunch. By the time dinner was over and I got cleaned up, it was close to 8 p.m. I had to report for work again at 6 a.m., so there wasn't much time to spend ashore.

Going south from Lima, our next port was Arica on the border of Chile. We stopped at Iquique, then Antofagasta, Chile. South of Antofagasta was Chanaral, where we stayed for several weeks. The town was very small but there were some large nitrate mines inland and here we finally unloaded our cargo of dynamite. At Chanaral, a sailing ship called the Lord Nelson was loading for England. Having read a book by Richard Halliburton who worked his way around the world, I decided to try to do the same thing.

The Lord Nelson was a square rigger. When I mentioned my interest to one of the stevedores who had been aboard, he told me that the ship I was on was luxurious compared to the Nelson.

Then I thought about riding freight trains from Chile across the South American continent to Buenos Aires. When I talked to the locals about this, they told me if I was caught riding a freight train I would be fined or put in a very primitive jail. Fortunately, I was discouraged by the information. Besides, someone told the captain what I was planning to do, and he refused to give me any more advances on my earnings.

Our next port was Valparaiso, the largest and best looking city we'd visited in Chile. We didn't stay long but we did pick up a stranded sailor named Ted Muth who had missed his ship. An able bodied seaman off a Grace Line cargo vessel which had called at Valparaiso before the Coya, he was being sent back to the U.S. by the American Consul. On the way back to San Francisco I told him about an expedition down the Snake River I had read about. The expedition was well-financed, with a custom-designed boat to negotiate the rapids. They started at Lewiston, Idaho and ended at Portland, Oregon on the Willamette River.

I convinced Ted that we could do the same thing with a fifteen-foot boat, and have a great time doing it. I'd have enough money to take the trip when I was paid off in San Francisco, and since he would have to wait for the money owed him from the ship he missed in Valparaiso, he might as well be floating down the river. Before we arrived in San Francisco, we were told that the Coya was going to be laid up as soon as the northbound cargo was discharged in Seattle. The mate said he would like to have us stay on while they were discharging along the coast. This was perfect for us, and we started planning our trip.

We hopped a freight train to Lewiston, Idaho, where the Clearwater and Snake rivers came together. We couldn't understand why there were no small boats around until someone told us that the surface of the rivers was covered with whirlpools. Only a fool would row a boat there, we were told, and no one was crazy enough to try to swim in the rivers. In spite of the warning, we asked around for a small boat we could buy. Someone told us about a hermit who lived on an island where the two rivers came together. The hermit had built several small boats with which he went to the mainland when necessary.

"How can we find this hermit?" we asked.

"Camp on the mainland and wait until you see him come down to the river," our source said, "then yell to him."

It was evening, so we went to a point on the mainland nearest the hermit's island and built a campfire. We had some second-hand blankets, and with some twine, a needle and sailmakers palm we made two sleeping bags. We had a little food, and we spent the night by our fire. Early the next morning we saw the hermit on the island. We yelled at him, asking if he had a boat he would like to sell. He said he had only one completed boat, which was old, and another which wasn't quite finished. He would sell one, but had to keep the other for transportation to the mainland. We asked him to row over to us towing the other boat so we could choose between the two. When he arrived it was obvious that the old boat wasn't going to make it through the rapids, but the new one had possibilities. It was 13 feet long and built like a scow with no sharp bow or stern, but it had a good shape which would allow it to be rowed easily. The sides were planked, but not all the way to the gunnel. Two or three more planks were still needed on each side.

He wanted twenty dollars for the partially completed scow. We offered him five and eventually gave in to ten. Ted had all his personal things in a seaman's canvas bag which we cut up and tacked along each side of the boat to cover the unfinished parts. We got four five gallon cans, cut off the tops and placed them under the seat for dry storage of food and the few articles of clothing we had with us. We folded our sleeping bags across the thwarts which made them more comfortable. The hermit gave us one oar with the craft, so we went looking for another. We found one

*Floating down the Snake River from Lewiston, Idaho,
destined for Portland, Oregon, 1931, age 19.*

in a second hand store and although it was slightly longer than
the one we had, we bought it. We picked up some cooking utensils, a canoe paddle and made a sail out of old canvas that we
hoped would push us along when we had a following wind. We
spent one last night at our camp across from the hermit's island
and departed at dawn the next morning.

I was nineteen years old. This was in early May, 1931, and there
was a good current during our first few days on the river. We
rowed and paddled once in a while, but for long periods we
drifted, watching the landscape as it slowly passed. There were
very few signs of civilization.

The first day on the river we didn't try to make good time. We
enjoyed being lazy and let the current take us along while the
changing landscape entertained us. We estimated our drifting
speed at approximately three or four miles an hour. With one of
us in the stern, we could with very little effort maintain a straight
course down the river using the paddle. If the need for speed became urgent, one person could row while the other paddled and
we could reach shore quickly. The boat's shallow draft and light
construction gave us excellent maneuverability.

As evening approached we looked for a good place to spend the night. We found a stretch of sandy beach and pulled the boat out of the water and built a fire. After we cooked our food and ate our fill, we cleared the fire area and placed our sleeping bags on the warm ground. We were up with the sun, looking forward to another day on the river. Before we left our campground, we got up the courage to take a quick dip in the icy water.

Pasco, Washington was the first large town we expected to see. It was approximately one hundred miles from Lewiston, and we didn't have enough food to last the entire trip, so we had to increase our food supply. When we saw a farm on a hill overlooking the river, we tied the boat to a tree and walked up. We bought some eggs and ham and had to extricate ourselves from the farmer and his family who wanted to know all about us, where we were from, and what we were doing on the river. I guess they were lonely sitting on their hill all by themselves.

It took us about seven days to reach Pasco. When we reached the Columbia, the wind started blowing hard upriver. To make headway, one of us paddled while the other rowed. This was too much like work, so we looked for a good place to go ashore. When we saw a deserted cabin on shore, we tied up and went to investigate. Half the cabin had fallen down or been washed away when the river was high and the open side was covered with scrap lumber. The door hanging on one hinge was no impediment, and we went inside. Half of the cabin floor was covered with hay, and in the center there was a pile of rocks on which a fire had been built. A hole had been cut in the roof above the pile of rocks, to ventilate the smoke.

The wind had now increased to a blast, so we brought our food and sleeping bags into the shack and gathered wood for a fire. The opening in the roof didn't get rid of the smoke completely, but we survived until morning. When we removed our sleeping bags from the straw we heard a strange rattle. An angry rattlesnake slithered out, and we quickly chopped it up with an old shovel.

The wind came from the east so we decided to try out the sail. We had two long poles, one attached to each side of the boat. We spread the sail between the poles. The sail was seven or eight feet high, as wide as the beam of the boat at the bottom and slightly wider at the top. We attached the sail to the double masts and rolled them up until we got away from the shore. As soon as there was enough clearance, we each grabbed one of the masts, spread the sail, and began raising the masts to an upright position. We secured each to the gunnel between blocks we attached to the bottom of the boat. As soon as we got the boat headed west, we really took off. After days of rowing, the sensation of effortless sailing was wonderful.

The wind gradually decreased, but we were reluctant to take down the sail so long as we were making headway in the right direction. Coming around a bend, we suddenly heard the roar of rapids. It was beginning to get dark, and the thought of sailing through rapids in the dark scared us. We struggled with the sail, while the boat headed for a rock. Then we shoved the masts and sail under the seat and tried to maintain our position in the midst of roaring water and rocks everywhere we looked. The noise was so loud we couldn't hear the warnings we shouted to each other. A couple of nasty looking rocks came so close I expected to see our boat shattered in the cold swirling water. A few rocks later we slid into calm water near a small town. It was pitch dark and all we wanted to do was rest.

A few days later, the river widened and we once again found ourselves lazily drifting along in the center. I was steering with the paddle when I suddenly heard a roar up ahead. We couldn't see anything along the surface of the water that might be causing the roar, but I started paddling hard toward shore and Ted started rowing. The roar increased. Suddenly it was too late to do anything, and we went over a dam. Fortunately it was only three feet high, but we still felt quite a jolt when we hit bottom. I let go of the paddle and started bailing as fast as I could. Ted grabbed one of our cooking pots and joined me. The only thing we lost was the paddle and it came floating up to us two days later.

One day as we drifted along, we saw a sign on shore indicating that we were passing an Indian reservation. We saw a few Indians on shore and decided to tie up the boat and explore. We followed a path and met up with a young Indian woman in tribal costume. She tried to tell us something, but we didn't understand what she was saying. She smiled and motioned for us to follow her. We followed her down the trail, with all kinds of ideas filling our heads. She took us to a wigwam and invited us in. Our hopes were dashed when we found out all she wanted to do was sell us her beads.

Soon after this disappointment, we awoke one morning to a good wind blowing downstream. We hoisted our clumsy sail and relaxed as the scenery went by. We left the shore at 9 a.m. and sailed all day. We enjoyed the sailing so much we continued until night fell. Rounding a turn we suddenly entered swirling water with rocks sticking up in midstream. The roar of the rapids filled our ears.

We furled our sail while pushing off rocks and trying to avoid the rough spots where the waves threatened to splash over our inadequate freeboard. It dawned on us that we were going through the John Day Rapids at night in a thirteen foot scow, but we were so busy we didn't have much time to think about it. After being knocked around and drenched with cold spray we passed the island at the mouth of the Deschutes River and drifted into calm water.

We knew there was a canal around Solilo Falls and as we got closer we wondered what would happen when we paddled up to the first lock. Would they let us through? No one heeded our shouts, until someone on top of the wall finally looked over and asked us what was wrong.

"Nothing," we said. "We want the locks opened so we can go through."

Several other men joined the first, and in an exasperated tone one of them said, "We are not going to lower the water level in the lock just to get you through. We will lower a line for you to make fast to your boat. Then we'll all hoist your boat up and lower it down on the other side of the lock." They didn't know how heavy the boat was, or how much gear we had on board. When the boat reached the next gate, the water level was the same as that of the canal, so it was opened without argument.

During the salmon season, only the Indians from the local tribe could use gillnets to catch fish fighting their way upstream to spawn near Solilo Falls. Other fishermen used conventional tackle, but they were restricted to selling their fish to a cannery buyer on the island. We built a lean-to on the island where we sat out a couple of rainy days. We were approached by several fishermen who wanted to use our boat to smuggle fish to the mainland, but we didn't give in.

As we continued through the canal, we came to another lock which was opened for us without argument. We tied up to the side while the water level was lowered. When the level was the same inside the lock as on the river, the lock was opened for us and soon we were on the Columbia headed for Portland.

We began to see more and more signs of civilization. From exploring a wild river to putting up with the various irritations associated with civilization, we found our mood changing. It was difficult to find a camp where we could cook and relax without attracting others who plied us with questions about where we had been and where we were going. If we needed to buy food one of us stayed with the boat so it wouldn't get stolen. Once we left the boat for an hour, and when we returned a bunch of kids were trying to launch it.

The next morning Ted told me he was going to Portland to get another ship. He was almost broke and he wasn't having fun anymore. I opted to continue for a few more days before I joined him at the shipping hall in Portland. Two days later I found myself in a delta of sorts between the Willamette and the Columbia with no current. I had to row constantly and the scenery wasn't very entertaining. I tied the boat to a tree, ate some cold food, then stretched out on the ground in my sleeping bag. The next morning I covered the boat with branches and went to buy a cup of coffee. When I returned, two boys had uncovered the boat. I asked them if they would like to have it.

"Yes," they said excitedly.

I'm sure they couldn't believe their luck when I said, "It's yours."

When I arrived at the shipping hall the next morning, Ted was sitting in the corner. He was completely discouraged. He told me that only one a.b. seaman job had been called since he'd arrived. I went out for a walk and passed an army recruiting sergeant. "Now there's someone who's trying to hire," I thought, "and such are few and far between these days." I made a U-turn and asked him if the army was really recruiting.

"Yes," he said. "We need just two more men to meet our quota for this month. If you're interested, go to the office upstairs and see the lieutenant in charge of recruiting."

The lieutenant was a good salesman and had me signed up in a few minutes. I passed the physical although I was underweight for my height. Because I was underweight I was sent to the barracks in Vancouver, Washington, where I could eat and sleep until my weight increased enough to be sworn in.

"This deal can't be beat," I thought.

Chapter Two ⚓

Landward Ho!

*A*t the Vancouver barracks they gave me another, more thorough physical and discovered that I had some minor defects. My jaws didn't come together just right, causing an overbite, and my hearing was not quite up to specifications. The overbite wasn't a problem, but my hearing was slightly more serious. The doctor cleaned out my ears, which had more than the normal amount of wax, and my hearing improved to the point that I passed the test. I was not yet twenty one years old so I had to get permission from one of my parents. I sent a telegram to Father in Houston, Texas and he quickly sent back his permission.

The only thing I needed before being sworn in was another ten pounds of weight. My only duty was to make my bed when I got up in the morning, so I figured that sooner or later I would gain weight. Merle, who occupied the bunk next to mine, was also trying to gain the minimum weight for his height before being sworn in. When I told him that I had been working on ships he said he had been offered a job on an estancia in Argentina but didn't have a way to get there. The job was offered to Merle by his former neighbor, Joe Gibbs, who had inherited the land. I quickly assured him that it was easy to get to Argentina, that I had been there less than a year ago and before that had lived there for two years.

"Will he give me a job?" I asked, excited by the possibility of returning to Argentina. He showed me the letter he had received from Joe, it was very explicit about the need for young men to get the estancia cleaned up and producing a good living. Joe didn't want to hire natives but he couldn't afford to buy steamship passage for American workers. I told Merle that getting to Argentina was no problem since almost every ship I had been on had a stowaway who was quickly put to work after being caught. The owners of the ships were usually glad to have some extra crew that they didn't have to pay.

Merle and I discussed at length what it would be like to work on an estancia in Argentina. After talking about it for several days, we decided to climb out the barracks window at night and go to San Francisco where we could stow away on a ship. We were on the second floor of the barracks but that posed no problem. At midnight we had our bags packed and as soon as all was quiet I climbed out the window, hung on the sill by my hands and dropped to the ground. Merle passed our two pieces of luggage out to me, then he climbed out and dropped to the ground.

When we arrived in San Francisco we checked the shipping news, but didn't find a ship going to Argentina. We were disappointed, but when we found a ship scheduled to sail the next day for Tahiti, New Zealand and Australia, we were excited again; we both liked the idea of going to Tahiti. We planned to go aboard at midnight, stay hidden until the ship was out of San Francisco, then give ourselves up.

While I was at Andover I used to go to the library and read the yachting magazines. I was so fascinated by the first installment of a serial about William A. Robinson that for a year I read every installment. Robinson was a single-handed sailor who sailed his 32' boat, called the Svaap, around the world. His description of life among the natives during his stay in Tahiti really impressed me and I decided that as soon as the opportunity presented itself I would be off to Tahiti. Now I was preparing to sneak aboard a ship headed for Tahiti but my ability to get aboard and remain hidden until the ship sailed was questionable. Also, the possibility of getting ashore and remaining in Tahiti was a gamble, because the captain of the ship might turn us over to the American Consul who could send us back to the U.S. Or worse, we could be arrested by the local police and put in jail.

The name of the ship we were preparing to board was the "Maunganui," named after a mountain in New Zealand. We walked down the Embarcadero until we found the ship, flying the national flag of New Zealand. It was a medium-size freighter for that time, and in fairly good condition.

The gangway was down and there was no guard but we had to find an inconspicuous way to get aboard. We noticed a more or less horizontal stern line running from the ship to the dock, eliminating the necessity for a steep climb to the ship's deck. The ship was scheduled to sail at noon the next day, so if we got aboard and found a place to hide, we could wait to reveal our presence for a couple of hours after sailing.

At about 10 P.M. we approached the dock where the ship was tied up. All was quiet, the cargo loading and discharging were apparently complete and the only person we saw on deck was a watchman, engrossed in reading a magazine at the head of the gangway. The eye of the stern line hung down from a cleat on the dock, then rose in a gradual curve up to the stern of the ship. We flipped a coin to see who would go first and Merle lost the flip. As he started up I remembered that there might be a rat guard on the line. I quietly explained to him from the dock how to remove the rat guard. He followed my instructions and the sheet metal guard swung down from the mooring line, then hit the steel hull of the ship. The loud noise brought the night watchman running down the dock. I climbed underneath the dock and held on to the bracing between the pilings until things quieted down. Fortunately, Merle had not been discovered.

I hung below the mooring line as I went up, swinging a little back and forth until I reached the stern rail. I quickly jumped over and started looking for a place to hide. I saw a gear box on deck with canvas hanging down over the front and made a dive to get in before I was seen. Unfortunately Merle was already in there and there was no room for two. I looked around for another hiding place, and since the gear box was too easily accessible, Merle joined me in my search.

There was a pile of potato sacks up against the rail with a tarpaulin over them, lashed down in a seaman-like manner which indicated to me that the potatoes wouldn't be moved until the ship was out to sea. We hid in the pile where we could lay without being seen and still get some air, but we couldn't see each other and had no way of communicating.

The hours dragged by, finally I detected some light and saw the sun coming up. I heard people walking back and forth and talking with Australian accents. I estimated the time to be nine in the morning. A tugboat came alongside and tied up to the ship; they were getting ready to sail.

I had to relieve myself so I let go on the potatoes hoping that my urine wouldn't run out on deck. Some of the crew came along, and a voice with authority, probably the bo'sun, said that the potatoes were to be dumped out of the sacks into the potato locker. I could feel the sacks being moved, and heard the crew talking mostly about the girls they had been with the night before. I felt something slide over my back but didn't move because I wasn't sure they had seen me. Suddenly there was complete quiet. "Blimey, it's a stiff!" someone exclaimed.

I still didn't move because I didn't know for sure whether they had seen me or Merle. I had my face up against a potato sack and when I moved my head a little I could see that the sun was shining on me. Five members of the crew were standing there looking at me with shocked expressions and bulging eyes. I realized that I had been found, so I sat up.

The bo'sun grabbed me and told one of the crew to take me to the chief mate. While we walked down to the chief mate's office the man with me said, "Don't ever try to stow away on this ship again because they'll work you night and day and give you only enough food to keep you alive."

The chief mate asked me why I had tried to stow away. I told him I lived in Tahiti and was trying to get home. He advised me to stow away on an American ship. I walked down the dock and waited outside to watch the ship sail with Merle. A few minutes later he came walking out. One of the crew had found him and advised him to get off.

Merle and I discussed what we would do next. With our sea-going attempt thwarted, we considered trying again to join one of the armed services. We chose the marines this time but our reputations for deserting preceded us, and they wouldn't even talk to us.

Merle suggested we go to his parent's place between Auburn and Grass Valley, California. He had an accordion there which he could hock to give us a little money for emergencies. In order to reach our destination, we separated and started hitch hiking. I had a good description of the place and the best route to follow, so I wasn't worried about getting lost. Merle got there first and greeted me when I arrived.

Merle's father owned a road house called Cottage Hill Tavern which he rented to a bootlegger who sold a little gasoline on the side. Across the road from the tavern there was a barn and a two-bedroom house where Merle's parents stayed when they visited the area. The country around Cottage Hill was very beautiful. In the early 1930's when I first saw it, there were no neighbors close by. Merle's younger brother, Paul, was working part time for the bootlegger, and another, even younger brother, Dude, worked for a ranch on the other side of the hills. The only thing to eat in the house was hot cake flour so we broke out the fishing tackle and caught a dish pan full of perch from the lake near the tavern.

I told Merle that I wanted to catch a freight train to Houston, Texas where father was staying with my grandmother. Merle said he had nothing better to do and would like to come along with me, so we hitch hiked to Oakland where we could get a train on the Southern Pacific to Houston.

I was supposed to be teaching Merle how to ride freight trains but when the train came out at a good clip and Merle got on, I didn't. By the time the train got to me it was going too fast, and I missed the ladder and rolled down the embankment. I dusted myself off and caught the next train, but it went the coast route, which was slower than down the valley the way Merle's train went. I was compensated when my train stopped near Point Arguello where I saw the beach lined with treasure hunters. They were searching for valuable objects washed ashore from the wreck of a passenger ship which had run onto the point in heavy fog at full speed. It was one of two ships, the Harvard and the Yale, which had been brought from the East Coast to provide fast passenger service between San Francisco and Los Angeles. After the wreck at Point Arguello the service was discontinued.

Merle and I had agreed that if we got separated we would leave messages for each other at general delivery in the Los Angeles post office. I met up with Merle there, he had found a place for us to sleep that night, and a job which we could start the next day at a camp for delinquent girls in Sunland. The job provided room and board, but no money. Our new employers gave us dinner, showers and cots in a dormitory for the night, and while we slept, they washed and sanitized our clothes.

The next morning we ate breakfast before piling into the station wagon to go to Sunland. Merle was given a job in the kitchen serving food and cleaning up after meals, but I wasn't so lucky. They put me to work in the 100 degree sun, building a stone wall. There were five of us gathering large stones, breaking them, and fitting them into the wall. When Merle finished his work, he sat on the shaded porch with the girls who cooked, and watched me build the stone wall.

Most of the men asked for jobs at Sunland because word got around that the delinquent girls sometimes sneaked out of the dormitories at night to visit with the male help. I figured this was just propaganda to make the job more appealing, but I admit I may have been influenced by the rumor, too.

The third night I was there, I was awakened by a lot of whispering and giggling near the door, followed about ten minutes later by the entrance of three guards. They went down the row of bunks pulling off the covers, rousting out the females who had sneaked into bed with the men in the bunks closest to the door. The guards returned the girls to their dormitories, and silence was restored.

While working on the stone wall, I noticed a man with a team of mules hauling irrigation pipe on the property adjacent to the camp. One evening, as I sat on the wall after dinner, the man came over to talk.

"Do you know how to drive mules?" he asked.

"Sure, I can handle a team of mules without any trouble," I said.

"I'll give you three meals a day and a place in my shack to sleep if you drive my team for me," he said.

"Throw in $10. a week, and you got yourself a deal," I said.

"I'll have to think about it," he said.

The next morning as I worked on the wall, he came back to tell me he would meet my terms if I could start the following day at 8 A.M. He also said that he wanted to get the pipe for his irrigation system installed as soon as possible, so if I could persuade another man at the camp to join me, he could use us both.

The next morning Merle and I started earning $10. a week and our room and board installing the irrigation system. In exchange for earning a little money, we gave up the opportunity for nighttime visits from delinquent girls.

After two weeks, with a jingle in our pockets, we decided to continue our freight train ride to Houston. It was a long, hot haul, and when we finally got there Merle got a job in a restaurant before I had a chance to see Father. When I did see him he told me that he and his old cronies were trying to establish an athletic club in Houston. I told him about my trip down the Snake and Columbia rivers, and he suggested I write a story about it. "You might be able to sell it to Boy's Life, or some other popular boy's magazine," he said.

With his help, I started to write, but soon found out that we had conflicting ideas of how it should be written, so I gave up.

At the time, Mother and Father had been separated for almost five years. Father introduced me to Esther, one of his young lady friends, the secretary of the Houston Chamber of Commerce. Shortly after I met her, she sent a messenger to Father's office with an envelope addressed to me. It contained two tickets to a new movie which had just opened in Houston. I phoned to thank her, and she told me the tickets were given to the Chamber by the movie company for publicity. Merle and I enjoyed the picture.

Once in a while Father sent me up to her office with the articles he wrote to publicize the Houston City Athletic Club. She was somewhere between 19 (my age) and 48 (Father's age), and I knew he went out with her occasionally, so I was surprised when she invited me up to her apartment for dinner. I told Father where I was going, and that I would be home a little later, but to complicate matters I didn't get home until after midnight. The next day, Father and I suffered through an uncomfortable silence; I couldn't convince him that we had been playing cards all evening.

The next day Merle asked me if I wanted to go back to California. He said hunting season was coming up soon, and he didn't want to miss it. He knew the foothill country well after living there for some time, and had always bagged at least one deer during the season. Besides, his father was in the hospital, so his mother wanted him to come home. She was living in the house across the highway from Cottage Hill Tavern with Merle's brother, Paul. Merle urged me to go with him, there was a lot of work to be done on the place, and he would welcome any help he could get.

While we were looking for a freight train to El Paso in the switch yards outside San Antonio, we spotted a slow-moving locomotive with a mail and express car and several passenger cars. The only place we could hop on without being seen by the train crew was between the engine and the mail car. We got aboard just as the train was picking up speed. We concealed ourselves by staying flat against the door on the front of the mail car. The train quickly got up speed and was soon going passenger train fast, which was a new experience for us. We worried about how we were going to get off before the train came to a station, because there were always guards at stations, and we didn't want to get caught. We pushed the door at the end of our car, and it opened. The mail car was empty. We lay down and fell asleep right away.

Speeding along on a quiet fast passenger train was a luxury, and if it just kept going non-stop until it reached Sacramento, we'd have it made! But we didn't know how we were going to get off at the first stop, or where the first stop was going to be. During the night we both suddenly woke up. We sensed a change in speed and being long time freight train riders we knew that it meant we were coming to a station. The train continued to gradually slow down until it stopped at the passenger station in Del Rio, Texas.

We opened the door a crack and saw an armed guard standing right outside the door. We rightly assumed that the U.S. mail was going to be loaded into our compartment. Luckily, someone called to the guard from the station. He turned and took several steps toward the station, and at the same moment I jumped to the ground and called for Merle to follow. While the guard was talking we walked toward him. When he finished and turned toward us I asked him if he knew of any restaurants in Del Rio that were open in the middle of the night. He said, "Yes, there is only one decent place." He told us how to get there. We thanked him and walked in that direction. He watched us for a few minutes, then turned away.

We arrived in Oakland, California by freight train a few days later. After getting cleaned up we hitchhiked to Cottage Hill where Merle's family welcomed us and asked us many questions about our adventures. The country looked like heaven to me, because I had always lived in cities. There was a cow in the barn which Merle and Paul took turns milking. I bought an old wreck of a car for $25. with $5. down. It was an old four cylinder Essex. We jacked up the rear wheels, ran a belt to a saw and soon were in the firewood business. Merle and I hunted and fished and sold firewood, Paul worked in the grocery store in Grass Valley when they needed an extra hand, and their mother manned the kitchen, serving us excellent country food. We never ate lunch, but we all returned to the kitchen in the evening where we went over the adventures of the day while we ate dinner. I will never forget how warm and friendly that kitchen felt after working in the woods all day.

My old Essex wasn't our only transportation, we also rode two horses, bareback. One was called Dynamite, rumored to have been a race horse; the other, called Ted, enjoyed tossing me off his back.

On Saturday nights we took baths in the stream and put on our best clothes for the dance at Le Barr Meadows near Grass Valley. Merle was frequently asked to sing along with the orchestra, he had an excellent voice and got a lot of applause. After listening to him sing, all the girls wanted to dance with him. At about midnight after drinking for three or four hours, some of the dancers got unruly; by 2 A.M. fights broke out all over the place and it was time to leave. Most of the people who lived in Grass Valley at that time were employed in the gold mines, and since the mines were prosperous, there was little unemployment.

Five miles up a country road from the highway was a large ranch with a huge barn overlooking a stream which swelled into a river during the spring. All of a sudden there was a great deal of activity in the vicinity of the ranch. A large black Cadillac sedan was frequently seen going up the dirt road leading to the ranch. Trucks loaded with building material were turning off the highway onto the road to the ranch and would come back empty after several hours. We asked the neighbors what was going on up there but either nobody knew or they wouldn't tell.

One day, Merle said he had heard that a still was being built at the ranch up the dirt road. I decided that it was time for me to investigate. I borrowed a gun to make it look like I was hunting in case someone saw me, and started walking up to the ranch. When I arrived at the gate, there were several men working in the barn. One of them walked over to me. "What do you want?" he asked.

"I need a job," I said. "It looked like there was a big project going on up here,"

"If you want a job, don't be caught hanging around here," the man said. "The boss is half way down the road to the highway. He's a short man in a black overcoat driving a black Cadillac."

I found the black Cadillac and the short man in the black coat and told him I was looking for a job. I asked him if he had any work I could do for him. He said he was building a sheep ranch up the road and asked me what I thought I could do to help. I said I could haul gravel from the stream, dump it on the road where it was needed, and dig drainage ditches to keep the road dry. He said, "All right, you have a job. I'll have a man down here to help you at 8 A.M. Monday. I'll pay you $200 a month to keep the road in passable condition."

Merle helped me convert my Essex into a truck by chopping off the back seat and building a truck bed where it had been. I was at the ranch road at 8 A.M. Monday with a load of gravel from the river bed on my "truck." The man who was sent to help me on the road was Andy Walker, the former bartender of Cottage Hill Tavern. According to rumor, Andy was an engineer with a degree from MIT.

While we worked, he asked me where I came from and what I had been doing all my life. I gave him a thumbnail sketch: born in Lincoln, Nebraska, lived in Dallas until about 1921, then in Buenos Aires until 1924. Spent a year in Houston, Texas, then three years in Brookline, Massachusetts until the fall of 1928. I entered prep school at Phillips Andover Academy in Andover, Massachusetts in the fall of 1928. I received a scholarship and worked my way through school until the spring of 1930 when, for lack of money I had to quit and get a job. I also intimated to Andy that I thought we were working for a still, not a sheep ranch. He pretended amazement and said, "If you ever mention that to anyone and I hear of it, you're fired."

Andy spent another day working with me, then I was on my own. I arrived every morning with a load of gravel on my truck and sometimes had to go back to the river bed and get several more truckloads during the day. On the day before Thanksgiving, I was working on the road when the big black Cadillac came around a bend in the road. It stopped in front of me, and the man with the long black coat stepped out with a roll of money in his hand. He peeled off two 100 dollar bills and gave them to me. I told him I would need another person to help me when the rainy season got going and he agreed to let me hire Merle as a helper at $150. a month. When I got home, everyone was waiting for me. They were feeling bad because we didn't have enough money for a Thanksgiving turkey. I said, "Let's get in the Essex, go to Auburn, and get a turkey."

"What are we going to do for money?" Paul asked.

I threw the $200 on the table. We all got into the truck, stopped at a ranch to buy a turkey, then drove to Auburn to buy all the trimmings. That was one of the most fun Thanksgivings I have ever had.

Merle and I left the house where we had been living because Merle's stepfather had been released from the hospital and was renting a house in Hayward with Merle's mother. Merle and I moved into an old cabin owned by a fellow named Jones. The cabin was near a river where gold prospectors had once lived, and although we had to share the cabin with Jones, we relished the rustic atmosphere.

Things went well until the rains started and the road leading up to the still got increasingly worse. One night at about 2 A.M., Andy knocked on our door and said a truck was stuck and we had to get it out before daylight. Merle and I found the truck up to its wheel hubs in mud. We worked frantically with help from the men at the still and got the truck out just as daylight was break- ing.

Andy told the still operator that he could design a large sled which could be towed by a tractor through the mud. It would be slow, but with the sled they could maintain a delivery schedule. Within a few days the sled was built; it held 60 five-gallon cans of alcohol. They tried it out with a rented tractor, it was slow but it worked, and no matter how bad the road got it would go on through. When I watched the new rig coming through the woods in the middle of the night with the tractor exhaust shooting fire up into the trees, lighting up the whole landscape, making noise that could be heard a mile away, I wondered how long it would take the authorities to find and destroy the still.

There wasn't much for Merle and me to do after the tractor and sled started to operate, so the man in the long black coat told us to take a couple of weeks off and see what happened. He thought that they might have to stop using the tractor if it tore up the road too much or if neighboring ranches complained about the noise. We didn't have to wait very long. About a week later, we were awakened in the middle of the night by loud knocking at the front door. It was Andy, screaming that the still had been knocked over and to stay away from it. About a week later, Pete, the foreman at the still, drove up in his yellow Marmon, which had a hidden compartment large enough to carry forty five-gallon cans of alcohol. Pete said he had been arrested when the still was knocked over, and was out on bail. He knew where a whole sled- load of alcohol was hidden and wanted to know if I would help him get it out.

I told Pete that the only way he could get the alcohol out of the woods and down to the highway was with a wagon and a team of horses. He said, "Okay, can you get me a team of horses and a wagon to help me load up my car?"

"Yes," I said, "but it will cost you $25. for the night."

He gave me the money and I made a deal with a local farmer to rent his horses and wagon. I couldn't find Merle, but his youngest brother, Dude, happened to be around and was willing to help. Dude and I had the team at the entrance to the road when Pete showed up in his Marmon. By this time it was pitch dark and pouring rain. A small white dog from the farm where we got the team and wagon decided to go along with us and bark all the way.

When we got close to the still we didn't know whether or not there would be guards around.

Pete said, "If anyone jumps us, get off the wagon and run like hell."

We arrived at the place, removed some brush, and uncovered 60 five-gallon cans of alcohol in a neat stack. Pete wanted to take them all at once, but it would have been impossible to get them all in the wagon even if the horses could have pulled it. Pete agreed to make two trips and we started off with 20 cans. The horses had trouble getting over the small hills, but with some urging made it back to the Marmon. We unloaded the alcohol into the Marmon and returned to the stash in the woods. To our surprise someone had removed six cans of what we had put aside for our second trip. Footprints in the mud indicated that two people had followed us and waited nearby for us to uncover the stash. When we left with our first load, they moved in and took as many cans as they could carry.

Pete was fighting mad. After we loaded the wagon for the second trip, he pulled out his gun and said he was going after the thieves. Dude and I started down the road with the loaded wagon, but the horses were tired, struggling over the uphill parts of the road. I didn't say anything to Dude, but one of the thieves' footprints looked like they were from the new pair of boots that Merle had recently bought. If one of the thieves was Merle, I hoped that Pete, with his gun drawn, wouldn't find him. When we were two-thirds of the way back to the Marmon, the tired horses stopped at a steep place in the road. I whipped them and they struggled but they couldn't quite make it. I told Dude we had to unload some of the cans and hide them close to the road, or the horses wouldn't make it. As we were unloading Pete came marching through the woods yelling, "What the hell are you doing? Get that alcohol down to the Marmon before the sun comes up."

I told him that the horses couldn't pull the wagon because it was overloaded but Pete ignored me, broke off a branch from a tree and started hitting the horses. It only made them more stubborn. "Well," he said, "take off ten or fifteen cans and get the rest down to the car as fast as possible." With that he headed back to the highway. We unloaded 15 cans and had no more trouble with the horses.

At the car we unloaded the alcohol from the wagon into the Marmon and accepted two cans each for our work. Before leaving Pete said, "I'll be back in a few days to get the rest."

When Dude and I walked into our cabin at dawn, wet and covered with mud, we were surprised to see Merle and Jones up and covered with mud. It didn't take me very long to figure that Dude had told them what I was doing. They had followed us and taken some of the alcohol. We were too tired, wet and dirty to do anything but crawl into our bunks and pass out.

We all sat around the next morning telling lies about where we had all been and what we were doing all night. The truth finally came out. Pete had found Dude first and asked him to find me so I could help him bring out the alcohol that had been hidden in the woods when they found out they were going to be raided. When Dude borrowed the team and wagon from the Locatelli's, he stopped to tell Merle and Jones what was happening. The rest was obvious.

Dude left the next morning so I told Merle and Jones about the twenty five-gallon cans of 190 proof alcohol hidden in the woods. I wanted them to help me move it a couple of miles down the highway before dark. Jones had an old model-T Ford truck that was so light it was ideal for going through the mud, even with a heavy load. They agreed to help me.

We picked up the cans, which were stashed only about a mile or so from the paved highway. Merle and Jones took the cans down the highway about four miles and then up a dirt road, which was in good shape. I followed them at a respectable distance, and after we unloaded the cans, I gave each of them two five-gallon cans for doing the job. I went up the hill, watched them until they were out of sight, and when they were gone, I hid the cans in different places along the side of the hill. I walked back to the cabin to pick up my car. Everything went as planned.

I drove down to Los Angeles and visited with Grandfather for about ten days. When I returned, the alcohol was still there, where I had hidden it. As I expected, Pete had showed up the night I left and came by the cabin and asked for me. He said he wanted me to help him get some more alcohol out of the woods. Merle and Dude told him I had gone to Los Angeles, so he got someone else to help him. They tried to go up the muddy road in his Marmon, got stuck and were unable to get out until the next day; they never made it to where the alcohol was hidden. It was the last time anyone heard of Pete around Cottage Hill.

I now had the challenge of trying to gain admittance to one of the local bootlegging establishments in order to sell my alcohol. They all had peep holes in their doors and when they saw how young I was, they wouldn't open for me. I talked to a man I knew who ran an auto repair business in Richmond, and frequently visited Cottage Hill. He claimed he knew all the bootleggers in his area and would have no trouble selling them my 190 proof product. He asked me to bring four five-gallon cans to him in two weeks and he would have them sold by that time.

A couple of weeks later, I loaded the cans in the back seat of my old Buick and headed for Richmond. After keeping me waiting for two days, my friend admitted that he had been unable to sell any of it. He offered to buy a can for himself, so I sold him one for $25., then made the trip back to Cottage Hill.

When I returned, Paul introduced me to Marmaduke Von Stermer. Jack, as I called him, came from Australia and had entered the U.S. illegally through Canada. He said he knew all the bootleggers around Grass Valley and Auburn and would have no trouble selling my alcohol for me.

Too many people knew I had a stash, and I felt that it was time to put it where I could keep an eye on it. Jack, Paul and I found an old cabin with an iron cooking stove, two bunks and a nice clear stream of water running right by the front door. We got some old sugar sacks from the former still site and lined the interior of the cabin with them to keep the wind from coming through the cracks. Then we pulled up the floor and dug a basement large enough to stow the alcohol. When we replaced the floor we put a hatch in the middle and covered it with an old rug. We found an old cot to supplement the sleeping arrangements and set it up next to the bunks.

We spent a lot of time at the cabin, experimenting with additives to convert the alcohol into gin, scotch or bourbon. We also used distilled water to reduce the alcohol from 190 to 80 proof. We hunted, fished and panned gold in nearby streams where people still lived in tents along the banks and stayed alive with what they earned from panning gold.

A different bootlegger now rented Cottage Hill Tavern. He was fairly well educated and I got along with him. He knew I had some alcohol to sell, but told me that if he bought anything from me and his present supplier found out about it he would not only be out of business but also could very easily be dead. I tried to find a way we could strike a bargain without disastrous results for the buyer. I finally worked out a deal to which he did not immediately say "no."

While Paul, Jack Von Stermer and I had been enjoying ourselves and living in our cabin which we had named the Hotel de Knothole, my liquor had slowly been evaporating. This no doubt was due to our experimenting with the various possibilities of concocting different drinks from 190 proof alcohol with different additives and colorings. Tasting was also an important part of the process.

Merle and I were ready to go seek our fortunes in Alaska. It was spring time in Alaska, Merle had a little money, and I offered the operator of Cottage Hill Tavern a well-planned deal he could not resist. At the same time Paul got a job in Grass Valley and Jack got a job on a ranch. We had a big party at the Hotel de Knothole, with a lot of the people from the neighborhood, and by the next morning the alcohol supply had been reduced enough that I could get it all into the old Buick and cover it with no trouble. I drove to the tavern at three in the morning, long after it was closed, when nobody was around. I parked the car in the garage under the tavern and left it there, full of cargo. I had no trouble finding the envelope containing the money and I was off to meet Merle at the Roseville freight yards which wasn't very far from Cottage Hill.

During the time I was a seaman on the San Felipe and the Coya, I had enjoyed visiting Seattle; I liked the city with all the water around it in spite of the fact that everyone told me it rained all winter and was occasionally very cold. Our inquiries about a job in Alaska brought replies that indicated it was relatively easy to get a job there during the summer but not in the winter. A lot of fishing boats went up there from Seattle, spent the summer fishing then returned to Seattle for the winter. Someone told Merle about job openings on a fishing boat operated out of Bellingham, Washington, just north of Seattle, so we hitchhiked up there. At sunset we were only half way. We walked down the highway for hours, then in the middle of the night we entered a barn and slept in the hay until a dog came and smelled us and started barking. The dog's owners must not have been home because we spent the remainder of the night there without being discovered. We left, half-frozen, as the sun came up.

Merle found the fishing boat captain, but he already had a crew for the coming season. We hitchhiked back to Seattle with one ride and decided to beg something to eat just for the fun of it. We each went a different way, and knocked on doors asking if they had some work we could do for something to eat. An elderly lady gave me a sandwich and an apple but said she had no work. Since I was in a residential neighborhood, I didn't want to sit on the curb, so I walked behind an apartment building to a vacant lot. I leaned against the apartment building to eat my sandwich when I heard a lady calling, "Young man, young man, I am right above you in the building you are leaning against. Wouldn't you like to come up and have a cup of coffee with your sandwich?"

I accepted her invitation. When I reached her apartment, I found out she had a daughter about my age. We talked while I drank my coffee. I told them I had just got off a freight train from California. The mother said if I would like to take a bath, I was welcome to use their bathroom. I accepted the bath, thanked them, and left with the phone number.

When I told Merle about the experience, he couldn't believe it. A week later I called the daughter and asked for a date. She accepted, so I rented a car and went to her apartment clean and neat. We went to a movie and I took her home. She told me she would cook dinner for me the following Wednesday if I was still in town.

"With that to look forward to, I will definitely stay," I told her.

When I returned from the date, Merle and I sat around our cheap room and talked things over. Merle was impatient to go to Alaska, and had bought a ticket on a ship to Ketchikan, Alaska which was leaving in ten days. Neither of us was sure of a job in Alaska, and even if we had been, the season up there was short, amounting to three or four months at the most. If we couldn't get jobs, we would have to come back in a month or two when our money ran out.

A few days later, Merle got a refund for his ticket to Alaska and I got tired of the girl in the apartment, so we headed back to California. While we were still in transit I decided to go on to Los Angeles where Grandfather was living. Merle got off at Roseville and hitchhiked back to Cottage Hill country.

I found Grandfather living alone in an apartment over a garage on one of the properties he owned. He was glad to see me. After I told him about some of the sights in Seattle he asked me if I would drive him there. He had just bought a new car and wanted to put some miles on it.

He was Mother's father, born in Oskaloosa, Iowa, where he went to school at a Quaker college, then ran a country store for many years. After selling the store he bought a flour mill in Tobias, Nebraska and worked there until he retired. He bought a three- story brick house in Lincoln across the street from the state capitol. My two uncles and mother all attended the University of Nebraska when they lived in the house. Grandfather bought several low-rent tenements in Lincoln and made a living from the rents. He was very active and took care of all the maintenance on the apartment buildings by himself.

When he was seventy years old, he told his wife he was going to drive to California. He gave her their home and his other rental properties in Lincoln. He estimated that the income from the properties would be sufficient to support her, and by this time his children were working at various careers, so he didn't have to worry about taking care of them. When he arrived in California, he bought property around Los Angeles. When the depression hit in 1930, he had trouble collecting rents. When tenants were broke he rented another house for them, paid a couple of months rent, and moved them out of his house so he wouldn't be responsible for them. Most of his southern California properties were single family dwellings which he personally maintained. I remember when he was 85 years old, he took a bucket of tar, tied a ladder to the top of his car and drove out to a property he owned which had a leaking roof on the garage. He repaired it himself.

I agreed to drive him to Seattle which gave me an opportunity to see my girlfriend. Grandfather and I spent about a week there. I had a couple of dates with the girl and spent some time showing Grandfather around. On the way back to Los Angeles, as I entered the city of San Jose, I got a speeding ticket. I had just passed the sign which read, "City Limits, Maximum Speed 25 MPH," when red lights flashed behind me. I pulled over, and a cop gave me a ticket for doing 45 miles per hour in a 25 mile per hour zone. I told him I lived in Los Angeles and had no way to get back up to San Jose to appear for the ticket.

Grandfather and I continued on to Los Angeles. One day, about a week after the trip to Seattle Paul showed up at the front door. His mother was now married to a man named Larsen.

Paul, Merle and Dude's father was named Barney. Paul had discovered that his father was in Arkansas and his aunt was in Hot Springs. He wanted me to go with him by freight train to see if we could find them. I looked at a map and saw that we would be near the Red River along the way. I asked Paul if he was unable to find his father, would he be interested in floating down the Red River to the Mississippi and on down to New Orleans, providing we could find an adequate boat. He said he would but that he wanted to try to find his father first.

Our first misfortune occurred after we hopped a train out of Los Angeles. As we entered the freight yards at El Paso, Texas, I was standing above the wheels of a dump car when I suddenly felt a sharp pain in my right eye. As soon as the train slowed down we jumped off and I washed out my eye but couldn't get the irritation out. It was early Sunday morning and there were few people around. In front of a nearby cluster of houses, I saw a sign on the front lawn, which showed that the resident was a doctor. I went to the front door and rang the bell. After a short wait, a Mexican man came to the door in his pajamas.

"Are you a doctor?" I asked.

"Yes, I am," he said.

"I have something very painful in my eye. Can you take it out for me?" I asked.

"Have you got any money?" he asked.

"Yes," I said, "I have fifty cents."

He took me inside and went to work on my eye in a professional manner. He told me I had a piece of steel embedded in my eyeball, and would try to remove it with a magnet, but if that didn't work, I would have to undergo an operation. Fortunately, the magnet worked but I couldn't endure the pain. He bandaged my eye completely and told me not to take the bandage off for at least two days.

Paul and I were very hungry so we looked for free food. Some workmen were loading cantaloupe into refrigerator cars, and when they left, we ate our fill of green cantaloupes which gave me a terrible stomach ache. It was just the beginning of my misery. I was wearing old shoes which were too small and had skinned my heels, and when we jumped on the next train I tore the seat of my pants. I was feeling miserable so I laid down on my back on the top of a box car and rode for miles with the hot Texas sun burning the part of my face that wasn't bandaged. As the train rattled and bumped across the plains of Texas I was completely miserable. I decided right then that I was taking my last freight train ride ever. When the train stopped at a small town, Paul ran over to the town where he could bum something to eat. I looked horrible, the seat of my pants was torn, the bandage around my head revealed only one eye, I hobbled on sore feet from tight shoes and my face was blistered from the sun. My looks wouldn't contribute to my ability to bum some food so I stayed on the train. When Paul returned he brought me a cupcake.

We arrived at Wichita Falls, Texas, late in the afternoon and with the Red River near at hand, decided to check it out before we did anything else. We walked through weeds up to our waists and found the river. Instead of a clean, fast flowing river like the Snake, we found a river so full of mud that it was actually red as the name implies. One look convinced us we didn't want anything to do with it, and we returned to town. On the way, we started to itch violently from our waists down and found that while walking through the weeds to get to the river we had collected chigger bites all over our lower bodies which now were driving us crazy. We had sent some clothes and money to American Express to hold for us until our arrival, and we dreamed of comfortable beds, hot baths, and some good food. We picked up our suitcases at the American Express office and asked them to recommend an inexpensive hotel. When we arrived at the hotel, they gave us one look and said, "We have nothing for you." However, they did give us the name and address of another hotel where we were able to get a room. The beds were comfortable and there was a wash basin in the room, but the shower was out the window on the roof. Fortunately, there was a gable between the shower and the view from the street.

After a shower, some sleep and clean clothes, I removed the bandage from my eye. Most of the pain had gone and my vision was normal. There was a public swimming pool not far from our hotel so we decided to stay for a few days, at least until we were completely rested, free from chigger bite itching, and the scabs from the sunburn on my face disappeared.

My decision to never ever again ride a freight train stuck with me; I haven't ridden one since.

Judging from the raucous male and female voices we heard in the hotel during the evening, we knew the place engaged in a business other than simply renting rooms to out-of-towners. However, it was inexpensive and our roof shower always worked. We spent a lot of time in the city swimming pool but didn't make any progress with the local girls. After we were rested and my infirmities had healed, we shipped our extra clothes to American Express in Hot Springs and started hitchhiking.

When hitchhiking on the highway we thought it best not to stay together. We were more likely to get a ride individually; the chances of there being room for two were not as good. If we started together only one would get out and ask. Paul got the first ride and I didn't see him until the next day. I slept in a barn on a farm and was just getting started when I saw a small truck slow down as it came near me. It stopped alongside me and Paul opened the door and let me in. As we rode along, I whispered to Paul, "How far is this guy going?"

"He is going all the way to where we are going," Paul replied.

Soon we came to a town named Hugo and the driver pulled over to let us out. Paul had misunderstood Hugo to mean where "you go." They were having a carnival in Hugo so we spent the evening there. I still remember seeing political signs all over the town asking people to vote for "Bent Henry" for sheriff. It looked like they wanted a crooked guy for sheriff.

We arrived at our destination a day or two later. Paul found his aunt and she telephoned his father who was in Los Angeles. Paul's father sent him a Pullman ticket for his return to Los Angeles. It was quite a change from freight trains. I had money with me so I hitchhiked to Dallas. I ran into a used car dealer who had bought a bunch of used cars and was recruiting drivers to take them to Los Angeles. Each car had a number on the windshield which designated the position the driver was to keep in the caravan. When a car broke down the whole line had to stop until the mechanic, who was in the last car, fixed it. The only time we were allowed to sleep was when a car broke down. The night before we reached Los Angeles, everyone was going to sleep at the wheel so the dealer hired a motel. We all slept for three hours, then it was non-stop to Los Angeles. It was 1933, traffic and road conditions were a lot different from what they are today.

I was glad to be back at Grandfather's house but I wasn't there for long. The morning after I arrived the doorbell rang. I heard the man at the door ask Grandfather if I was there, so I went to see what he wanted. It was a plain clothes cop who wanted to arrest me because of the ticket I had received when I was driving Grandfather's car back from Seattle.

He said he was taking me to jail in Los Angeles, then I would be taken to San Jose for the hearing. I told him I'd get a sweater and be right back. I took my wallet out of my pocket and hid it in the lower drawer of Grandfather's dresser while I got a sweater. My wallet had quite a lot of money in it, and I didn't want it to get stolen while I was in jail.

I spent three days in the holding tank at Los Angeles. The first day I was there most of the men in the cell were white, so one of the older and larger of the prisoners said we must draw a line on the cell floor and require all the blacks to stay on the other side of the line. In the middle of the night they threw about five more prisoners into our cell. They were all black and big so the segregation that the racist man had imposed was no longer enforceable. On the third morning I was released into the custody of a deputy from San Jose. He told me he was taking me back to San Jose for the trial. His wife and her girl friend were with him, the latter sat in the back seat with me and we struck up a nice friendship. She said that she knew the judge and would see that I received a short sentence. During the trip, I watched the speedometer over the deputy's shoulder to see how many times he exceeded the speed limit. I didn't have a very good view of the speedometer, and my count may not have been very accurate, but I counted fifteen times.

We arrived at the San Jose jail in the late afternoon. I was put in a cell with two other prisoners; one had hit his boss over the head with a crowbar and the other had been convicted of beating up his girlfriend. In spite of their crimes, they were congenial cell mates. The following day I was taken to court for sentencing. I told the judge that I had not returned to San Jose to appear for the speeding ticket because I had no money for transportation. I also reminded him that I had already been in jail in Los Angeles for three days waiting to be brought to San Jose. He said, "Okay, you stay here for three days more."

My next question didn't go over very well. I asked him who was going to pay for my transportation back to Los Angeles.

"If you can't get back to Los Angeles," he said, "you're welcome to stay here in jail as long as you like."

"The alternative is so unappealing, I'll find a way to get back."

The scene in the courtroom was late in the afternoon so that counted as one day. I stayed all the next day and was released at 8 A.M. the third morning. I still had a problem because I had no money but I remembered that Merle was now living with his mother and stepfather in Hayward which was not far from San Jose. I found the phone number and called collect. Merle answered and said I could stay with them until Grandfather could send me some of the money from my hidden wallet. In order to pay for my keep I waited on the table and washed all the dishes for Merle's mother and stepfather until my money arrived. Merle and I discussed some adventures he was considering, but I told him that if riding freight trains was involved he could leave me out.

At Grandfather's house again I had to find something to do that would support me. I had been noticing that many signs were appearing in hotel lobbies for "share expense cars going to all destinations." The cars were owned by individuals who paid the travel bureau a commission in exchange for passengers. I decided to buy an Oldsmobile sedan which I could get for a small down payment and try my luck at driving. After shining up my used car I bought a set of retread tires and stopped at a travel bureau to ask for some passengers. The first travel bureau offered me three men who wanted to go to San Francisco. It was late in the afternoon, the passengers had their luggage with them and were ready to go. I loaded them up and took off for San Francisco. I delivered them to a hotel in Oakland early the next morning. I noticed that the hotel where I unloaded them also advertised a travel bureau in the lobby.

There were a few flaws in the system because the car owner could collect the money, and after taking the passengers down the road a ways, say he was sleepy and was going to stop at a motel and get some rest. The passengers would get a room, everyone would go to sleep and the driver would take off, drive down the road to the next town and pick up more passengers. If he got caught, his name, license number and description of the car would be given to the police, but the person driving the car might turn out not to be the owner and would get away with money from two or three loads of passengers. In addition, most of the car owners engaged in this business had no insurance and the luggage strapped onto the top or rear of the car wasn't insured either.

After several trips between Oakland and Los Angeles, I got a family going to Fargo, North Dakota. The trip showed me that long hauls paid better than running back and forth between Los Angeles and Oakland. From Fargo, I went to Oklahoma City where, after unloading my passengers in the middle of the night, I parked my car near the railroad tracks and went to sleep. After a couple of hours I was awakened by two policemen who said they were taking me to the police station. I convinced them that I was not a law breaker, but one of them said he was going to keep the small billy club which I had bought in Haiti and had the name of the Martinique carved on it. I told him that if he didn't give it back to me I was going to give him a lot of bad publicity. He gave it back to me, and I left town, but I learned I couldn't park in a deserted place and expect to be unmolested by the police.

The Oldsmobile was getting beat up so I traded it for a Buick. Paul joined me and we made a few long trips taking turns driving. We made deals with the owners of some of the small restaurants along our route to give us something to eat for free if we brought our passengers in. We didn't pay for many of our meals.

We made a trip to Houston, Texas, and while we were there, I went to see Father. He was having a tough time. The club that he and his friend were promoting wasn't making much headway. While we were talking I casually asked if he knew anybody in the steamship business who could give me a job on a ship. The long distance driving was wearing me out. He picked up the phone and after a few minutes talking turned to me and asked if I would be interested in a trip to North Africa and Italy on a Hog Island ship sailing in two days. I thought about the offer for two seconds before I said, "Thanks, I'll take it."

The name of the ship was the Liberty Bell, and after parking my car in Father's garage, I joined the ship in Galveston.

Chapter Three

The Albuquerque Flyer Express

I signed on as an ordinary seaman at $47.50 per month. The ship was operated by Lykes Brothers Steamship Co., and had a two watch system. We worked twelve hour days instead of eight (on a three watch system). When I joined the ship, Paul left for southern California, where his grandparents lived. The Liberty Bell stopped in New Orleans and Tampa before heading for Oran in North Africa.

After a few days in Oran we went to Algiers where one of my shipmates and I went ashore. We visited the Casbah, the native quarter made famous by a movie. We were advised by the ships agent never to go into the Casbah unless there were at least three in the party. I bought a fancy dagger, which I still have, and both of us were solicited by local women.

At our next port, Genoa, Italy, we stayed to unload cargo for about three weeks. The exchange rate for the American dollar was very good and we found we could enjoy a five-course dinner in a fancy restaurant on our measly earnings. The Dixie Home Bar at the harbor became our headquarters when we went ashore. The name was designed to attract the sailors from the ships whose home port was in the southern U.S. Our final port of discharge was Venice with its Grand Canal, an attraction for tourists from all over the world. On my return to the U.S. I decided to stay on for another trip, which, according to my discharge, ended on March 28, 1933.

After sailing from Venice on the second trip, one of the engine room gang got sick with pneumonia accompanied by a high fever. We visited him daily, but we had no doctor aboard so we didn't know how serious his sickness was. As we approached Gibraltar, we asked the captain to stop and put the sick man in a hospital where he could get medical attention. Instead, the captain radioed the owners and told them about the sick crew member. They told him to keep going, because the ship would lose a cargo if it didn't get back to New Orleans on time.

The next night, the seaman died. The captain was ordered to put the body ashore for burial at Funchal on the island of Madeira. We arrived early in the morning and I had to admit, in spite of the solemn occasion, it was a beautiful little town on an interesting island. An undertaker came aboard and put the body in a metal casket which was soldered shut before being taken ashore. We told the captain that we wanted to go ashore and see the burial place, but he only allowed ashore the men who were not on watch. We wanted an opportunity to, at least, have a drink to ease our sorrows, but the local bar wouldn't accept American money because it was during the U.S. bank holiday. We resorted to a money-changer who only offered us half the usual exchange rate. We had no choice so we took what we could get.

The third mate was with us to make sure we returned when we had seen the burial plot but he participated in our attempt to drown our sorrow. As we sat drinking, the American Consul showed up with three armed police and ordered us to return to the ship immediately or be put in jail. We knew that our day ashore was over, so took the waiting shore boat back to the Liberty Bell. The ship was our home and looked pretty good to us after we thought about the kind of quarters we would have had in the native prison. The captain showed us his displeasure by logging us for disobeying orders. I reminded him that we were back in time to stand our watch and that he could only log our pay if we missed work or damaged the ship. He wasn't swayed by my logic and logged us anyway.

I left the ship in New Orleans, and since I had enough time in as ordinary seaman I went to the office of the Shipping Commissioner to take the examination for able bodied seaman. If I passed the examination, I could work as an able bodied seaman at a higher wage. The office manager said that they were no longer giving the examination because there were thousands of unemployed seamen in every port. If a ship needed an ordinary seaman there were plenty of able bodied seamen who would be glad to have the job. I decided that although I enjoyed going to sea, I would concentrate on something else for the time being.

At my grandmother's house in Houston I found out that my father was away. There was practically no food in the house and my Buick had been given to the man who held the mortgage on the house, to prevent foreclosure. The car was broken down so he let me have it but I had to pay a repair bill before I could get it.

I took my car to a mechanic who fixed it enough that I could trade it in on another used car. Since I intended to go back into the "travel bureau" business, and I could make more profit with a seven passenger car, I bought one that was in apparently good condition. I got a phone call from Paul, who said his father got him a job with an insurance company but it wouldn't start for several months. He asked if he could join me until he started his new job. I was agreeable to it, because one of us could drive while the other slept. We could drive night and day, even though sleeping while sitting in the small jump seat might be uncomfortable and difficult. Before we left I filled up my grandmother's kitchen with enough food to last her until my father returned.

That year the World Fair was held in Chicago and there was a lot of travel between Chicago and the West Coast. We took a full load from Los Angeles to Chicago. We wanted to see the fair but instead of paying admission, we tried to save some money by climbing over the fence. The first time when we went over the fence a cop was waiting there for us and we were escorted out the front gate. The second time we made it without getting caught, and spent the afternoon and evening exploring the interesting exhibits.

Paul had never been to New York City and I thought it would be fun to see it again so we took a load to New York City. We spent a few days there, then returned to Chicago. Back in Chicago Paul got word that his job was ready so he left for Arkansas. Shortly afterwards I got a full load for San Francisco. I was trying to make it non-stop and had been driving all night when, early in the morning, I went to sleep at the wheel. I woke just as we were going over the bank into a ditch. When we hit the bottom of the ditch my six passengers woke screaming and grabbing for the wheel. I got up speed in the ditch and gunned it right up the bank and back on the highway. I kept going until we came to a restaurant. I stopped there, told my passengers to go into the restaurant, get breakfast and stay at least one half hour. "When you return," I instructed them, "Bring me a large cup of black coffee."

I delivered all of them to San Francisco in good condition and my car showed no evidence of the detour I took in the ditch. I had some money in my pocket and needed some rest so I went up to Cottage Hill. Merle's stepfather had rented the place to a family they had known for a long time and Merle was living there with them. He was in love with Mary Farrell, the daughter of the man who was renting the place, but he didn't have a regular job so Mary's father wasn't agreeable to the marriage. Merle and

Mary asked me to drive them to Reno for the marriage ceremony and keep it secret for the time being. I agreed, but we were caught in a snow storm and didn't get back until the next day. Merle explained our late return. Mary's father bought the story, and everything went back to normal.

What happened next is even hard for me to believe. My grandfather had some friends of long standing named Farrell, who, strange as it may seem, had a daughter named Mary. The Los Angeles Mary Farrell disappeared from home about a year before the Cottage Hill Mary Farrell was married to Merle. The parents of the Los Angeles Mary Farrell were well to do and hired several detectives to find their daughter. One of these detectives got word that a Mary Farrell had been married in Reno and told the parents of the lost girl. They told him to find their daughter at any cost and report back to them.

One day a strange car drove up in front of Cottage Hill Tavern and stopped. Merle and I were not there, so Merle's father-in-law greeted the strangers and asked what they wanted. They asked if Mary Farrell lived there. Her father said, "Yes, would you like to speak to her?"

When they said yes, he called to her and she came out. The strangers immediately accused her of running away from her poor parents who were in ill health and almost going crazy with grief. She quickly told them that her father was standing right there and that her mother had passed away a year before. They then pulled out a newspaper clipping of Merle and Mary's Reno wedding announcement. Mary had to admit in front of her father, that she was the one who had been married in Reno.

It had become my custom that in the evening when Merle and I came back from cutting wood, I would have a drink with Mr. Farrell. On the day Mr. Farrell found out about the wedding, Mary met us before we could get to the house and told us what had happened. Merle was worried about what Mr. Farrell would do, he was big and tough, having started out in life as a miner. Mr. Farrell ignored Merle and asked me if I was ready for my evening drink. I said that I was and he poured the drinks. After gulping down his drink he looked me in the eye and asked, "What mean, low-down, dirty trick have you played on me?"

I thought that he was accusing me of marrying his daughter, so I told him that it was Merle who had married Mary. He said "Yes I know but you took them to Reno in your car." With that he stood and took a wild swing at me which I managed to dodge and his fist hit the glass of the door behind me, breaking the glass and cutting his hand.

The next morning I drove to Sacramento to find Andy, the man who helped me get the job at the still. He was working for an elevator company installing elevators and working with architects who designed buildings with elevators. Andy and his wife really liked my seven passenger Buick so although I was one month behind on the payments, I offered my equity in trade for their old Pontiac coupe.

I called my grandfather in Los Angeles and he told me that mother had called with good news. An old friend of the family in Minton, Nebraska told her that his brother owned the West Oregon Lumber Company, and would give me a job if I wanted one.

I headed my Pontiac for Linton, Oregon, just outside Portland on the Willamette River. I arrived late in Portland, and got a room in an inexpensive hotel near the port. The next morning I went to the West Oregon Lumber Company and asked to see the president. I only waited a few minutes before I was escorted into his office. He asked me where I had stayed the night before. When I told him, he gave me a lecture about the evils of associating with the no good, International Workers of the World members who were trying to destroy our way of life, attempting to overthrow capitalism in favor of communism.

I told him that I was tired when I arrived late in Portland the night before and had gone to bed rather than talk to any members of the IWW. With that he called his foreman and told him to put me to work in the planing mill. The noise in the planing mill was so loud, it was impossible to talk in a normal voice and be understood. The lumber came through the planing machine in various lengths and my job was to stack it in piles of the same length. In order to keep up with the planing machines I had to judge the length in one look, then put the piece on a pile of the same length. I had to keep up with the machines or the pieces would pile up at the end of the conveyor.

A lot of the people who worked in the mill lived in company houses and bought all their food from the company store adjacent to the mill. During the summer they were able to pay off the debts they accumulated during the winter when they didn't work regularly. In the winter when the mill received an order they would blow the whistle and the employees would hurry to the mill and start work as soon as the lumber began coming through. Three quarters of the time they were in debt to the mill, they could never quit their jobs and were practically prisoners. They all lived in rows of company houses and appeared content. There were many who, because of the nature of their work, had lost fingers, hands, or arms in the machinery.

When winter approached work was cut down, and we worked shorter days. After a couple of months we were told to stay home until the whistle blew. When the whistle blew, we went to work, when the whistle blew again, we went home. The order was complete.

I lived in a boarding house with several others who worked in the mill. My Pontiac coupe had a rumble seat so I took them to work at the mill every day. When the work at the West Oregon Lumber Company slacked off two of my riders began talking about going to the Coos Bay Lumber Company where one of them had worked before. I was spending more money than I was making so I decided it was time to move on. When I told my two riders I was leaving they asked for a ride to Coos Bay. We took off the next morning, I for Los Angeles and they for Coos Bay.

My grandfather was glad to see me because he was still living alone. I decided to stay and look for work in Los Angeles. Mother's cousin was married to a man who owned a lumber company in Los Angeles with yards all around southern California. I called him first thinking I might be of some value since I had worked in the planing mill of the West Oregon Lumber Co. Unfortunately he had all the workers he needed. I had read some ads in the paper asking for owner-drivers to work for a new truck line called the Albuquerque Flyer Express, starting up between Los Angeles and Albuquerque, New Mexico. The owner-driver was paid a percentage of the freight charges that the cargo earned. I took my Pontiac coupe to the GMC truck dealer and asked if he would take it as down payment, but he said no.

My grandfather talked to the operators of the Albuquerque Flyer Express, Nick Glaviano and his brother-in-law, Bruno Guardia, and was convinced it was a good deal. He put up the difference and I bought the truck.

I needed a freight body on my new truck, and gasoline tanks large enough to eliminate the necessity of buying gasoline in New Mexico and Arizona. Nick and Bruno badly needed another truck, so they built the freight body and installed two extra gas tanks made out of old water heaters which had been cut in two, sandblasted inside, then welded back together. Bruno rode with me on my first trip, we took a full load to Flagstaff, Arizona, then returned empty to Los Angeles. I was all right on the trip out but I needed enough back haul to pay for the return trip. If I had another driver with me, I could make round trips without stopping (except to load and unload cargo). One driver could sleep while the other kept the truck moving. I called Paul, his job selling insurance had petered out and he was glad to have some work.

We enjoyed being out on the road and driving through the beautiful desert country. The other trucks were owned by the company and the drivers hired. On the other hand I was out to make as much money as I could, and getting cargo to haul back to Los Angeles was the way to do it. In a short time I had lined up enough cargo to keep me at least half loaded coming back.

This was during the early days of the long distance trucking business. Any one could start a truck line and haul freight to any destination in the United States without a license from the Interstate Commerce Commission. With a truck, a driver, and shippers to fill up the truck with freight, anyone could haul freight. It wasn't against the law to charge any rate, or charge one shipper a lower rate for larger quantities. When shippers called asking for rates on cargo we had not handled before, we told them that our rate clerk was out of the office for a few minutes and would call back. We asked the railroad for their current rate on the specific cargo, reduced it by ten percent, and quoted it to the customer. We learned from experience that the railroad could handle some light bulky freight at a lower rate than a truck line and still make a profit. On the other hand trucks could deliver small quantities directly to a retail store while railroads could only unload on rails.

The city of Los Angeles was a natural supply center for the country between the Arizona border and Albuquerque. The towns we served were mostly along old Highway 66 en route to Albuquerque. We handled a lot of freight for Babbitt Bros. and Arizona Wholesale Grocers in Flagstaff.

We started our route at the end of the day, leaving Los Angeles, and driving all night to unload our first shipments at Prescott, Ashfork or Williams, Arizona early the next morning. In the afternoon we typically got as far as Winslow and Holbrook.

The second morning we unloaded in Gallup or Albuquerque, although sometimes we turned around at Holbrook and returned to Los Angeles. I developed a backhaul that consisted of empty drums for the oil companies supplying the service stations, tires from the Greyhound bus terminals being returned to Los Angeles for re-treading, and engines from Ford dealerships being returned to the Ford plant in Long Beach for rebuilding. I also worked out a deal with a copper smelter in Jerome, Arizona which shipped copper ingots to France. The smelter ran 24 hours a day so we could pick up any quantity in the middle of the night and deliver it on our return trip to the Port of Los Angeles or Long Beach.

It was my first experience soliciting freight and I found out that the most important thing was to keep on schedule. The shippers could always rely on me.

As Nick and Bruno prospered they continued to put more and more trucks on the run which decreased my ability to be fully loaded on the return trip. When there were five trucks soliciting backhaul individually my share declined, and to make matters worse, the new drivers cut the rates. One afternoon I was loading for Arizona at about 4 P.M., I didn't have my minimum of 10,000 lbs., and although there was supposed to be more freight coming in I saw no sign of it. Finally Nick (who was Sicilian with a hot temper) told me to secure my freight and take off. I called his attention to the contract that I had with him which guaranteed me a minimum of 10,000 lbs. before I was obligated to go anywhere. "Well," he said, "you have got to be flexible."

I told him there was no flexibility in my contract. He told the men who loaded the trucks to unload my truck. When the truck was empty I went home.

The next morning at 9 A.M., Nick called me. He said that if I returned, he would give me a full load. A lot of freight had come in early that morning and there were no other trucks available. I knew then it was time for me to get out of the business. I put an ad in the paper offering my truck and contract for sale. Two prospects showed up and they wanted the deal but said I must take them with me on a trip to show them the route. At the end of the trip one of them was sold but the other wanted out. Nick offered to finance the deal since the remaining buyer didn't have enough money to do it alone. I'd been driving back and forth for over a year with no vacation or time off so my first reaction was one of relief.

I had a relative who owned a printing shop and offered me a job there. After being on the truck for over a year outdoors doing heavy work and with never a dull moment the printing shop was, to say the least, boring. The owner had presses that could print clear plastic wrappers for spaghetti and macaroni and fancy Christmas wrapping paper. I stood beside a table for hours sorting the stuff, pulling it out from the presses and trying to get the presses running again when they jammed. On the way to and from work I stopped by the truck terminal to talk with the drivers and occasionally Nick and Bruno. On one occasion there was a truck loaded and ready to go to Arizona but no one to drive it. Nick came out and said "How would you like to take that truck to Flagstaff and back?"

It didn't take me more than a second to say "I am on my way." On the return trip I thought about what I was going to do back at the printing plant. When I walked in, everyone greeted me and asked where I'd been. I apologized to the owner and explained what happened but he said, "Don't worry about it, we didn't need you."

The next time I stopped by the truck line office Nick called me in to the dock. He told me he had hired a manager for the Albuquerque office but he wasn't getting any results. He asked if I'd be interested in taking over the office on a commission basis. I quit my printing job and drove to Albuquerque. It was spring of 1935. After a few months in Albuquerque Nick called to tell me he was going to have to take me off the commission salary deal because I was making more than he and Bruno. He said that if I didn't agree to a salary, he would have to replace me. It was the first time I had the opportunity to run things the way I wanted without any arguments or suggestions. I wasn't going to give it up for a few dollars one way or the other. I enjoyed myself so much I probably would have stayed with no salary.

We had two competitors; the Santa Fe Railroad, and the truck line for which Nick and Bruno worked before they started their business. I wasn't concerned, I scouted around Albuquerque for new accounts.

The Anchor Liquor Company had started in Albuquerque right after prohibition ended. Anchor had about 75% of the wholesale liquor business in Albuquerque. I watched truckload after truckload arriving on the Los Angeles Albuquerque Express line trucks and vowed I was going to get that account. My chance came when Nick told me to rent a warehouse building on the outskirts of the town because we needed an office with warehouse space to accumulate freight for outbound trucks. I also got a pick up truck and driver. I rented a building from Anchor Liquor with the understanding that they would route their cargo from Los Angeles on our trucks.

I had been going with a girl who was a reporter for one of the Albuquerque daily papers and she arranged a nice story which contained good publicity for us with the headline "Albuquerque Flyer Express Expands Operations in New Quarters on New York Street." Everything was going well. I had secretarial help and my own pick up and delivery truck and driver. My secretary and pickup driver had both lived in Albuquerque for a long time and would bring me leads every day about who was shipping to or receiving freight from Los Angeles. My secretary's father made and sold headstones for graves, and received all his stone on the Albuquerque Flyer Express.

We were handling double the amount of cargo in and out of Albuquerque, and I was happy with my job, even a year later. But a letter from Nick changed everything. Nick didn't want more than one driver on the trucks anymore. To him it meant more money for the company, since he would only have to pay one driver to haul the same amount of freight, but to us it meant that we wouldn't be able to maintain our delivery schedule. With two drivers, we could make a straight shot, without sleeping along the way, but if only one driver took each route, he'd have to stop to sleep. I guaranteed second morning delivery in Albuquerque, and I'd lose shippers if I couldn't guarantee my shipments. I should have been more calm, but I got carried away when I answered Nick's letter. It took ten days for Nick to reply—with the name of the man who was hired to replace me, Al Russell. Nick asked me to introduce the man to my customers and prepare a final accounting before turning over the office.

I told the manager of a competing line that I was looking for a job. He said he would get back to me, and I didn't expect to hear from him again, but the next day he told me I could run their new Flagstaff office.

Everything was checked out, and my accounting was accepted in Los Angeles, so I turned over the Albuquerque office to Al. When I arrived in Los Angeles a few days later, I went to see Nick. He was very friendly, told me that his accountant said the Albuquerque office accounts had checked out to the penny. Still in an affable mood, he asked me to continue to work for the Albuquerque Flyer as traffic manager in Los Angeles. Further, he said that while I was in Albuquerque the westbound freight volume almost overtook the eastbound; everyone thought it was impossible. However, the revenue from the eastbound freight was substantially higher.

I told Nick I would consider the traffic manager position, providing he wouldn't force the drivers to do their routes alone. Fortunately, he had already seen the error of his decision, and decided not to go ahead with the plan.

I felt pretty good, my services were in demand, both of the truck lines running between Los Angeles and Albuquerque wanted me to work for them. I decided to take a few days off and let them wait. In considering the matter it became clear to me that Nick and I had a good working relationship.

Nick was vicious when angered, but easily calmed by his wife. He got along well with people who were honest and hard-working. He had more physical energy than anyone I have ever known. He'd work all day in the office, then spend the evening and part of the night repairing a truck engine or building a truck body. On the two occasions when he caught someone stealing, he took them behind the office and beat them up so badly they had to stay home for a week. I knew Nick came up with some unrealistic ideas, but now I felt confident that I could talk him out of them if I persisted.

On the other hand, I didn't know anything about the owner of the competing line. I didn't know if he'd trust me to run things my way or force me to play by his rules. I decided to go back to work for Nick.

I heard that one of Nick's former truck drivers was selling cars in Huntington Park, so I went to see him and ended up buying a fancy convertible Plymouth from him. He was well known in Prescott because he fell asleep at the wheel as he drove his truck up a long hill into town. He rolled the truck down a canyon, covering the side of the hill with cans of Dutch Cleanser, satisfying the local cleanser demand for the next ten years.

Some people from Wichita came to town and told Nick they were organizing a coast to coast truck line. They wanted to take on the owners of the existing lines as stockholders of the new transcontinental network. They already had an operator who applied for Grandfather rights between Albuquerque and Kansas City via Denver and would join his system with Nick's to provide service between Los Angeles and Kansas City. These people were promoters and snowed Nick under without a protest. The name of the Albuquerque Flyer was changed to Kansas City-Los Angeles Flyer, and Nick ended up with non-voting stock in a company controlled by people who knew nothing about the business—they were stock brokers.

Originally the new Denver office was supposed to come under the jurisdiction of the Wichita office. Six months after they hired a man with no past experience to run the Denver office, he was only getting about 2,000 lbs. a day out of Denver. Nick had a big argument with the promoters. He told them that he wanted to send me to Denver to take charge.

When Nick asked me if I would be willing to take over the Denver office, I said yes. Then he asked how much freight I thought I would be getting out of Denver by the first of January. It was October already, and I had never been in Denver, so I was reluctant to guess. Nick said, "If you are averaging 10,000 lbs. a day by January first I'll buy you any tailor made suit you pick out."

By modern standards 10,000 lbs. seems like a small load, but in those days we were just starting to use semi-trailers between Los Angeles and Albuquerque. 10 to 12,000 lbs. was about standard for a truck with no trailer.

I drove my new Plymouth convertible to Denver and rented a room. The Denver office was in a building owned by a warehousing and storage business whose loading dock and trucks we used for loading and pick ups. The office force consisted of a freight solicitor, a secretary and a manager.

I didn't have much time to get things going in order to collect the new suit from Nick, so right away I fired the so-called freight solicitor and the secretary. I gave the manager two weeks notice, and brought in Dave, a fellow who was active in the Twenty-

Thirty Club in Albuquerque, to stay in the office during the day when I was out calling on freight receivers and shippers.

We had a good system worked out. Dave got the shipping papers from the pickup drivers when they brought the freight to our dock and immediately started typing the freight bills and delivery documents. He also answered the phone and supplied information about our rates and services. Sometimes while I was soliciting, I saw a nice shipment on a dock, and with the shippers consent I would call Dave to tell him to get a truck out there before the shipper changed his mind. I returned to the office at about 4:30 P.M. every day, and both of us would type freight bills and manifests until all the paperwork was ready. Then we woke the driver who slept during the day and the three of us would load the truck.

Usually, by 8 P.M. we were finished for the day, went to dinner and talked over the days successes and failures.

By Christmas I had received the new suit and was loading a truck and sometimes two trucks a day. I had my own pickup truck and driver, the same man that worked for me on the pick up truck in Albuquerque. Nick and Bruno were gradually eased out as the new owners in Wichita found out how to run the business and took over the operation. One by one they fired the people Nick and Bruno had working for them and replaced them with people from the Wichita and Kansas City offices.

I knew that they were ready to get rid of me when my salary check started arriving late. First it was late a day or two, then a week or more. When I complained they said they were losing money and did not have enough cash to pay on time. I let it be known around Denver that I was looking for a job and within ten days I had an offer from Campbell & Speers Freight Forwarding Company. I went to work there at the same salary I had been receiving but my only responsibility was soliciting freight between Denver and Kansas City and from Denver to Oklahoma City. My new employer ran directly from Denver to Kansas City without going through or stopping at Pueblo and Wichita so I had little trouble switching accounts from the Kansas City Los Angeles Flyer to my new employer. The manager of the Denver office was the son of Campbell—the president and owner of the company. He spent most of his time playing poker with the truck drivers so he didn't interfere with what I was doing or, for that matter, know what I was doing. I frequently sent a bunch of routing orders signed by cargo receivers in Denver to Kansas City requesting that all shipments consigned to them be routed over Campbell & Speers.

I asked the office manager of a large wholesale grocery to route his truck shipments out of Kansas City with Campbell & Speers. He pointed to his secretary and said, "Talk to her, she types up the orders." When I asked her about their shipments, she specified Campbell & Speers. She was a nice looking blond and when I asked her for a date she said yes.

A year later I was offered the job of manager of the Campbell & Speers office in Oklahoma City. They told me that the office was not doing very well but that was an understatement. The office wasn't doing anything but unloading the freight sent to them, collecting the freight charges and complaining that they needed more help. The office was small, dirty and in the wrong part of town. The only person who had been there for more than a couple of weeks was the billing clerk.

I moved the office to an old building in the new Civic Center. The owners of the building homesteaded it to foil the efforts of city officials who wanted to condemn the building and tear it down. One of the provisions of the homestead was that the owners must spend the night there at least once a month. The two owners, both in their 80s, came around once a month, went up to the second story where they had a double bed in a vacant area, and spent the night.

The place was ideal for our use, there were openings along one side and in the front where we could back in three trucks at one time. All the trucks coming to Oklahoma City were semi-trailers with at least 20,000 lbs. capacities. We had enough space on the first floor for operations and there was a freight elevator to the second and third floors, where we could store freight when necessary without paying any storage.

Mr. Campbell started in business with the help of the traffic manager for Colgate Palmolive Peet. As a result he practically had a monopoly on their freight from Kansas City to Denver, Minneapolis, St. Louis and Oklahoma City. We sometimes got three truck and trailer loads in one day, but we had to produce back hauls to Kansas City for all those trucks. Before I went down there most of the trucks would go back empty or nearly so. Some commodities were seasonal but we had plenty of storage space to accumulate seasonal product before the season and were ready to ship immediately when the season started. We were soon loading commodities that none of the other truck lines had ever moved by truck. One was poultry feathers packed in sacks, the other was hides from the meat packing houses which required the interior of the truck body to be steam cleaned after discharge. One week-end we loaded five steel oil storage bolted tanks, which had been taken apart, on seven empty trucks with the help of a small truck mounted winch and boom. The Illinois oil field was booming and the Oklahoma field had quieted down.

When the manager of the Tulsa office quit I was instructed to take it over along with the Oklahoma City office. Mr. Campbell was aging, so he let the business run itself. The Kansas City to Oklahoma City route was going great but the rest of the operation was going down hill. I developed a working arrangement with the Houston & North Texas Motor Freight Lines to exchange freight from the Kansas City area to points in Texas at Oklahoma City. They began soliciting northbound cargo to points we served. When I went to the bank one day to cash my salary check, I was surprised when the teller asked me for a deposit before he could cash my check. I was upset because I was planning to get married to Noradene, the nice blond girl who routed the orders for the wholesale grocery in Denver. She had moved to Oklahoma City and was working there.

One afternoon Pin Smith, the manager of the Houston and North Texas Motor Freight Lines, came to my office and told me he had been promoted to take over the Houston office of H. & N.T. Motor Freight. His company had asked him to recommend someone to takeover the Oklahoma City office. He had recommended me and they wanted to know if I would take the job. I told him I would consider it and let him know in the morning. That night I called A. W. Campbell at his home in Kansas City to discuss it with him. He said he was trying to sell what remained of Campbell & Speers Freight Forwarding Company. I told him I was taking the Oklahoma City job with H.& N.T. Motor Freight and he wished me good luck.

The owners of H.& N.T. were also in the warehouse business with a large warehouse in Ft. Worth and another in Dallas. I knew I wouldn't have to worry about whether or not I could cash my salary check. The corporation owned all the trucks and trailers so there was never any arguing with the drivers about whether or not they would take a load. The trucks usually arrived from Dallas early in the morning and parked against the loading dock. The three pick up truck drivers came to work at 7 A.M. and opened the road truck to unload the cargo. I arrived at 8 A.M. and soon after that they left with the pick up trucks to deliver cargo. I had an office manager and two clerks in the office to answer phones, quote rates and do the billing and manifesting. I spent a good part of my time calling on shippers and receivers of freight, coordinating the office work and handling of the freight.

*Abbott as terminal manager, Houston & North Texas
Motor Freight Lines, Oklahoma City, 1941.*

Everything went well except that Noradene gave up waiting
for me and went to Wink, Texas where her sister lived. I was so
busy working for H. & N.T. that I did not have time to think
much about it.

The traffic manager for Black, Sivalls & Bryson, one of my
regular freight sources, graduated from night law school and
had passed the Oklahoma Bar examination. I was interested in
law, but I told him I had not graduated from Andover and
doubted I could be admitted to law school. He told me all I had
to do was apply to the Board of Bar Examiners and they would in-

terview me. If, in their opinion, my business experience made up for the lack of formal education, I could attend law school in Oklahoma and take the bar exam when I had satisfactorily completed four years.

When the next Oklahoma City College of Law class formed I was a student and enjoying it. My grandfather had been a charter member of the American Bar Association and was involved in some history making cases in Nebraska. Not long after I had started law school I decided to go to Wink, Texas to marry Noradene. It was a long drive across west Texas from Oklahoma City and when I arrived all I could do was sleep. We had an appointment with a Justice of the Peace for the wedding ceremony. When the ceremony was over we were on our way back to Oklahoma City. I drove as far as Abilene and then we stopped and got a room. We were a little late getting back but no one seemed to object. Back in Oklahoma City I continued working for H. & N.T. and going to law school. I got a break when the truck drivers union called a strike on us and the owners of the business wouldn't negotiate. Instead they laid off everyone except the managers, put the trucks in storage, and wouldn't talk to anyone. The owners decided to wait to negotiate and let the union get a little bit hungry. I never missed a day's pay and my wife, Noradene, went to work for a food broker in Oklahoma City right after we returned from Wink, Texas.

After about three months the truck drivers decided to come back to work and two of the three clerks also returned. I had to hire one new clerk and we were ready to go. Mine was the only terminal on the line whose freight volume the first month after the strike was, at exactly the same level as that of the last month before the strike. Some of my best customers tried to make me look good by giving me more than my share of shipments into the territory we served to compensate for the additional freight my competitors had handled while we were on strike.

About this time I heard from Paul, now working as a scaler for a logging company in Idaho. He invited me to come to Idaho and do some fishing when I took my vacation. We hiked through the Idaho primitive area and fished in the streams and rivers. Wherever we threw our lines into the water, we caught fish.

As the months went by the war in Europe came closer as we heard more and more about it. Everyone was planning in which service they would enlist in order to get the best deal. With this in mind I went to the airport outside Oklahoma City for flying lessons. My first lesson was in an old, open cockpit Stearman with a radial engine and streaks of oil along the fuselage from the engine to the tail. The instructor handed me a leather helmet, told me to put it on and started walking out to the plane.

At the plane he said, "I'll control the plane on take off and when we get to a safe altitude I'll hold up my hand. That is the signal for you to take the control stick. We'll be over a highway intersection when you take the controls, and I want you to fly figure eights over the intersection until I hold up my hand again. When I hold up my hand release the controls to me." We took off, and when he raised his hand, I flew figure eights over the highway. After a few minutes I learned to maintain my altitude and fly in a good figure eight. When he raised his hand, I released the controls and he landed the plane.

I took three or four lessons, then one day I went out to the airport and found my teacher sitting in his office looking glum. He told me that one of his students had crashed the plane in a corn field and there would be no more lessons until he got another plane. For the moment, I gave up my imagined role as a bomber pilot and started thinking about the navy since I had quite a lot of experience at sea.

The Merchant Marine had an officers school but entrance requirements would make it necessary for me to serve additional time as a seaman before I would be eligible.

I told my employer that I was trying to get a pilot's license so I would be assured of a commission in case I was drafted, and he looked upset. He told me not to worry about being drafted, he had enough political power in Texas to protect me from the draft, and besides, transportation within the United States was critical to the war effort. My anxiety about being drafted was relieved, but I still would rather take my chances in the war if I could be assured of receiving a commission.

I was sitting at my desk at home one Sunday studying my law books when a friend called to ask if I had been listening to the radio.

"No, I've been studying." I said.

"The Japanese have attacked Pearl Harbor, and sunk most of our navy," he said.

"You're kidding, right?" I said.

"Go turn on your radio," he said, and hung up.

When I turned the radio on, I realized it had happened. The next morning I called the head office in Dallas. "Don't worry," they said. "Transportation is very important to the war effort. All you have to do is keep up your good work. We'll protect you from the draft."

A few days later, I received a letter from mother in Wellesley, Massachusetts. Betty had married Frederick Adams, the son of cousins of the Roosevelts, and she and her husband and in-laws had been weekend guests at the White House on December 5th, 6th and 7th. Mother forwarded Betty's letter on to me to read.

Dear Mother,

Shall I tell you all about the White House? The first thing that impressed me was the facade and portico. The upstairs was like a barn, compared to the really beautiful downstairs dining and reception rooms. My next impression was the number and omnipresence of guards, aides, ushers, butlers, maids, police and secret service. Freddy laughingly said it made him feel as though all the Secret Service in Washington were notified whenever we went downstairs.

Friday night there was nobody there but family and Harry Hopkins. The President was told of my approach, "Here is the new member of the family." He opened his arms wide and greeted me with a hug and a big kiss. I wasn't a bit scared or even self-conscious after the first moment I saw him. He was, I knew, the dearest, wisest, kindest, jolliest person I ever met. I just sat there thinking what fun he was and how I liked him, unable to realize that he carried the responsibilities he does. Conversation flowed rapidly from Japs, to Campobello, to priorities, to sailing, to cocktails, to education, to the West Indies, etc. Prexy as Freddy called the President, dominated the room with his big personality, quick fluid change of expression and mood, compelling voice, strength and beauty of mind and speech. He was so easy and natural, it seemed no different from meeting any other man in his library in a smoking jacket and sitting down for a cocktail with him. We had dinner Friday night with 150 or so people whom Mrs. Roosevelt wanted to interest in the Open Road, a travel education project in connection with colleges. An aide came while we were at cocktails, bowed and said, "Excuse me, I am sorry to interrupt the President, but it is time for the President's guests to go down to dinner." Prexy's answer was, "Goodness! I won't let you go yet, why you haven't had your second cocktail." Then to the aide, "I'll send them down in time." As he filled Mr. A's (that's my father- in-law, Mr. Adams) glass up, Prexy said, "You can't go down and talk to uplifters until you have gotten uplifted yourself." We had another drink and a good time for twenty minutes, then went down in plenty of time. The Friday night dinner was good, we all sat together at a small family table with lots of other small tables around. Louise Rainer and Helena Rubinstein both impressed me to be all I expected each of them to be. When Mrs. R spoke she was really lovely looking, she is gay, capable, warm and a lovely person. After dinner speeches were dull and Freddy and I skipped out early.

Saturday morning was breakfast in bed—We felt very grand in the four poster in the "Queen's Room"—and a thrilling morning at the Mellon Gallery. Lunch with about fifteen people at the White House was most exciting: Mrs. R, whom I decided again was lovely all over, enhanced by a touch of childlike, nervous laughter and awkwardness, only enough to be human and lovable, was really made beautiful by speech, lively interest in all things, and sound judgment, perfectly expressed.

Saturday evening was cocktails with the President again—just as much fun—then to dinner, a small one of about fifty people. I sat next to Jimmy Roosevelt, who struck me as charming, natural, friendly, good at conversation and full of interesting stories. His new wife, whom I liked tremendously sat next to Freddy.

Sunday—late sleep—quiet over the house. When we returned from a visit with friends for the day, Mr. A was pacing the hall before the President's library as we flew by to our room. His appointment with the President was overdue and he said, "Those damn little Japs are still in there." As it was dinner time he came down with us.

After dinner Mr. A skipped coffee and went right upstairs to see if he could talk to the President. In about half an hour, Freddy and I were on our way to our room when we met Mr. A coming out of the library. I watched him close the door behind him, tense and almost shaking. He waited for us to come up close then he said, "The war is on—Japan is attacking Pearl

Harbor." A few quick questions and answers about it, then Mr. A went into his room, quite unstrung.

Freddy and I stood in that large, silent, empty, Sunday afternoon- calm hallway, outside the President's library door, with the full meaning of war for the United States crashing into our senses. We reached for each other half-trying to protect and half-seeking refuge. When I looked up, my eyes fell on the title of a book in the long rows of shelves that line the hall: "Blood, Sweat and Tears."

We went to our room and finished packing, and were back in the hall no more than ten minutes later to find it swarming with activity. Knox, Stimson, Marshall, Hopkins, and scores of others, all gathered outside the library door, tense, hushed, excited whispering. Stephen Early sent out the news to the press and radio from a desk right in the hall. We listened to Mr. A's story. He had gone in to see the President just after the news of the attack, heard him phone Knox and Stimson, only Hull had been phoned before Mr. A's entry. They had their talk, (Mr. A and the President) about allocations and Uncle Carl Adams heading a committee. While Mr. A and the President were still discussing, Litvinoff phoned from New York and wished to pay respects and present credentials at earliest convenience. The President made an appointment with him and told him to tell his government that Japan had opened fire. Mr. A said the answer from the other end of the wire was a long silence, then a few words before the receiver fell.

The upstairs hall was electric - in ten minutes we watched it change from a peaceful home into the most important executive office in the world. There was a sense of relief - almost hushed exaltation - for the end of the long period of doubt, discussion, dissension, watching, waiting, sitting on the proverbial powder keg: for the event that made the one road so clear - when you know exactly what you have to do - there is a certain thrill in getting about it - no matter how grim the task. And those boys realize fully what war means to every family and every person.

When we emerged from the front door, we found ourselves faced with solid phalanxes of news cameras and flash bulbs on each side of the narrow lane to the car. You should have seen what a disappointment we were to them! But the layfolks on the sidewalks snapped us like mad, and Mr. A's remark that if we never do anything else, we will live in many a family album, is a fitting one on which to end this letter.

In spite of the assurances from my employers that they could protect me from the draft it was not long before I received "Greetings from the President." I was drafted. I asked for a meeting with the draft board and a date was set for a few weeks later. When I was allowed to speak to the draft board, I told them that the Merchant Marine was advertising for experienced seamen to man the laid up ships that were being fitted out for war service. Further, I showed them my discharges from the vessels on which I had been employed. One of the female members of the draft board looked at me like she didn't know what I was talking about. She said, "Do you mean you want to join the Marines?"

After more discussion I told them that I had to go to Galveston, get my seaman's papers brought up to date, get a physical, and take an examination for an able bodied seaman's certificate. I also had to join the seamen's union and then wait in the shipping hall until an able bodied seaman's job was called. They passed the newspaper ads around so everybody could read them, then they asked me how long it would take me to be ready for a job, if one was called. I said I would like to have a month because I had to find a place for my wife to live while I was gone.

They told me I had two weeks to either prove to them I was in the Merchant Marine or report for the draft.

I notified H. & N.T. that I was leaving, and my wife and I drove to Galveston. I got all my papers in order, said good bye to my wife and at 3:30 in the afternoon on the Friday before Labor Day went up to the union shipping hall. It was my last day to get on a ship. I told the dispatcher that if he did not get me on a ship that day I would be drafted into the army. At about 4:30, a bo'sun from an army transport ship in the shipyard came into the shipping hall. The dispatcher told him my plight, "Surely you can use one more man?" he said. It worked and I missed being drafted by about ten minutes.

Chapter Four ⚓

Narrowly Escaping the Draft

I boarded a dry-docked Eastern Steamship Line passenger ship called the Evangeline, which was in the process of being converted to a troop transport. There were only five crew members on board since, with the shipyard workers all over the place, we didn't have much to do or any place in which to do it. In addition to our salaries we were paid for hotel rooms ashore and the cost of eating in restaurants. We all slept in passenger cabins and took our meals ashore.

Before being converted to an army transport, the Evangeline had carried passengers between Boston and New York. According to my discharge, I signed on Sept. 2 1942, almost ten years since my last trip, which was on the Liberty Bell. It took a little time for me to adjust.

Most of the seamen had graduated from a maritime training school, but had little experience on a seagoing ship. When we were finally going to be moved from dry dock to a regular dock, the inexperience of the crew became apparent. Because I was older and had some actual sea-going experience, the captain who had already been torpedoed, appointed me as chief quartermaster. I relieved the other quartermasters in the middle of their watch for a twenty-minute coffee break and steered whenever we left or entered port.

The chief mate was a retired admiralty attorney who wanted to help the war effort but was too old and nervous to be going to sea. The second mate had lost his last ship which burned in Australia. The third mate was on his first voyage as an officer. I had a cabin right below the bridge so I was always available if they needed me on the bridge. We joined a convoy outside of Galveston and before all the ships were in position we got a submarine alert from one of the escort vessels. It was early in the war and no one had much experience in convoys so when the escort vessel reported the presence of a submarine the convoy commander hoisted the signal that required the convoy to start a zig zag course. The captains of the ships had little experience running a zig zag course so the result was pandemonium. We narrowly avoided three collisions when finally the zig zagging was called off.

We arrived safely at the entrance to the Mississippi where our captain, on a previous voyage, had been torpedoed so close to shore that he was picked up out of the water by the pilotboat. About twenty minutes after we took the river pilot on board, I was eating breakfast in the crew mess room when a man came from the bridge yelling for me to get up to the bridge immediately. The man steering was unable to keep the ship on course and was zig zagging up the river with the pilot almost out of his mind. I took the wheel on the bridge at 8:30 A.M. and wasn't relieved until we were at the dock in New Orleans at 4:30 P.M.

On the way to New Orleans, I ordered the other helmsmen to stand by and watch me while the pilot was still on board, then I let each one give it a try while I stood by. I wanted to avoid missing breakfast and lunch again.

We loaded stores and a few troops in New Orleans, as well as a captive German submarine crew. "A Streetcar Named Desire" was playing in several movie theaters.

From New Orleans we sailed in convoy to Guantanamo Bay, Cuba, and from there, to Colon, Panama. The harbor and entrance to the canal was covered with barrage balloons to discourage an air attack. We visited all the dives in Colon and thought it would be interesting to take a life boat from the ship, and cross the bay to see the jungle on the other side. We disguised our adventure by telling the captain that the crew needed some lifeboat training. He said we could go but must take one of the officers with us, so we invited the third mate. He was eager to go.

A lifeboat is awkward to handle with oars unless you have an experienced team of rowers. The Evangeline life boat was probably built in about 1932 and had none of the refinements of a more modern one. It was certified to carry 30 people with no engine and all the oars were badly warped. We headed for the other side of the bay and made pretty good time with the wind behind us. It was evening when we finally arrived at our destination, so after a hasty look around at the jungle, we started back.

We struggled to make headway into the wind, worrying about the sun going down. With the war going on there were no small boats allowed on the bay after dark, and a patrol boat, seeing us with no lights, had a right to open fire if we didn't immediately answer a hail. We were struggling along when a beam of light shone on us. It was a patrol vessel, it's gun aimed at us, ready to fire. We called out that we were the life boat off the troop transport Evangeline docked in the harbor. They came alongside and carefully looked us over. We asked them if they would give us a tow to our ship, and they talked among themselves for a few minutes, before giving us a line. They kept their guns aimed at us until we were in sight of the Evangeline. When we came alongside our ship the captain and chief mate were there to greet us. I might add that their greeting wasn't friendly.

Unloading troops is a lot faster than unloading cargo so after a few days we took on passengers, the wives and children of Panama Canal employees being sent back to the US for security reasons. During the passage from Panama to New York there were many liaisons between the female passengers and the ship's officers and crew. The hundreds of unoccupied passenger cabins could be opened with little experience at lock picking. It was good for morale, wartime can be a desperately frightening experience.

Before we arrived at New York my wheelsmen were steering like experts. My only job was to relieve them for twenty minutes in the middle of their watches, but the captain still wanted me to steer when we had a pilot on board.

Upon arriving at New York I had the necessary sea time to qualify for admittance to the Merchant Marine officers school. I passed all the tests and was told to report at the school on January 5th. Betty was living in New York City, mother was still working at Dana Hall, and Charles was living in Washington, D.C., so I split up my holidays between them.

The Merchant Marine officers school was modeled after a military school but we were actually civilians. The first test was one of intelligence, designed to segregate us into groups of the same intellectual ability. We were all in the 6th class (whose numbers ranged from 601 to 608). My group consisted of those who had received the second highest marks on the intelligence test, so we were placed in class #602. There were four of us in each barracks room with four bunks and four desks.

I was elected to write a monthly column in the school paper about things that happened in class 602. We started the course around the first of February 1943 and finished on the last day of May the same year. My roommates were Bird, Borecky and Carr, all younger than I. I was always the first one up, so I mopped up the snow that came in the window during the night. Bird claimed to be a communist, and Carr was a nice guy, a hard worker. Borecky was the most relaxed and overslept every morning. I told him he was going to have to work harder to pass but he said, "I'll pass—but just barely." Which he did.

The smart guys in 601 caused quite a ruckus one night when they smuggled several girls into their quarters. They dressed the girls in spare uniforms and sneaked them under the fence at the place were we all came in when we were late. They had a few drinks and got noisy, attracting the attention of the MPs who raided their quarters. That was the last we saw of them.

The most difficult courses were celestial navigation and morse code, they took a lot of concentration. After the first month we all relaxed a little and took some time off on weekends to go visit New York or Boston. The day of the final exam finally came and we started early. My three roommates all passed, even Borecky who, as he predicted, just barely passed. Only one cadet of class 602 flunked. I didn't want to take any chances, so I stayed in the room and went over everything once more just to be sure. I got the highest mark of anyone in the school. They tried to persuade me to stay at the school and teach but I couldn't wait to get to sea.

The next day I flew back to Oklahoma City to spend a week with my wife. From there I went to New Orleans and looked for a ship. The Army Transport Service, for whom I worked when I was on the "Evangeline," said they would put me on the payroll immediately if I would agree to sail on their vessels. I agreed.

After a week, at the request of the War Shipping Administration, I was told to report to the Josephine Lawrence in Mobile, Alabama. The Lawrence was loaded but unable to sail for lack of officers.

I rode all day and well into the night on a dirty, hot, slow train to Mobile. The next morning I dressed in my new uniform and went to the Josephine Lawrence. It looked like what the West Coast called a lumber schooner. The house and bridge were on the stern with nothing from the bridge to the bow except space for loading lumber. One mast was right in front of the bridge and the other at the bow. There were two cargo booms at the base of each mast. The ship looked like it had been built at the turn of the century. Unlike the traditional lumber schooner, the hull was steel instead of wood but only 250 ft. long.

After awhile another seaman showed up, then a third man (I was the only one in uniform) who said he just got an original second mate's license. There were two others, dressed in dirty dungarees, waiting for the port captain. The few crew men running around on the ship behaved as thought they were at least partially under the influence of alcohol.

The port captain finally showed up. There was some confusion between two of the prospective mates about who was going to sign on as second mate and who would go as chief mate. The man who had an original second mate's license had just received it, but had no experience navigating. The other man had been in jail for stealing cargo, but was released on the condition that he would go to sea on the first ship looking for a mate. After listening to the conversation for a while I stepped up and said "I will take anything from captain to third mate. Let's get this thing settled."

At that the port captain pointed his finger at me and said, "You're going as third mate!"

The man recently released from jail became the second mate and the one with the original second mate's license became the chief mate. The die was cast. I asked the man at the gangway where the third mate's cabin was and he said, "What do you mean cabin? The third mate's bunk is at the end of the passageway."

This was quite a "come down" from the Evangeline. We loaded 60 ft. pilings on deck and various supplies below deck for the new navy base under construction in Trinidad. We went in convoy to Guantanamo Bay in Cuba, reorganized the convoy, then continued to Trinidad. There was nothing for me to do while we were in port so the gunnery officer took me to the navy BOQ and a beautiful beach on the east coast of the island frequented by navy nurses. When the ship was ready to return to Mobile I rejoined.

My second trip on the Josephine Lawrence was pretty much a repetition of the first except for one night; we fought against a head wind which reduced our speed. We were going as fast as we could but trailed the convoy about as far as a German submarine would trail before attacking. A navy plane above us, watching for submarines following the convoy, dropped a flare to identify us, and lit up the area as if it were daytime. It was quite a shock, as we were on the bridge in pitch darkness, to be suddenly flooded with brilliant light. The captain was sound asleep in his cabin below the bridge and when he was awakened by the light of the flare he came out yelling "Turn off that light!"

Upon our return to Mobile we were told that the Josephine Lawrence would be converted to a floating machine shop. Most of the crew and officers lived in Mobile and left the ship after we were tied up. The port captain asked me to stay aboard that day to receive supplies and answer any questions the new crew might have about the ship. I was supposed to be available from 8 A.M. until 5 P.M., but there was no lunch served because the galley crew had left the ship. I abandoned ship and went to the Masters, Mates & Pilots shipping hall to ask for a third mate's job. They told me there was a Liberty ship, the Duncan U. Fletcher, fully loaded, on its way from Florida which would arrive in Mobile around midnight to refuel and pick up a third mate. The ship was brand new, bound for Puerto Rico.

I boarded the next morning at 6 A.M., found the third mate's quarters and turned in for a nap before I took over the bridge at noon. We were still in Mobile Bay in nice weather. The bo'sun was securing the gangway with the deck crew, when suddenly the bo'sun came running down the deck so he could see the flying bridge and yelled "Man overboard! man overboard!"

I went immediately to the engine room telegraph and rang "STOP." The captain was Italian and quite temperamental. He had heard the engine room telegraph and as he came charging up to the bridge, I was giving turning orders to the helmsman. The men on deck had already thrown about five orange colored life rings over the side, and we immediately dropped two motor life boats over the side, one with the second mate and one with the chief mate in charge. They found the life rings that had been thrown overboard but no sign of the man.

The captain told the radio operator to call the navy base and ask them to send a search plane. The navy said they were sending a training plane with two men aboard. The plane arrived and started flying in circles around the two life boats. Suddenly the plane dove into the ocean and broke into small pieces. The life boats converged at the spot where the plane went down, and we could see them pull the pilots into the boats. We called the navy, told them their plane had crashed and that the pilots had been picked up without apparent injury. The navy asked us to change course and head for Mobile as soon as the rescued pilots were on board. The navy would send a fast crash boat to meet us and pick up the pilots.

The pilots had told our men in the life boats that they each thought the other had the controls when the plane crashed, but when they came aboard our ship they said the controls in the plane jammed and neither could free them.

The captain of the Duncan U. Fletcher was very gloomy and superstitious about losing a man overboard. It was the first time he had lost someone overboard in the ten years he had been master and he thought the ship was very unlucky. He was determined to leave the ship at the first opportunity.

After discharging at San Juan, Puerto Rico, we went to Mayaguez, on the west coast of Puerto Rico to load sugar in bags. The entire under deck capacity of the vessel was full before we sailed.

During the loading operation we dragged anchor in the middle of the night which strengthened the captain's certainty that the ship was "unlucky."

From Mayaguez we went to New York City and loaded landing craft on deck. The captain's request to be taken off the unlucky ship was granted and we were given a Norwegian captain. He'd been going to sea all his life, and had twenty years experience as a captain. He didn't talk much, but when he gave an order the crew promptly responded. On the last vessel he had commanded, a drunken member of the crew came at him with a fire ax. He waited until the attacker was within hitting range, then shot and killed him with his revolver.

When we sailed from New York after taking on a deck load of landing craft, we weren't told our destination, as was the custom in wartime. We joined a large convoy with an aircraft carrier in the center and it was obvious we were going to be crossing the north Atlantic in the winter with the added threat of bad weather. It was September of 1943.

I had a new experience on this voyage. We were in the middle of a convoy of about seventy ships in a fog, so thick, that we couldn't see another ship. We kept our position at night by watching the water thrown up by the fog buoy towed by the ship ahead of us.

Keeping a ship in its assigned position in a convoy of up to 100 ships is not always an easy job. It involves constant phone communication with the engine room to speed up or slow down in order to maintain the required safe space between ships.

I was on the 12 to 4 watch on the Duncan U. Fletcher during our transatlantic voyage in convoy from New York to Liverpool. Because of the inexperience of the other two mates, the captain slept only when I was on watch on the bridge from midnight to 4 A.M. and from noon until 4 P.M. The fourth mate had the watch before me from 8 until 12, A.M. and P.M., the captain usually stayed with him until his watch was almost over. As soon as the captain left the bridge, the fourth mate would usually tell the engine room to slow down because he was worried about getting too close to the ship ahead.

When I took over one night, the rest of the convoy was so far ahead I couldn't identify the ship we were supposed to follow. The fourth mate pointed to a ship on the horizon, saying it was the one, so I called the engine room to increase our speed enough to put us close in three hours. When we got close it was obvious I was following the wrong ship. I went up between the columns and found the ship we were supposed to follow. It was three columns over which we had to cross through to reach our position. While I was crossing between ships of the last column the second mate came up to the bridge to relieve me. He couldn't figure out what was going on until I explained it to him, but then he refused to take over until I was in position. Fortunately, we were soon in our column, and the captain was none the wiser. I returned to my cabin with relief, but before I could get to sleep, I was called back to the bridge. The ship behind us was cutting between the columns to regain its position. Lucky for me, the captain didn't come up to the bridge until all the ships were in their assigned places.

It took over thirty days to reach Liverpool because we followed a circuitous route to avoid submarines. The only land we saw was a quick look at one of the Azores through a hole in the fog. Finally, we went up the Mercy River into the port of Liverpool. The English people greeted us, entertained us and thanked us.

We had to be on board the ship during the day in case a failure occurred that required us to replace cargo gear. Evenings we were free, and we usually went straight to the Adelphi Hotel where the American Bar was located.

"Why do you call it the American Bar?" I asked the bartender.

"Because we put ice in the drinks." he responded. British drinks are served at room temperature.

Liverpool had been badly bombed. Four walls was all that was left standing of the customs house, a building that had occupied a city block. Inside, there was only rubble. There was more rubble across the street from the Adelphi Hotel where once a large department store had stood. Empty spaces on either side marked where destroyed buildings had been cleaned up.

After a few evenings ashore we began to get acquainted with some of the natives, and before long they were inviting us to their homes. We had a little trouble getting around in the darkened city, but on almost every corner there was an English policeman to direct us. There were few cabs and the bars closed early, so we sometimes had a long walk back to the ship.

When the vessel was almost empty of cargo, we began to wonder where we would be sent next. The chief engineer had survived one trip to Murmansk and was hoping he wouldn't have to undergo another. He told us that if they installed additional radiators in the cabins it was a sure sign we were going on the Murmansk run.

When they started loading sand ballast in the cargo holds, we heaved a sigh of relief, assuming we were going home. But then they started discharging the sand, and we didn't know what to think. Finally we were told we were going to take part in the invasion of Italy! We figured it would take about two weeks to load the cargo, so we began telling our friends in Liverpool that we wouldn't be around much longer. In spite of the food shortage several of these new friends gave us going-away parties.

The convoy we joined after sailing out of the Mersey River was much larger than the one we had crossing the Atlantic. A storm was brewing as we milled around searching for the column we were supposed to join. As darkness gathered, the wind kept increasing. When we finally got a course and speed we found that the course was directly into the wind, which had risen to more than 60 knots. Like the other Liberty ships in the convoy, we didn't have the power to overcome that kind of wind, so we fell off enough to give us a sufficient speed to steer by. During the night we stayed with two other Liberty ships and one escort vessel. At times, the tremendous seas caused solid water to slam down on the flying bridge, requiring us to duck behind the forward rail and hold on to escape being washed down the deck.

A couple more ships had joined us by morning, and our escort vessel, in contact with the commodore, gave us a course to follow. The storm had nearly blown itself out and ships were scattered all over the area. Other vessels joined us and radio messages indicated that at least two vessels had been sunk by torpedoes.

The next day the escort vessel ordered us to turn to an almost opposite direction in order to join the main body of the convoy by the following day. Joining with the other ships we noted that the convoy we were in numbered fewer vessels than those with which we had originally departed from England.

Before we reached Gibraltar, we were told to notify our gun crew members that a British submarine would be joining our convoy in about two hours. Before we went through the straits of Gibraltar in the middle of the night, all vessels equipped with barrage balloons were ordered to put them up to discourage strafing. One barrage balloon went up in flames putting on quite a show and giving any lurking German plane a bird's eye view of the whole convoy.

We received orders to anchor in Augusta, Sicily, and the rest of the convoy continued on. The bay was full of allied ships waiting for orders and there was very little room left for another vessel. However, our captain was an expert ship handler and squeezed us in. The remains of several German fighter planes along the shore indicated that the invasion of Italy was going well.

Two days later we were ordered to Salerno, Italy which had just been secured by the British Eighth Army. Half of the city had been completely destroyed and many homeless, starving people came to the ship begging for food.

I wanted to see the ancient ruins of Pompeii, so I managed to get a day off, and hitchhiked on military vehicles. At Pompeii, I met a few guides who had survived the invasion by hiding in the ruins.

After discharging at Salerno we were sent to Bizerte, Tunisia. This part of North Africa had been under allied control for some time, so we were curious why we had been sent there. The next day we loaded land mines and high explosive shells. The second mate and I had the following day off so we planned to look for an officers club. A Red Cross girl in a jeep on the dock said she would take us to an officers club. She let us off within a short walk from the club and we asked how we could get back to the ship.

"You do what everyone else does," she said. "If you see an empty jeep and can get it started, drive it back to your ship."

About 7 P.M. we started walking in the direction of, we hoped, our ship. By 8 P.M. we were still walking, more turned around than when we left the club. Finally we saw in the distance what appeared to be a large garage for military vehicles. When we got closer, we noticed that there was a stream between us and the garage. It was a sluggish looking stream with a lot of mud around it. We got across, but not before we had both fallen and got covered with mud.

We saw jeeps and trucks coming and going around the garage, but technically we were civilians and we didn't know whether or not they would help us. We brushed off the mud the best we could and walked into the garage. I didn't know whether to demand a car like I had some authority or beg for help. Still undecided I walked up to the sergeant and said, "Sergeant we have got to have a car to take us to our ship."

He looked at me and said, "What do you mean, got to have one?"

I changed my tune in a hurry. "Sergeant," I said, "our ship is at the dock and we would sure appreciate some transportation. We aren't supposed to be ashore after eight, but we're lost and don't know which way to go."

"That's better," he said, then ordered one of the soldiers to take us to our ship in a command car.

At the Duncan U. Fletcher, the soldier drove up to the gangway and stood at attention after he opened the door for us. Most of the crew watched from along the rail. We made quite an impression.

Our gunnery officer, a navy lieutenant said, "Gee they only gave me a jeep ride when I came back from the Navy Officers Club."

The next day a hospital ship came into port and tied up just ahead of us at about 4 P.M. It had only been tied up for about half an hour when we noticed military vehicles going to the gangway and picking up nurses. First, high ranked officers in their command cars picked up commissioned nurses, then an array of vehicles all the way down to jeeps went to the gangway to collect their dates. Even a few motorcycles and some foot soldiers showed up.

We couldn't find out where we were going to discharge the high explosive shells and land mines we were loading. We weren't taking on a full load, so they spread the cargo out with approximately the same amount in each hold. It looked like an invasion beach would be the destination of our cargo to be discharged in the shortest possible time.

We sailed to the port of Naples, Italy, a few days after it had been taken by the British 8th Army. Two days later, we joined several other Liberty ships anchored in a small bay near the town of Pozzuoli just north of Naples. A couple of hours after we anchored, a small patrol boat started dropping depth charges in the bay. Our captain came out on the wing of the bridge and asked what was going on.

When we asked the officer in charge of the patrol boat, he told us that a swimmer had been seen in the water, and one ship had already been sunk after a swimmer attached a bomb to the bottom. He directed our captain to issue side arms to all deck officers, and if they saw a swimmer, they should shoot without asking any questions.

The next day one of the Liberty ships heaved up their anchor and departed. Two days later we received orders to proceed to the Anzio beachhead under cover of darkness. We had several army LSTs with us to show us the way, and anchored there at sunup. The same Liberty ship that left Pozzuoli two days ahead of us was in two pieces; the bow was on the beach and just the top of the mast stuck out of the water from the stern section. A boat brought army stevedores to unload our cargo, and as the men walked down the deck, a shell exploded alongside the ship.

Seven men were hit by shrapnel and fell on the deck. Blood ran down the deck. We took the injured men to the officers mess and laid them on the tables where we dressed their shrapnel wounds, put them on stretchers and returned them to shore.

Another gang was sent out from shore to unload the explosive cargo, but an enemy gun on shore fired shells near the ship, splattering the side with shrapnel. Periodically one of our planes took off from the beach to spot the gun's location, but as long as the plane was up the gun was silent, and as soon as it came down, a shell exploded beside us. When the shells got too close for the army stevedore's comfort, they were sent back ashore, anticipating the ship's impending destruction.

I suggested to our captain that we heave up anchor and move down the beach a ways. The gun would have to find the range again and we could relax for awhile. The captain agreed and asked for volunteers to operate the anchor windlass on the bow.

The gun stopped firing, as soon as we started moving. We dropped anchor about two miles down the beach. A small power boat with a man standing in the bow approached us from the beach. The boat pulled up near the captain who was on the wing of the bridge, and the man on the bow yelled, "I am in command in this area and I order you to take your ship back to where it was before you moved it. I will take full responsibility for loss of your ship."

"I'm not worried about the ship, sir," the captain replied. "It is the people aboard that I am worried about."

The small boat returned to shore and we discussed what we should do next. Since it was near sundown, we decided to slowly heave up the anchor and take our time going back to our former position. By the time we got back, it would probably be too dark for the enemy to see us, and we could sleep peacefully knowing we had lived another day.

Usually, one or two German bombers would fly over at daybreak and drop a couple of bombs but they didn't land close to us. One morning, after several days of discharging while shells exploded alongside, we received word that if we finished unloading the ship by nightfall, we could sail for Naples. As soon as the army barges were alongside us we started discharging without waiting for the army stevedores. Every crew member not on watch went into the cargo holds and worked very hard all day to get everything out. In the afternoon, even the captain and chief engineer came down to help, and by six we were empty. As darkness fell we were out of the bay, on our way back to Naples, and still alive. We learned afterwards that the gun was mounted on a rail car and moved into a tunnel when allied planes were near.

It was spring time, the mild sun and beautiful days made our return to the U.S. much more comfortable. There were several ships full of German prisoners in our convoy, so we were on alert for German subs. As we sailed close to the coast of Portugal at night, a neutral ship, all lit up, saw us ahead, turned on a powerful search light and raked the entire convoy. If a German submarine had been in the vicinity we would have known it. When we picked up the pilot to come into Baltimore he noticed that the canvas on the flying bridge was torn from shrapnel while we were in Anzio.

After we docked in Baltimore, an FBI agent boarded the ship looking for me. My draft board had told the FBI that I had not reported for the draft. I told him where I had been and what I had been doing ever since I left my job and went back to sea. He was surprised that I had gone through Merchant Marine Officers School because my records didn't show it. I didn't want to be trailed by the FBI again, so I went to navy officer procurement in Baltimore and applied for a reserve commission in the navy.

I had enough time in as third mate, so I enrolled in Merchant Marine Officers School to prepare for a second mate's license examination. It was a two week course, and I called Noradene in Oklahoma City to ask her to join me in Baltimore while I was going to school. She arrived a couple of days later and stayed for two weeks but something wasn't right between us, I guess we had been apart too long.

The upgrading school was easy, I had no trouble with the examination. I received my second mate's license and notified the War Shipping Administration I would be ready to go back to sea as soon as my leave time had expired. I spent my last week of leave with Noradene in Oklahoma City, then flew to New Orleans, ready to go back to sea with the Waterman Steamship Company. Waterman had nothing for me, so I went back to school to learn to maintain a gyrocompass while I waited for a ship. This was part of the second mate's job.

The temperature in New Orleans in the middle of summer was too hot for my comfort. The gyrocompass school had been set up in temporary quarters on the top floor of an old warehouse with no air conditioning. The sun beat down on the roof, making it so hot in the class room that we all fell asleep in the middle of lectures. The teacher had a French horn, and when he saw a student sleeping, he blew the horn by his ear. Just when I was about to take the final examination, I received notice that Waterman had a ship waiting for me in San Diego. Because I'd done so well in class up until then, the instructor gave me my gyrocompass operator's certificate without an examination and I hopped a plane for San Diego.

I signed on as second mate of the Azalea City in San Diego on June 20, 1944. It was a cargo ship converted to a troop transport with bunks installed four layers high in the cargo spaces. They added air ducts to keep the soldiers from being overcome by lack of oxygen. The ship was a C-2 but not a standard one, the standard C-2's were designed by the Maritime Commission, but this one was designed by Waterman Steamship Company and built in a shipyard in Alabama. The engine was a standard C-2 high pressure steam turbine enabling the ship under normal conditions to cruise at 12 knots, but all our special equipment for air conditioning cut our speed to about 10 knots.

It was my first trip as navigation officer. Every day at noon, I recorded the official position of the ship, the days run in nautical miles, the amount of fuel used and the amount of fuel remaining. In addition to the noon position I took star sights at dawn and at sunset if the sky was clear. Sun sights were taken when the sky was clear at about ten in the morning and mid afternoon. My navigation duties kept me busy when I wasn't on watch.

Our first trip was to Saipan, with troops trained to build aircraft runways for B-29 bombers. We carried one lower hold full of dynamite which was to be used for runway construction. We stopped in Eniwetak on Kwajalein Island on the way, and from there we went directly to Saipan, to a dock in Garapan where we unloaded the troops and the dynamite. When all troops and cargo were off the vessel we went out to an anchorage. We were still at the anchorage a couple of nights later, when at 2 A.M., we heard a tremendous explosion. The wind scoops at my two port holes were blown across my cabin against the bulkhead opposite the ports.

I thought we'd been torpedoed, but as soon as I went outside, I realized that the dynamite on the dock had been exploded by some Japanese soldiers who were hiding after the invasion.

We returned to San Francisco, took on another load of troops and cargo and returned to Saipan. This time the neighboring island of Tinian was being invaded. Battleships, cruisers and destroyers were everywhere. We lay at anchor watching the action and hearing the noise. After three days the navy said the island was secured. We took a load of troops to Saipan from the nearest end of Tinian Island. They came out on a small vessel and tied up alongside. A lot of Japanese who had been driven off the end of the island, killed themselves before they jumped into the water, and their bodies were floating all around us.

We went on to Guam where we unloaded personnel and cargo and then returned in a small convoy of about five vessels. We had a navy commodore aboard and watching him take sights was funny. He had a CPO stand on one side to keep the wind off, and a lieutenant on the other, taking time with the stop watch. When he had his sight he handed the sextant to the CPO to read and work out the sight. The captain or a mate on a merchant ship takes his sight, starts counting while he walks to the chronometer, notes the time, then goes to the chart room to work it out, strictly a one-man operation.

We returned to San Francisco but missed Christmas at home because we had to start the next voyage on December 12th, 1944. While in San Francisco I received notice from the navy that I was granted a reserve commission as an ensign. I would no longer have to worry about the draft board bothering my wife.

Our first stop was at Eniwetak on Kawajalein where we spent a day or two getting orders. This time we went to Tinian Island first and unloaded men and supplies for the B-29 bomber base which was already in operation. A group of pilots and navigators came out to our ship to talk to me about marine navigation. They promised to take me on a practice run over the uninhabited Island of Rota not far from Tinian. I later found out that when they came to get me our ship had sailed.

From Tinian we went to Guam where we unloaded a few men and supplies but didn't go ashore because we were anchored out. Our next port was Espiritu Santo where we picked up several navy nurses who completely changed the life on our ship. There were parties in the captain's cabin every evening. When I took over the bridge at 4 P.M., I heard feminine voices in the captain's cabin below the bridge. By 8 P.M., the party was well on, and usually lasted until midnight. I felt sorry for myself up on the bridge alone with all the merriment going on below. A couple of times one of the nurses brought me a piece of cake with ice cream on it, but the teaser only made things worse.

Our next port was on Guadalcanal where the nurses left us to return to the U.S. by air. There were still a lot of troops on the island but not much going on. From Guadalcanal we went to Milne Bay, New Guinea. I remember this port well, because of the Russian ship anchored close to us which had a number of female crew members. From a distance the New Guinean natives looked like they had red mud all over their hair.

From Milne Bay we went up the coast making a few stops along the way, to Hollandia where the fleet that brought the invasion force to the Philippines started. Navigation along the coast of New Guinea was difficult because the charts were not accurate. There were notations such as, "This portion of the coast has been reported to be five miles further east than shown," on the charts we used.

While in Hollandia the Evangeline came in with a load of WACs. Troops came aboard our ship looking for liquor and offering $100 for a fifth of scotch. Since the invasion of the Philippines was successful everyone felt the war was almost over. We picked up troops in Hollandia and Finchhaven, and returned them to the United States. At the beginning of the war, most of the troops were sent to Australia, then moved up to New Guinea for the Philippine invasion.

While we were in Hollandia a cargo vessel came in with a full load of beer. It was funny to see how the troops helped themselves. Every kind of military vehicle loaded up from the dock.

I will always remember the full load of troops we took back to San Francisco, most had been away from the United States for three years, and some longer. The week before we were scheduled to arrive in San Francisco, every time I was on deck for any reason, the soldiers asked me, "When are we going to arrive in San Francisco?"

I gave them an approximate answer, allowing for weather conditions and currents. When I was able to tell them, "tomorrow," their eyes lit up, and they asked, "What time?"

"It depends on the weather," I answered, "but I would guess it will be in the morning." Their eyes got large and they said, "In San Francisco tomorrow! I can't believe it."

The troops were not the only ones who got excited about returning home. The chief engineer came up to the bridge a couple of days before we were due to arrive home and asked, "How many knots do we have to make to arrive at the pilot station by eight tomorrow morning?"

I figured it out, and he went back to the engine room. Pretty soon there were a couple of new rattles in the wheel house windows and the knot meter showed that our speed had increased by one and a half to two knots. After a while the captain came up, walked around a little, looked at the knotmeter, and said, "Look at that speed! If I told him to make twelve knots he would say it is impossible. That speed will tear the engine apart."

The weather was good the morning we saw the Farallons and the deck of the Azalea City was covered with troops from the bow to the stern. We picked up our pilot and headed for the Golden Gate Bridge. The decks were packed, they had climbed up the mast ladders and crowded in the gun tubs. As the bow went under the bridge a roar went up from the bow and rolled down the deck past the house and on towards the stern as the ship forged ahead into the Bay. There to greet them were a fleet of small boats and two San Francisco fire boats shooting plumes of water into the sky. The memory of the scene and the sound effects stays fresh in my mind.

March of 1945, I ended my last trip as second mate and as soon as I was off the ship, I applied for admission to the Merchant Marine Officers Training School to prepare for my chief mate's license examination. It was great to be back in San Francisco with some time off. Schoolwork wasn't very demanding and I had a room in the El Cortez Hotel on Geary Street about two blocks from the school. The school was well-organized and the teachers were ex Merchant Marine officers, so they knew what they were teaching. I called Noradene to ask her to take off a couple of weeks and come to San Francisco, but she said her boss was traveling and she couldn't leave.

It was often very difficult to get a room in a decent hotel in San Francisco or any other large port city in the U.S. during the war. The first time I visited San Francisco, mother told me that one of her distant relatives was on the board of the Palace Hotel. I went to see him in his office, introduced myself, and told him that I was having difficulties getting a decent room.

"We always have something we can give you," he said. "All you have to do is call me. If I am not here, call my secretary."

I got a kick out of walking in off the street, asking the desk clerk if they had any available rooms, and listening to him ex-plain how full the hotel was and why he couldn't help me. Then I called my relative's secretary, who told me she would leave instructions with the desk clerk to get me a room. I waited a few minutes, then went back to the desk clerk. He said, "Yes sir I can give you room so and so, the occupant just vacated the room."

The Palace was a little too rich for my blood, but for the first few days ashore it was a wonderful feeling to go there after I'd been living for two or three months in a small dingy cabin that constantly pitched and rolled. For my long stays, such as when I attended upgrading school the El Cortez was preferable.

After three weeks of school I faced an examination that lasted four or five days given by the Coast Guard. The exam was thorough and I really had to know my subjects in order to pass. Navigation was most difficult for me, it involved long complex computations in which the altitude and bearing of stars and or the sun were reduced to a specific longitude and latitude. Ship handling, ship construction, cargo loading and even first aid were included.

Examination papers were graded as they were handed in, so when Friday afternoon rolled around, I wondered if I was going to finish that week or had to return the following week. I was lucky and walked out Friday night knowing I had passed and didn't have to come back. I was licensed to sail as chief mate.

Waterman Steamship Corporation had opened a new office in San Francisco so I reported to them for a job. After three days they put me on a Liberty ship, the Michael Kerr, anchored near the Bay Bridge off the San Francisco waterfront. There was no crew aboard yet, and I didn't have much to do, but they wanted to keep me on a Waterman ship so I spent each day on the ship and returned to the El Cortez for the night. I found out that the officer I was replacing was the son of the president of the San Francisco Stock Exchange.

After ten days on the Michael Kerr, the Waterman port captain left a message for me to call him. He sent me over to Bethlehem Shipyard to the Eagle Wing, a C-2 type cargo ship just returned from the South Pacific. A captain and half a crew were already on board. The chief engineer suspected that the propeller shaft was cracked, and recommended that it be removed and inspected. I went aboard and started looking around the ship. The few crew members aboard told me that while the ship was in Hawaii the captain had invited the bo'sun up to his cabin to beat him up because he had refused to do something the captain told him to do. The bo'sun went to the captain's cabin but when he found out what the captain intended to do, he tried to escape through the bedroom. The captain, in hot pursuit, having fortified himself with a couple of drinks, stumbled over the watertight door sill, and broke his ankle. As he lay on deck, the bo'sun returned and started kicking him in the head. The chief mate heard the noise, pulled the bo'sun off the captain, and called for help. The captain was taken off on a stretcher and the bo'sun was taken off in handcuffs. There being no other licensed captain available the chief mate had brought the ship back to San Francisco from Hawaii.

When checking the lockers in the crew and officers' quarters I found hundreds of cartons of cigarettes in their original packages, stowed in every space available. When the chief mate, who had made the previous trip, came aboard, I asked him about the cigarettes. He told me the crew had stolen them out of the cargo but the guard gate at the shipyard prevented them from smuggling the cartons ashore. I gathered up the cigarettes and put them in the slop chest where they stayed until we had sailed on the next voyage. When the crew wanted to buy cigarettes, we gave them the ones I had stored from the previous voyage cargo.

We finally got out of the shipyard with a new propeller shaft and tied up to a dock. We received notice that the ship would move to Encinal Terminal to load cargo the next day, but I told the messenger from the port captain's office that my entire crew only consisted of three men.

"I'll see what I can get for you, but you may have to use the mess boys to help tie up," he said.

"We must have some one that knows how to run an anchor windless. Can you get me a bo'sun from the seamen's school?" I asked.

Two of the mess boys said they could handle mooring lines and the second cook said he could throw a heaving line. The so called bo'sun from the seaman's school was husky but he didn't impress me. He didn't even know how to let go the anchor and read the markings on the chain. My inexperienced crew and I let go the stern lines and then ran up to the bow and let go the lines forward and heaved them in. As we entered the channel between the Encinal dock and the surrounding land I could see that the only available vacant space was between two ships already at the dock. The pilot stopped the engine as we entered the channel. "Let go two shots on the anchor windlass," he called out.

At my order the man who was supposed to have bo'sun papers proceeded to let go the anchor, then stopped the chain from going out. The ship didn't slow down as it should have, with the anchor dragging on the bottom. As I stepped over to the windlass controls the pilot yelled, "Two shots in the water now!"

I pushed the bo'sun away from the anchor chain release and as the chain went out I saw the 1 mark go by and finally the 2 shot mark appeared and I started applying the brake so the chain would stop with the 2 mark in the water. The pilot shook his head as we changed our pace to a slower speed. The line handlers were on the dock, so I told the man who could supposedly handle a heaving line to throw it to the dock. He threw it so hard it went up on the roof of the shed but came back down to where the lines men could get it.

With the rudder turned right and the starboard anchor dragging, the Eagle Wing swung her stern into the dock and stopped a few feet from the stern of the ship ahead of her. Lines from the bow and stern were quickly run out and she was secure. The pilot got a few additional gray hairs but revived quickly.

We started loading cargo for Tinian, the origin of constant bombing raids over Japan. We were instructed to keep #3 and #4 holds empty for a special cargo to be loaded later. We were asked about the availability of spare cabins for military officer passengers. We offered two cabins, two bunks in each, with private baths. They told us we would have three army officer passengers for the voyage.

All working parts of the cargo gear at the holds which we were not now loading was to be doubled up and the pins on all shackles secured in preparation for the upcoming special cargo. The two empty holds with the double gear would be loaded at Port Chicago, California, where all explosives were stored and loaded. There had already been one disastrous explosion there.

After we finished loading at Encinal Terminals, we went up Suisun Bay to Port Chicago. We noticed that the stevedores handled the cargo with extreme care. It took three days to load at Port Chicago, then we returned to San Francisco.

Before sailing we acquired two more crew members. One was an army cargo officer and the other was an army intelligence officer. I was instructed to take the temperature in the two special holds twice daily and to inform the cargo officer.

We were all a little worried about the secret cargo, but as one day followed another at sea and nothing happened, we began to relax. One evening an army officer found a bottle of whiskey in his luggage and invited several of us to celebrate. After quite a few drinks the army intelligence officer said, "I am willing to bet anyone here that this war will be over after we unload this cargo on Tinian Island and it is delivered to Japan by the B-29 bombers."

S.S. "Eagle Wing" delivered the first Atomic Bombs to Tinian Island from Port Chicago, California, in July of 1945.

Nobody took him up on the offer but it got everyone to thinking. Several people in the group made the remark that, in their opinion, the war could go on for two more years.

"When the special cargo on this ship is delivered to Japan the war will be over," said the intelligence officer. He went on to say that an amount of that stuff the size of a cigarette package can eliminate a city, if exploded.

We finally arrived at Tinian Island and started unloading our cargo. The first thing I noticed was that civilization had arrived. There was an outdoor movie theater and an officers club as well as good roads and swarms of B-29 Bombers coming from and going to Japan. I was on the midship section of the ship watching the secret cargo being discharged and after a large crate had been landed on the dock, I said, "I will sure be glad when that stuff is all away from the ship."

*Abbott, at left on the bridge of the "Eagle Wing" with Captain Pugh,
Chief Engineer Pesek, Lieutenant Hummeland, a gunnery officer,
and Lieutenant Dezell, the cargo security officer.*

The army officer standing next to me said, "That cargo would
have to be beyond those mountains on the horizon when it ex-
plodes for you to be safe."

About that time the Indianapolis arrived at the dock in Tinian.
She was rumored to carry the warhead for the new explosive we
brought from Port Chicago. Several weeks later, while we were at
sea, we received news by radio that the Indianapolis had been
sunk at sea with a terrible loss of life. When we got back to San
Francisco, after other atomic bombs had been delivered, we
heard that Japan had surrendered.

Soon after Japan surrendered, we received official notice that
we could now ignore black-out regulations at sea. After four years
of being at sea during which all portholes had to be closed with
the metal covers, and all exits and entrances had to have closed
doors with two layers of black curtains which wouldn't reveal any
light, we suddenly were free again. The fresh air in the cabins
made everybody feel good and easy to get along with.

My second trip on the Eagle Wing started in Los Angeles
where we loaded a complete cargo of aviation gasoline in drums.

When we sailed, our orders were to go to Okinawa. When we got there, they were expecting a typhoon so we joined a group of vessels under the command of a commodore and went to sea for two days. When the weather cleared we returned to Okinawa for orders.

Our new orders directed us to go to Wakayama, Japan, but before we departed I found out that the vessel anchored next to us was operated by Waterman. It was captained by the man who was second mate on the Josephine Lawrence when I was on as third mate. He invited me and my crew to come aboard for movies the night before we sailed for Japan. We lowered a lifeboat, took about ten or twelve men over, and had a great time.

Wakayama was a thriving steel mill town before the war, but when we got there it had been so thoroughly bombed, the steel mills were completely destroyed. The typhoon we avoided had hit Wakayama and wrecked all the small boats in the harbor. Therefore we had to put a life boat over the side to go ashore, pick up the pilot, and bring him to our vessel before we could enter the harbor. We were the first American merchant vessel to enter since the war started. For that reason, we were wondering how we would be received when we went ashore.

We tied up the life boat, walked over to the first street and started towards what was left of the town. The first Japanese we met all bowed to us as we passed them. I didn't know whether to bow back or to ignore them, so I did a little of both. Soon a Japanese man came along on a bicycle, and in his broken English, invited us to his home. We accepted his invitation and followed him to his house, where we were met by his wife and two daughters. They asked us to take off our shoes before we entered, then served us refreshments: tea, and a section of tangerine. The man said he had taught in the U.S. before the war. After a few days, the locals stopped bowing to us on the street but they never showed us any animosity.

We made regular afternoon explorations of the small fishing villages along the coast in our lifeboat. Before long, the navy established an officers club, and it became a popular destination for our life boat cruises. The first few times, when we sat down at a table in the club, the Japanese waitresses would kneel behind our chairs and say nothing until we beckoned to them, after which they came, bowing, to the table. We pointed to the item on the menu that we wanted and they brought it. When the club had been established for a few weeks the Japanese waitresses learned how to handle Americans. When we came in they would walk up and throw one arm around us and say, "Hi kid, what you want?"

After we had been in Wakayama for about three weeks the navy unloaded our cargo, but we saved a few drums for fuel for our lifeboat expeditions. A floating post office was set up on a navy ship in the harbor, giving us the perfect excuse to take our afternoon lifeboat cruises—we were going to pick up the mail.

During one of our excursions, we found an old building on the waterfront where we could trade cartons of cigarettes for cultured pearls. As the harbor filled with navy and merchant ships the price of the pearls went up until the sellers demanded American money instead of American cigarettes.

Finally the navy started to load us with cargo bound for the United States. We asked them for a list of the cargo so we could make out a stowage plan but instead they started dumping cargo into the ship without giving us weights or cubic measurements. After the lower holds were full it was obvious that the vessel was getting tender. The captain stopped the loading until we could get some fuel in the double bottoms for stability, but the navy tanker who refueled us only gave us half of what we had asked for. The captain refused to take any more cargo until he received the weight and cubic information he had requested. Apparently, they didn't have the information, because they ordered us to sail.

Our instructions were to go to Hawaii and fill up with fuel oil, but before we got there we were unstable. We would take on a list which got worse until fuel oil was pumped from tanks on one side to tanks on the other side. Soon after the list had been corrected the vessel would flop over the other way. In addition, we were burning more fuel as we went along which made correcting the list increasingly difficult.

A week before leaving one of our seamen was killed in a Japanese recreation club. According to the men who were with him, he was wearing a sheath knife in a scabbard on his belt. When he was doing a hand stand the knife fell out and he fell over on it. The blade went through his back into his heart. Several of our crew were with him and verified the story. I was assigned the unpleasant task of calling on his parents when we returned to the U.S.

We stopped in Hawaii, and while we were filling up with fuel, we received orders to change our destination from San Francisco to Los Angeles. Arriving in Los Angeles our pilot told us he was taking us to an anchorage just inside the breakwater. The pilot took a long time getting the anchor to hold but was finally satisfied and left the ship. The captain was in a hurry to get off to see his wife and left me in charge early the next day.

Before light the next morning I heard a lot of shouting and ran out on deck. A Liberty ship was dragging anchor, going slowly by us. The wind had increased considerably and was gusting up to a high velocity. I took some bearings on lights and found out that we had dragged from our original position. I woke the chief engineer and asked him how long it would take him to get up steam for maneuvering. "Two hours," he said. I told him to get started immediately.

At daylight it was obvious we had dragged anchor quite a ways and would end up on the breakwater unless something was done right away. The bo'sun was on the fo'c'sle head with the second mate and as soon as the engine room notified me that the engine was ready, we started heaving up the anchor. As soon as the anchor was off the bottom I rang "slow ahead" and threaded my way through the anchored ships to the area where we first anchored. It was the first time I had been in charge of maneuvering a 500 ft. cargo ship through a crowded anchorage, and can't say I was completely at ease, but we re-anchored in a spot where we had room to swing and since the wind was steady from one direction we dropped both anchors for safety.

At about noon the captain returned in a small boat. Noticing that we were in a different location he yelled, "What happened? What happened? The ship has been moved."

I told him what happened, and he said, "You should have called a pilot."

"We were dragging through a packed anchorage and we didn't have any time to call a pilot and wait for him to arrive." I answered.

He understood.

After a couple of wind changes, the two anchor chains got fouled and the next job I had was to get them untangled and heave one up.

I found out my old friend Paul Barney from Cottage Hill was on R & R at a camp in Orange County. He had been a glider pilot in the Battle of the Bulge. We got together and had a three day celebration.

Chapter Five

The War is Over

When the war was over, Noradene had a job in San Francisco, working for the Hawaiian Pineapple Company. I couldn't decide whether or not to take another trip on the Eagle Wing. If I did, I would have enough time in to take the examination for a master's license, if I didn't, I could benefit from the large number of jobs being advertised in the daily papers. My decision came when ships were being laid up, and on January 11, 1946, I signed off the Eagle Wing.

I answered an ad for a freight solicitor placed by the New York, New Haven & Hartford Railroad and was given the job. In a truck line office, the man who yelled the loudest got his way, but the atmosphere in a railroad office was entirely different. Ruled by hierarchy, the agent was in charge, and everyone else was there to make him look good, increasing the freight carried was secondary.

The railroads had more freight than they could handle during the war, so they put little effort into attracting business, but in peacetime the freight solicitor was under the gun. I had no difficulty getting freight, but when I had to tell officials who visited our office from Boston that the agent had done all the work, I ran into trouble. Before long I was transferred to Los Angeles, and was responsible for southern California, New Mexico and Arizona. I was much happier there, working by myself.

I especially enjoyed taking trips to New Mexico, where I knew a lot of people from my Albuquerque Flyer Express days. I went there to romance the wool buyers from Boston wool companies who bought carloads of wool from wool traders on local Indian reservations. On my first trip I met a wool buyer in the hotel at Gallup, who told me to never mention where I had seen him. The same went for all the wool buyers, they had their secret sources and didn't want the other buyers to know.

My son was born in the early morning hours of April 9th, 1948, after a night of labor for Noradene, and a night of worry for me, at the Cedars of Lebanon Hospital in Los Angeles. That day, I was told that the New Haven Railroad was forced into bankruptcy. My job was eliminated, but I had seniority so I was offered a job as chief clerk in the San Francisco office, and the poor guy who had the job would be laid off. I didn't want to take the job in San Francisco, because my wife and I had just relocated to Los Angeles, and bought a house on Maltman Street with a rental on the first floor. With a newborn, and our new house, we didn't want to leave just yet. I spent the next few nights walking the floor with my infant son who didn't want to sleep, and spent the days looking for a job.

One day, as I walked downtown trying to scrounge up some leads, I ran into a man I knew from the railroad business. He said "I was wondering where I could find you. I was just offered a job as a freight solicitor with a steamship company, but I turned it down. I've worked for the railroad for a long time, and I have too much invested in retirement benefits to change jobs. If you want the job, go to the Sudden & Christenson offices, and ask for Mr. Richards, the manager."

I thanked him for the information and headed for the offices of Sudden & Christenson who were agents for, among others,

Waterman Steamship Corporation. I reported to Lloyd Richards, who was also my contact when I arrived in San Diego, in September of 1944, to take the second mate's job on the Azalea City. He remembered me, and I briefly told him what I'd been doing since we had last seen each other. When I said that I was interested in the freight solicitors job, he immediately said "If you want the job, you have it." After we discussed the salary, I accepted.

Within a week I was offered a freight solicitor's job at a higher salary with Pacific Far East. I told Lloyd about it, and without hesitation he said, "I'll meet it but you'll have to wait longer for a raise." That was okay with me, and I stayed on with Sudden & Christenson.

There were about four inter-coastal steamship lines running between East and West Coast ports at the time. They had all been shut down during the war when ships were critical to the war effort and couldn't be wasted on inter-coastal traffic that could be handled by rail. Many of the shippers that I had called on for the New Haven Railroad were also my accounts for Waterman. When we had a ship loading or discharging cargo in port, I took my customers aboard for lunch. We ate with the captain, and he showed them how their cargo was loaded and discharged.

Sudden & Christenson started out in the West Coast lumber business and operated their own ships. They were still lumber brokers, with one salesman working out of the same office as I, but their principal business was as a steamship agent, representing foreign and domestic lines in ports where it was more profitable for steamship companies to use an agent than open an office. When I went to work there, they had two principal lines; Waterman, and Klavness who, although Norwegian, operated between the U.S. West Coast and the Orient.

When my son was almost three years old, we sold our house on Maltman and bought a small house in Arcadia, closer to the good schools.

When I was confronted by the draft board in Oklahoma City at the beginning of the war I had already finished two years of law school. I found out that there was a night law school about two blocks from my office in Los Angeles, so I asked a few attorneys if they knew anything about it. The school had a good reputation among the lawyers I questioned, so I enrolled. I attended regularly, and to maintain my grades, I spent most of every Monday at the Law Library. It worked out well, because Monday wasn't a good day for calling on customers. My Bachelor of Law diploma was issued in 1950.

I had a little more time on my hands, developed an interest in boats, and joined the Power Squadron where I taught a seamanship class. I also went to Newport Beach every weekend (after I got the lawn mowed) and rented a small sailboat. Sailing in Newport Harbor was an excellent way to learn, and I made up my mind to buy a boat as soon as I could afford it.

Klavness Line opened their own office in Los Angeles, and Sudden & Christenson closed up. Waterman took over the office and sent a former stevedore with no management experience to run it. He had met one of the Waterman family at a military installation during the war and they had promised him, in return for a favor, that they would give him a job if he ever needed one. They knew he would need a lot of help, so they made me assistant manager. I ran the office and at the same time taught him how to run it. He made horrible blunders like passing out in the car after taking a shipper to lunch, but no one in the head office in Mobile knew what was going on.

In 1952 Jane, a student in my Power Squadron seamanship class, introduced me to a millionaire named Allan Guiberson who she had met in Acapulco where her sister lived. He had an 85 foot yacht in Acapulco, called the Sea Rider, that he wanted to bring to Texas, but he needed someone to bring it around through the Panama Canal. I didn't think much about it at the time, but about a year later, I received a phone call from Jane. She was in Guiberson's room at a hotel in Beverly Hills and he wanted to talk to me about bringing his boat to Corpus Christi. I told her that I couldn't get away from the office right then but would call back as soon as I was free.

Before I called back I gave it some thought. I decided that if I could make a deal with Guiberson, I would ask my employers for the time off without salary to do the job. I met Guiberson and Jane at the hotel, told him the fee I expected to receive for the job, and asked that the boat be in acceptable condition. He agreed to everything, and hired me.

All I had to do was get my employers permission to take some time off. It would be useless to ask the manager of the Los Angeles office, so I called the San Francisco office, which was supposedly in charge of the whole West Coast. First they couldn't decide, then they told me they wanted to think about it and would let me know. I had told Guiberson that I would be in Acapulco on the Fourth of July, and it was almost the end of June. I finally received word from San Francisco. They said if I was sure everything would run smoothly in my absence, they would allow me to take the time off.

Before Jane went to Acapulco to visit her sister, she told me that the Club de Pesca Hotel would be a good place for me to stay, because it was close to the shipyard where the Sea Rider was being prepared for the voyage. I flew to Acapulco and took a cab to the Club de Pesca. When I asked for a room they told me there were no vacancies. I called Jane, who said that her brother in law, a resident of Acapulco, would come down and straighten things out. He walked into the lobby shouting at the desk clerk, who apologized to me and brought out the room register for me to sign.

The following week I was busy getting the boat surveyed, arranging for a haul-out, deciding what stores to buy for the trip, and hiring a crew. The engineer sent down one or two men every day for me to interview for jobs, and of them I hired a cook and three seamen. When I asked the cook if he knew how to cook American food, he asked, "What do Americans eat?"

When the boat was hauled out, I could see that the hull was in fair condition, but both propellers were bent. Guiberson said he would send me two new ones, but when they arrived, the boat yard workers noticed that the hole for the propeller shafts was off center. The Mexican Navy shipyard was the only place where we could find drills to correct the defect, so we had to negotiate a little, but the problem was eventually solved and the new propellers were installed.

I called Guiberson in Dallas to tell him I was ready to go, only to discover he had decided to go along with us, and would be in Acapulco the next morning. All the bills were paid, but getting the crew list changed to include Allan's name and a proper clearance took a little time. Guiberson had once owned a hotel in Acapulco and spent a lot of time there, so we were invited to the beautiful, luxurious homes of some of his acquaintances while we waited for clearance. At dawn we swung ship to find the compass error, 20 degrees on some headings.

Between Acapulco and Corinto, Nicaragua, we crossed the Gulf of Tehuantepec, known for its rough weather caused by northers coming out of Texas and blowing across the narrow strip of Mexico into the Gulf. The crew asked me if we were going to hug the land along the coast or go across the Gulf. I told them that we had a deadline, so we'd go straight across. They were worried, repeatedly coming to the chart room to ask me to show them where we were. We had huge swells left over from the last storm, but no wind, and made the crossing without any trouble.

After a refueling stop at Corinto, we arrived at the entrance to the Panama Canal, and the first thing we did was have the compass corrected.

While we were in Panama, Guiberson tried to sell Sea Rider to a hotel for passenger excursions in the Gulf. While negotiations were in process, I looked around a little and had lunch with some of the people from the steamship agency that handled Waterman ships. On the day we were supposed to leave, Guiberson received a phone call from the people who were drilling an oil well for him. The well had turned out to be a dry hole.

Before he left for Dallas to deal with his dry well, he asked me when I would arrive in Corpus Christi. I did a little mental arithmetic and named a day. He said, "If you hit a rock back off and hit again—hard— so the boat will sink and I can collect my insurance!"

He didn't tell me how I was supposed to get back to civilization after sinking the boat, so I decided to keep it afloat.

I had reluctantly agreed to Guiberson's request that Jane continue on with me to Corpus Christi, and as he left for Texas, Jane and I transited the canal and headed for Puerto Cabezas, Nicaragua.

I asked Waterman's Panamanian agent if I should clear for Puerto Cabezas or Corpus Christi. They said, "Clear for Corpus Christi, and if anyone says anything at Puerto Cabezas, tell them you ran low on fuel because of the weather and had to refuel there." When we arrived at Puerto Cabezas, we tied up at an old wooden pier. I had hoped to get fuel and get out that night.

Jane and I walked down the pier to the port captain's office and reported our arrival.

"You have entered illegally, and there will be serious consequences," the port captain said.

"We'll take fuel this afternoon and leave before dark," I said.

"You have broken the laws of Nicaragua, and I can't let you leave this office unless you are under armed guard," he replied.

We left the office and walked up the dock, followed by a rather young boy holding a rifle. At the end of the dock there were three beat up cars, and when the drivers all accosted us at once, I realized they were taxis. One of Waterman's Panamanian agents had told me that the bartender in the American Club ran the weather station, and I needed a weather report before I left port. I made a deal with one of the drivers, we got in the car and I told him to take us to the American Club. The poor, young soldier didn't know what to do, so he just stood on the dock and watched us ride away.

At the American Club, Jane talked to some Americans while I made arrangements to get a weather report. The bartender said he would prepare a three-day weather report for me as soon as he finished his bartending shift at 5 P.M., so I could have it first thing in the morning.

Jane had found out that the Americans in the bar were employees of an American lumber company with headquarters in Mobile, Alabama, and they knew some of the same Waterman Steamship people in Mobile who I knew. When we got ready to leave the bar, they invited us to an all-night party, and we happily accepted the invitation. It was so hot that most of the time we partied on the porch that encircled the house.

At 8 A.M. my engineer started taking on fuel and I went to see the port captain about getting released to sail. He wasn't angry that I ditched the young guard, but he said we had to make a formal legal application in Spanish to leave the port, then bring it to him for approval. I asked him where I could find a Spanish speaking lawyer to write the application for me. He said he knew an attorney who charged $50.00. I gave the port captain $50.00 of Guiberson's money and went back to the Sea Rider. We sailed at about 4 P.M. heading for the port of Progresso on the north coast of Yucatan. It was our last stop before crossing the Gulf of Mexico to Corpus Christi.

In order to clear shallow water along the coast we headed out in a north-easterly direction, then turned north. Our course would take us close to the Albuquerque Reef, so the next after-noon, when I thought we were close to the reef, I went up on the bow to take a look. About ten minutes after I got out there I saw discolored water ahead and signaled the helmsman to reverse his course immediately. When we had cleared the obstruction we re-sumed our course.

Twenty-six years later I was on one of two boats heading for the island of San Andreas, and the other boat ran on this Albuquer-que Reef in the middle of night. I tried to reach his position by talking to him on the radio, but got into shallow water myself. I went to San Andreas and sent a small boat down to help, but be-fore it got there my friend was off the reef and had made it into San Andreas on his own.

We arrived in Progresso at nightfall and anchored until the next morning when we went to the dock to take on fuel. The engineer and one man stayed on board, but I gave the others the day off to go ashore. When the last of the fuel was on board I let the engineer and his assistant go ashore too. I had told all of them we were sailing at sunset, so they should be back to the boat well before then. At sunset I rode down main street in a taxi, stopping at every bar to round up the crew, and we still got away on schedule.

As we left the harbor of Progresso I laid down a course to Cor-pus Christi, for the trip across the Gulf of Mexico. I had to re-member my celestial navigation and use Jane's sextant. About half an hour before local apparent noon, I pre-computed the al-titude and the local time that the sun would cross our meridian. By taking one sight just before the sun crossed our meridian, and another just after, I plotted two lines of position that would cross at, or very near, our noon position. At noon on the third day we could not yet see land but, by our position, we knew we would see it within a few hours. First we saw a large ship coming out, then the buoy marking the entrance to the channel. Soon we saw a string of low land ahead of us, the crew were happy and relieved.

We were a day earlier than the arrival date I had given Allan Guiberson off the top of my head. We were in the channel for some time before seeing any sign of the city and had made a wrong turn. A navy escort vessel gave us directions to the yacht harbor, and as the sun set we tied up. I got a hotel room for the night and called Allan in Dallas. The first thing he said was, "You are not supposed to be here until tomorrow!"

The next day we went through the formalities of entering, sent the crew off to Mexico with letters of recommendation, and Jane and I flew back to Los Angeles. It had been eight years since I was a chief mate on a merchant ship but I proved to myself that I could still navigate with a sextant.

When I returned to the Waterman office, everything was running normally, and because I felt secure in my job, bought my first boat. It had been a fishing boat and living quarters for two fishermen and a fisherwoman. The interior was filthy and I had to install a new engine, but I knew it would be worth it. I worked on the boat every weekend for several months before I took my first trip to Catalina Island. My converted fishing boat looked out of place in the harbor at Avalon with all the million-dollar yachts, but I had more fun than anybody. I ran a speed trial with it and my top speed was only 7 1/2 knots. Some of my customers loved to spend weekends on the boat, and when I entertained them, Waterman paid for part of the costs.

In 1954, Waterman Steamship Corp. applied for additional inter-coastal permits between the East and West Coasts of the United States. I was asked to oversee the application process because of my experience with truck lines applying for new routes before the Interstate Commerce Commission. I became well-acquainted with Captain Nicholson, president of Waterman, who attended some of the hearings. He often took me to dinner to discuss strategy.

When Waterman received their inter-coastal permits, Sea Land bought them out, taking possession of their inter-coastal routes and vessels. Sea Land sent their own employees to the West Coast to run their offices, and all of the Waterman employees, including me, were unemployed. It was 1955, I had a boat to pay for and a family to support, my son was seven years old. The chief clerk in the Waterman office went to work for another steamship line, and with the help of a friend from the Power Squadron, I got a job as office manager for a newly organized company called American Electronics.

Electronics was something completely new to me, so I went to night school to learn as much as possible in a short time. It was not long before the salesmen were calling me for advice on how to complete a tough sale. When the sales manager found out that I had been instrumental in closing a couple of deals he fired me, accusing me of trying to get his job.

I went to an executive placement agency who sent me to Western Gear Corporation, a large manufacturer of engine transmissions, aircraft actuators and many related products. They had bought out a small manufacturer of electronic equipment in order to get into the electronics business. They hired me as a salesman, and the first call I made was on an engineer I met through the Power Squadron. He mentioned that his company was designing a tape recorder that required special reel motors that operate with a lot of slip. I got a copy of the specifications, took it to one of the Western Gear engineers who had designed a similar motor for General Electric when he worked for them. We built a sample, they tested it, and gave Western Gear my first order for $40,000.

Six months later I was promoted to national marketing manager for the Electro Products division of Western Gear. I appointed commission sales agents to cover every part of the country and worked with them until they learned our products and capabilities. The Electro Products division made a profit for the first time since Western Gear bought it. I hired a Chicago area representative who handled several lines that were not competitive with Western Gear, and brought him out to Los Angeles to introduce him to the owners. They didn't like him because he was loud and coarse. I said, "In my opinion, that is the kind of person you need in the Chicago area. I have checked with some of the companies he represents and they all say he is a top producer."

They let me keep him and he became the top producer for Electro Products.

While talking to some people at a bar one night I heard about a requirement for a dc electric motor that would raise a fin on a prototype atomic bomb after it was released by the pilot. When stowed on the plane the fin folded flat. As soon as it was released, the motor automatically started raising the fin. Rumor had it that Rheem Aircraft had the contract, but I couldn't find anyone at Rheem who could tell me the name of the engineer in charge of the project. One of my local salesmen had worked at Rheem, so I told him to go out there and find out who was in charge of the atomic bomb project. My salesperson came back the next day and told me an air force officer was in charge but he didn't have the man's name. After more sleuthing, I finally found him. He was only a couple of years older than I, and easily entertained. I invited him to come to Catalina Island with me on my boat for a weekend. He asked if he could bring his girlfriend and I said, "Yes, of course." I had a newer and larger boat that went faster. I made reservations for them in a luxurious island hotel and I slept on the boat.

The weekend was calm and beautiful so no one got seasick. By Monday morning I knew as much about the atomic bomb project as anyone. In order to get the job for Western Gear they had to be approved by the Rheem engineer in charge of the project. I had lunch with him Tuesday after the trip to Catalina, and listened to a sad story. He was earning a good salary at Rheem, and started to build houses on the side. He made money on the first few, so he decided to build a large, luxurious one and make more money. The large, luxurious one was designed and built at a much greater cost than he had planned and he was unable to sell it. He was deeply in debt to a lot of people, but if he could get a pay off from the atomic bomb motor contract, his problems would be solved. He told me that the first contract would be in the neighborhood of $1,000,000.

He said he had the greatest respect for Western Gear and wouldn't hesitate to give them the order if they could arrange to help him get out of his predicament. A few days before the order was supposed to be signed, he got sick and was taken to the hospital. From the hospital, he gave his assistant instructions to give the order to Western Gear. When I visited him at the hospital, he told me that his wife had inherited a lot of money from her family, but he couldn't ask her for help. His condition got worse, and five days after entering the hospital he passed away.

An engineering firm in upper Pennsylvania got the job of building the prototype atomic bomb, and Western Gear had the only approved design for the motor, one that would automatically raise the fin when the bomb left the plane. I called the company in Pennsylvania and talked to the president. He flew to Los Angeles to inspect our facilities, and I introduced him to the manager of our plant in Pasadena.

Because we had the only approved design for the motor, it didn't take much effort to get our first $500,000. order. There were a couple of minor problems with some of the motors so we sent an engineer to Pennsylvania, and he quickly corrected them.

I spent about four years with Western Gear in their Electro Products division and they allowed me to do things I loved to do, like taking a bunch of engineers to Catalina Island on a 85 foot yacht. I chartered and operated the Esterina myself, and it was

the most successful entertaining I ever did. I had sold the Esterina to Allan Guiberson to replace the Sea Rider, still doing survey
work in the U.S. Gulf. I later negotiated the sale of the Esterina
for Guiberson to another person who lived in Los Angeles.

There were sales people in Western Gear who had been there
for twenty years, and at first they didn't want to have anything to
do with starting up a new division, but when the new division
prospered, they all were eager to get involved. The vice president
in charge of marketing at the main plant, and the sales manager
for the Aircraft division both wanted to take over the Electro
Products division. Besides getting new business I had to defend
my rear from the vultures in Western Gear.

I discovered that my job had been advertised by someone in
Western Gear, and handed in my resignation. When they asked
me why I was leaving, I said, "When the company you work for ad-
vertises for a replacement it's time to look for something else."

The president of the company asked me to have lunch with
him. He told me that as soon as he found out who put the ad in
the paper, he would fire them. It turned out that the vice president in charge of marketing had placed the ad and he did get
fired.

When all this was going on, Warren Heningsgard, a man who
worked for me when I was at Waterman Steamship called to tell
me about something he had read in the paper. A Yugoslav steamship line was going to start a new around-the-world-service and
was looking for someone to act as agent on the U.S. West Coast. I
told him I would check it out in a few days when I was in New
York. I asked him if he would be interested in leaving his present
job and joining me as a partner if I could get the agency. Warren
jumped at the offer, and wished me luck in New York. I spent
about three hours with the Yugoslavians, and when I left their office I had the agency. The first ship wasn't scheduled to arrive in
Los Angeles for three weeks but we had a lot of work to do, pre-

paring for the representation, finding out who our competitors would be, and who was shipping what cargo to the Mediterranean.

I always wanted to have my own steamship business. The agency was my opportunity to do something I'd wanted to do for a long time, and I wasn't going to miss it. We rented an office near 7th and Spring streets in Los Angeles where the rent wouldn't put us out of business. The Port of Los Angeles was glad to have more business, they appointed us the official hosts for the city when any Yugoslavian VIP's visited, and we entertained them at the expense of the city.

We started with one ship a month discharging and loading at Los Angeles and at San Diego. When I read in the paper that an anti-communist organization in San Diego said they were going to prevent one of the Yugoslavian ships from entering the port I called the Coast Guard for help. After I explained the situation, the man who answered the Coast Guard phone said he would have the officer in command call me back. About half an hour later a Coast Guard captain called to say that he would be down in San Diego with several Coast Guard cutters when our vessel arrived, to prevent and clear away any obstruction that developed in the entrance channel. That was good news. The captain of the Yugoslavian vessel called the harbor officials by radio, asked for permission to enter, and was immediately given clearance.

As the Yugoslav vessel started down the entrance channel a group of small boats left shore with flares going off right and left, the crew members yelling and singing as they tried to get in front of the ship. The Coast Guard cutters reacted immediately, effectively ending the demonstration. Some of the demonstrators yelled "Don't let this vessel deliver airplanes to Cuba." The demonstrators had secured a cargo list from the stevedores, but they hadn't read it right; Yugoslavia had purchased surplus planes, but they were sending them to Yugoslavia, not Cuba.

After the ship docked in San Diego, reporters came aboard and interviewed me in the captain's cabin for TV. They asked me how I knew the planes weren't destined for Cuba. I explained that the ship was calling at three ports in Europe before discharging in Yugoslavia and that the cargo for the European ports was on top of that for Yugoslavia and could not be discharged in Cuba. If the ship even stopped in Cuba the U.S. would know immediately and all aid to Yugoslavia would end.

The TV reporters interviewed the captain, asking him what he thought when he saw the small boats trying to stop him. He said, "Oh it looked just like carnival time in Venice."

The Yugoslavian steamship line was named Splosna Plovba and had a route around the world running eastward. Leaving the U.S. West Coast, they ran directly to the Mediterranean by way of the Panama Canal, stopping in Spain, France, Yugoslavia, Greece, India and the Orient. On the U.S. West Coast they discharged in San Diego or Los Angles and went as far north as Seattle. Then they loaded as they came down the coast, Los Angeles usually being the last loading port. Most of the crew on the first ships were Slovenian although later we had some crew from Montenegro.

Splosna Plovba's vessels were built only a year or two before we became their agents in southern California, so they were still in excellent condition. The officers and crew bent over backwards to be pleasant and cooperative. When I boarded the vessel the first time, the captain wanted to know what plans I had for discharging and what type of cargo I was loading. I went over everything with them, explaining why I did it that way. I had to make a stowage plan for the outbound cargo to guide the stevedores' loading. Although the captain and the chief mate had the authority to overrule me, after I explained my logic they let me do it my way.

When the first vessel arrived in port, I thought it would be a good idea to invite the shippers aboard for a dinner party. When

I received permission from the captain, I asked, "Do any of the crew have musical instruments to provide some entertainment?"

"Oh yes," he said. "They all sing or play some instrument."

The party was terrific, the crew and the guests enjoyed themselves so much that from then on we had at least one party while each ship was in port. Later, when I called on the shippers, the first thing they asked was, "When are you going to have another ship party?"

One of the Yugoslavian captains told me that when salesmen came aboard to sell ship supplies they always gave him a business card. He said, "I would like to have a business card to give them in return. How much would it cost to have some printed with my name and title?"

"Only about $20.00," I replied.

"Twenty dollars?!" he said. "Do you know what my monthly salary amounts to? I get paid $55.00 per month."

"Don't worry," I said, "I will have our printers make some for you at no charge."

When I delivered the business cards, he looked at them, then with a big smile said, "Now I feel like an American business man."

When I was in the steamship agency business, the Yugoslavian captains and crews were the most easygoing, cooperative people I worked with.

When we handled them, the Yugoslavian ships always had a full load of cargo when they sailed from Los Angeles. On each ship they had four or five nice passenger cabins, usually empty when they sailed from Los Angeles, so we asked the head office in New York if we could book passengers. They agreed, and after a few sailings, all of the cabins were full on departure from Los Angeles. A good selling point was the wine tanks built into the hull; wine was served at every meal except breakfast.

Our most interesting passenger cabin booking was to a retired couple who bought an around-the-world trip on the condition that they be allowed to take their piano with them. The captain gave permission, and the couple set out on their trip. When the ship returned to Los Angeles, I went aboard early to find out how things went. They had had so much fun, they (and their piano) were going around the world again.

As time went on, other ship owners and operators came to us for help. PAXMO was a broker and dealer for copra, for many years they controlled the sale and distribution of this commodity produced in the Philippines. Copra is coconut meat, used by pressing plants that produce vegetable oil, one of the principal ingredients of soap. The economically efficient transportation of copra must be done in bulk carrier type ships. A Norwegian ship owner with two old cargo ships, not the type that could transport copra economically, convinced PAXMO to sign a two-year charter party for the two ships. After one voyage it was obvious that the ships could not profitably handle copra. The new president of PAXMO was frantic to find employment for the ships, because they were bound to pay charter hire monthly for two years.

He was referred to us, and we told him that we could load the vessels on round trips between the U.S. West Coast and the Orient. The ships were old and slow because the engines broke down frequently and they were twin screw which made them use more fuel. One of the ships was in Los Angeles and needed cargo bound for the Philippines so it could load a cargo of copra back to Los Angeles. We filled it with cargo for Japan and Taiwan, and from there it went in ballast to the Philippines. Several others had told PAXMO that they could get cargo to the Orient, but they weren't able to produce anything. On short notice we filled the ship with cargo, minimizing their loss.

For two years we had Sunny Duke and Sunny Lady operating between California and the Orient. PAXMO could count on minimizing their loss by allowing us to handle the ships, and once in a while they even made a profit. Others told PAXMO that they could do better, but when given a trial, the results were always disastrous. We always got our commissions because we collected the freight charges.

After a couple of unusually profitable voyages of Sunny Lady and Sunny Duke, the president of PAXMO asked me to take a trip to Norway and spend some time with the Norwegian owner to further cement our relationship. I flew to Oslo on one of the early SAS polar flights and spent a few days with the ship owner. We talked of ways to improve the operation of his two ships, and he showed me around Oslo. Before returning to the U.S., I decided to call on the Italian Line's main office in Rome, to try to get more agency business for us. I got stuck there for a three-day layover before I could call on the Italian Line, but the time wasn't wasted because the stewardess on the flight from Oslo was also taking a three-day layover in Rome, and we spent the holiday together.

The president of the Italian Line heard me out over lunch, but because they had retained their agents in San Francisco for a long time, they weren't interested in making a change. I asked him to call me when he visited San Francisco and he said he would. I called the president of PAXMO to check-in before I left Rome, and he asked me to continue around the world, calling on our agents in Hong Kong, Taiwan and Japan. That was what I had been trying to do ever since I first went to sea on the Coya, after reading Richard Halliburton's story of working his way around the world. The end result was the same, but my trip was certainly more comfortable than Halliburton's, and PAXMO paid for it. Of course it took me a little longer than it did Halliburton to make it around the world. I left Andover in 1930, and now it was 1960.

I flew from Rome to Beirut, Bangkok and Hong Kong. I spent two days in Hong Kong, then went to Taiwan. What had been

China Merchants Steam Navigation Company was now in Taiwan and my call there resulted in our handling their ships on the West Coast for several years. We also represented Taiwan Navigation for a while before they discontinued operations.

My next stop was Japan where I spent a week working with our agents. In 1960, Japan and Taiwan were very different than they are now. The first time I was in Taiwan, in the early 60s, there were still many rickshaws on the streets. During my first trip to Tokyo, I was looking for an address and asked a Japanese man where a street was located. He looked at the address, took me to a bus, got on with me, paid my fare and delivered me to the address. I tried to at least pay him for the bus fare but he wouldn't take any money.

We named our two Norwegian ships the Scandia Pacific Line. As shippers began to see our consistently dependable operation, they sent more cargo our way. We developed a business with less desirable cargoes, such as green hides and alfalfa pellets in bulk which some of the lines would take only if they desperately needed cargo and could not find anything else. Less than full cargoes of scrap were not attractive to the lines who ran fast ships, but they fit our operation. We analyzed and adjusted our rates to produce profit for us and still allow the shippers to sell at fair market prices. Before long our ships were booked full several weeks before sailing dates. Brokers who sold alfalfa pellets to Japan found they could no longer get orders unless they used our ships because we had a slightly lower rate and kept our schedules. Unlike some non-conference operators who might cancel a firm booking just before sailing if they were offered a higher rate from another shipper, we made honest, fair deals and stuck to them.

During the two years that we handled Sunny Lady and Sunny Duke, we became known in the shipping world. Foreign ship owners called us to secure return loads when they had tramp ships scheduled to discharge in California. I made another trip to Oslo and spent some time with the owners of the Sunny Lady and Sunny Duke, trying to convince them that we were getting more out of the ships than anyone else could. As a result of that trip, they left the ships with us until they were sold for scrap.

With a one-year contract to haul scrap for a dealer in San Diego, we chartered a large Norwegian bulk carrier named the Balto. We had the outbound cargo, but in order to make a profit we needed return cargo from Japan. Our agents in Tokyo had offices in other Japanese ports, representing other steamship lines that weren't in competition with us. I spent two months in Tokyo to ensure consistent backhaul from Japan.

The Japanese agents gave me a private space in their office and I lived within walking distance at the Imperial Hotel. Before I left, I had the next two sailings booked full of eastbound cargo. When I made calls on shippers, I took the manager of the agency with me, so he could carry on when I left.

Shortly after I returned to the U.S. a movie company called to ask if we had a World War II cargo ship. They wanted to use it in a movie they were filming in our area and around Catalina Island. The script called for a fully loaded ship, so we found a ship, the Blue Dolphin, and loaded it with scrap for Japan with the understanding that the cargo would not leave the U.S. West Coast for at least one month, two months at the most.

Moratori starred Yul Brynner and Marlon Brando, and during the filming, they lived on Catalina Island. Since 1953, I had owned 5 successive power boats that I used to make regular trips to Catalina, so I knew most of the people who owned businesses in Avalon, the principal town on the island. Because of the movie company living there, all the businesses on the island were doing well. When they found out that I had set up the deal between the ship owner and the movie company, most of the bar owners wouldn't allow me to pay for a drink. Everyone in our office was allowed one day on the ship to watch the filming.

Marlon Brando came and went inconspicuously, but Yul Brynner got acquainted with everyone, often inviting his Hollywood friends to elaborate Chinese dinners on the Blue Dolphin. Yul had been raised in China and the crew members on the ship were Chinese. The crew would do anything for him because he spoke Chinese and treated them well, learning their names and getting them what they needed.

One scene in the movie put the ship at a dock in the Orient. For this scene, the movie company redecorated our dock with signs in Chinese and crates and boxes stenciled with Chinese words. We leased the dock to them with the stipulation that the lease would end when the dock was returned in its original condition.

During filming, the ship lost an anchor, later found by a local diver after running up a large diving bill. When the script called for a fire on the ship, the charterers placed gas pipe with holes in it around the main superstructure connected to gas tanks. When they were ready to roll cameras, they turned on the gas and lit it. The fire was so realistic that someone reported it to the Los Angeles harbor department who sent three fire boats to put out the fire. The fire damaged the paint, so the owner of the ship demanded a new paint job before he would accept re-delivery.

We finally lost Sunny Lady and Sunny Duke to a scrap yard in Taiwan. The Balto was still running, but the scrap dealer in San Diego had taken over the operation himself after we had taught him how to do it. We weren't hurting for money because the movie deal had paid well, but we knew we should get something else started before our money ran out. It was just our luck that Glen Howard came to us with a tanker converted to a cargo ship that he was trying to operate. A new bank in Los Angeles gave him a line of credit that enabled him to charter a ship, and he had hired a man who said he knew all about running ships but turned out to know nothing, and had made a mess of Howard's business.

No one around Los Angeles knew anything about Howard except that he was from Dallas and owned an office building there. My partner and I told him about our experience, showing him records that proved we had profitably operated vessels in the Transpacific trade. He had manifests with him showing the cargo that his ship, Belo Horizonte, had aboard, and asked us for a quotation to discharge the ship in Los Angeles or Long Beach harbor. I told him that the stevedoring companies don't make firm quotes on loading or discharging cargoes because they never know how the men are going to work or even how many gangs they will be able to get. He insisted that the bank required a quote, so I made one up and he gave it to the bank.

I was able to discharge the ship at a cost slightly below the amount I quoted, which made a good impression on the bank. They told Howard that if he hired us on a regular basis they would extend his credit line. When Howard approached me with the proposition, I told him that I required a one-year contract to handle all his ships. I wrote a contract detailing the amounts of all commissions and agency fees, so there would be no arguments or haggling, and he signed it. He chartered ships as we needed them and I appointed agents in Japan who I knew and had worked with before.

My crowning achievement for Glen Howard was chartering Belo Horizonte to the United States government to carry military cargo from the Long Beach army docks to Vietnam. In order to use Belo Horizonte, a foreign flag vessel, there had to be some compensation. The freight rates we collected were computed to adequately compensate an American flag cargo vessel for their considerably higher, made in the U.S.A., vessel cost and high union labor costs. I sold the War Shipping Administration extremely large hatch openings to speed up loading and the availability of cargo booms capable of handling 25 tons. The deal cost me two trips to Washington and a contribution to a political fund but it was worth it.

My partner, Warren, spent most of his time working on houses he bought to fix up and rent. I decided that I needed to get away from the office so he would pay more attention to our business, and the opportunity presented itself in the form of Dr. Lawton.

Dr. Lawton ran a school for medical and dental assistants in Beverly Hills, and was so successful that he decided to sell franchises, so he came to me for help. I was sold on the idea, and suggested that my partner join me to start a school for medical and dental assistants in Santa Ana. I found a suitable building that needed some alterations for which the owner agreed to pay if we leased for a minimum of one year. With Dr. Lawton's help, I hired one dental and two medical instructors and planned a big opening reception. One week before the opening, the furniture company said they couldn't deliver when promised. The invitations had already been sent out, so I had one week to dig up used furniture to fill our school. It was the busiest week I had spent in a long time, but fortunately for me, there was a good local supply of used school furniture available at considerable savings.

The reception was successful; prospective students, their parents, local doctors, dentists and members of the local press were there. The school wasn't far from my home in Newport Beach and was a convenient stop on my way to our office in Los Angeles. Our fourth month was the first profitable one and thereafter the profit gradually increased. My partner wasn't very interested in the school, but with me out of the Los Angeles office part the time he gradually took over more than he had before.

We had done a little business with Jim Chen, owner of a few World War II freighters and tankers that he operated as tramps. We had provided cargo for a couple of his ships and acted as cargo brokers for him, securing cargoes for his vessels at ports in the U.S. Gulf and Canada. He told us he intended to run several ships between the U.S. West Coast and the Orient on a regular basis. This gave us a more or less continuous service to work on and advertise in our local schedules. The ships were slow but his rates were low and he took almost any type of cargo. Chen's account kept my partner busy and away from his real estate.

After a few successful months I noticed that the manager of Dr. Lawton's school was spending a lot of time at our school, visiting my dental instructor. The next thing I knew she came to me and asked for a raise. When I turned her down, she said she was leaving the first of the month, giving me two weeks to find a new instructor. It didn't take me long to figure out that the other school had offered her a job at a higher salary. The franchise agreement specified that the original school would find employees for me and instead they were hiring my employees away from me. I complained to Dr. Lawton that he had broken my franchise agreement and I would no longer pay the monthly franchise fee. He agreed to meet with me, and brought his attorney. After the meeting, I didn't hear from Dr. Lawton or his attorney again, and I didn't pay any more franchise fees.

Over the years we had run an office in San Francisco, in addition to the head office in Los Angeles, staffed by a man and a secretary. Occasionally when I tried to call the office, no one answered the phone. On one trip to San Francisco, I went to the office at 10 A.M. and it was locked up. Jim Chen told me that he was only going to run his ships to San Francisco, canceling his service to Los Angeles. At the same time my partner said he wanted to buy my interest in the Lawton School. He wasn't interested in the steamship business anymore, he wanted to make his living from the school and his real estate. I greeted this news with relief, because my wife had filed for divorce, the house in Newport Beach was up for sale, and my son was in his last year at U.C. Santa Barbara. It was the perfect time for me to start a new life in San Francisco.

My new office was at 260 California Street and I leased an apartment in the Golden Gateway with a view of the Bay where I could see my ships before they went under the Bay Bridge. My office was only two blocks away and I had an office phone extension in my apartment so people in Europe or the Orient could call me during their day. Jim Chen said he would let me handle all his San Francisco bound ships, approximately one a month. I had also booked cargo for a Norwegian bulk carrier, expecting to hear more from them, and I was trying to get started in the cargo and ship brokerage business. I applied for a foreign freight forwarder's license, issued by a U.S. government office, which permitted me to do business documenting foreign shipments and opening bank credits and sight drafts in foreign countries.

My businesses were all related and worked together. Ship owners in Europe and the Orient called me regularly when they had space to fill or needed an agent for a ship discharging on the U.S. West Coast. Foreign owners were tough, they never gave away a penny. If the price wasn't right, no amount of persuasion influenced them. On the other hand, if they made money they didn't expect to make, they didn't hesitate to show their appreciation. On one occasion a Norwegian owner reluctantly accepted a price he thought too low, but after the cargo was delivered he made much more out of it than he expected. He sent me a check for $1,000.00 as a bonus.

I heard rumors that a Russian line was starting a ship service between the Orient and the U.S. West Coast. I made some inquiries and found out that they intended to operate passenger ships as well as cargo ships in the trade. One afternoon a Russian who spoke perfect English came into my office. He introduced himself, saying that his government was considering operating Russian ships between the U.S. West Coast and the Orient. He had been in charge of Russian shipping in England for a number of years, which explained his fluent English.

I outlined my experience, giving him the names of ship owners and operators I had represented. He seemed interested, but I got the impression he was gathering information for his superiors, who would make the ultimate decision. I talked to other people in the business and the story was all around. He came back a second time to ask if I had friends or relatives who were close to politicians who could be helpful for a new national steamship line. I told him my sister was married to a relative of President Roosevelt, but that I didn't know if the connection would be helpful. I got the name of his immediate superior in Moscow and asked if my going to Moscow would help. He said he would let me know.

My attorney was well known in the water transportation business. When I mentioned to him that I was considering a trip to Moscow to try to persuade the Russians to appoint me their U.S. West Coast representative, he said, "Just pay my transportation, I'll go with you and represent you."

I waited a couple of weeks, then phoned Moscow to make an appointment to visit the shipping group.

We had to pay for our hotel rooms in advance and buy tickets for food in designated hotels and restaurants. We met with the shipping officials for a week, then went sightseeing with a female guide for another week. Our tour guide spoke perfect English, but she had never been outside Russia. I asked her to visit me in San Francisco where I could be the guide and she could be the tourist, but she wasn't enthusiastic about it. Even so, the week of sightseeing with her was unforgettable.

We didn't get the job to represent them because they wanted to work with a larger organization. When their first passenger ship called at San Francisco they sent me an invitation to dinner and a show on board. Their Russian dancing in costume was something I will always remember.

One weekend, after working night and day for ten days I needed a rest, so I went to Lake Tahoe with a young lady who had worked for me in our San Francisco office when I was still in Los

Angeles. On Monday I was still in Tahoe, so I called my secretary to tell her I would be returning a day late. She told me I had a call from Jim Chen who was looking for cargo for a ship that was loading in New Orleans. I called Wiborg, a San Francisco broker, who offered 2000 tons of wood pulp to Kobe, Japan at a workable rate. I called Jim back and he booked the cargo on the phone without any dickering. He trusted me, and knew when he had a good deal.

As I became better known, new business came to me from some of the most unexpected sources. A consolidator in Brooklyn, N.Y. had been accumulating knocked down houses in his warehouse, intended for shipment to Saudi Arabia in containers. The containers had to be a special high cubic size that was difficult to find in large quantities. The KD houses would be erected in Saudi Arabia for a village of American workers, employed in the construction of an oil refinery. The shipments were slated to move over a six month period, and the rate was high enough for the steamship company to buy fifty or sixty high cube containers that they could also use for other cargo. I told the caller that I knew a company that would take the business, a Saudi Arabian steamship line managed by a retired American admiral.

I had been introduced to the admiral at a social function the day before. He had recently been appointed as the U.S. manager of a Saudi Arabian steamship line, but there had been several managers before him who allowed their eastbound business to slack off. The admiral knew nothing about the business of running a merchant shipping company, and he was feeling the heat from Saudi Arabia because their ships were still returning with little cargo. The one shipment I was setting up for him would provide a steady stream of back haul for six months, and I knew he would do anything to get it. I dictated a contract to him over the phone, outlining the terms under which he must deliver the cargo and furnish the containers. "I must have a yes or no answer now because if you are not interested, I'll have to find someone else today," I said.

He put me on hold, and when he came back to the phone, he said yes.

"I'll be in New York tomorrow afternoon between three and four with the contract ready for your signature," I said.

When I got off the phone from talking with the admiral, I called the consolidator and said, "I have the cargo booked, and the high cube containers will be furnished by the steamship line."

The manager for the consolidator was a retired Brooklyn police officer with a lot of interesting stories to tell about the life of a Brooklyn cop, but all I wanted from him was his signature on the contract.

In New York City the next day I got a cab at the airport and went straight to the offices of the Saudi Arabian steamship line. They were waiting for me and we went through the contract I had read to them over the phone. There was some disagreement between the admiral and some of the others about the wording, so I reminded them that I had read the contract over the phone and they had agreed to it. They left me in the lobby and went to their private offices to discuss it. They returned with the signed contract but they had changed two words. I guessed that it was meant to show that they were in charge, because the two words they changed had absolutely no effect on the meaning of the contract. When I went back to the waiting cab, I asked the cabbie how much he would charge me for the use of his cab for the rest of the day with an hour off for lunch.

"$100, if the last stop is the airport," he said.

I paid him the money, took care of all my New York business and got the consolidator's signature on the contract.

On the flight back to Los Angeles I estimated my commissions on the deal to be $40,000. Not bad pay for a days work! The Saudi

Arabians made me wait about thirty days for each payment, but with a deal like that, I couldn't complain.

When Warren and I formed the Pacific Steamship Agency, an unknown in the steamship business started Retla Steamship Company. The name Retla derived from Walter spelled backwards, and for this reason it was rumored that the owner was receiving financing from Walt Disney. I watched Retla grow and concluded that they must have had financing from somewhere. When they first started they only served Los Angeles, but after I moved my office to San Francisco, they asked me to handle their ships in San Francisco. I wasn't soliciting cargo for them, my only concerns were operations loading and discharging, so I was paid a flat fee per vessel. It came in handy when I was first getting started in San Francisco, but I gave it up after a while because I was required to be up night and day during discharging, and their demands became a constant irritation.

In 1972 I married Sandy, and we bought a house in Alameda adjacent to a yacht marina. We decided to buy a sailboat since San Francisco had plenty of wind and I had learned to sail about ten years before with rental sail boats in Newport Beach. Our first sail boat was a 30 foot Dufour made in France. We took delivery right off the ship, and dropped it into the water alongside.

We kept Sagitaire in a slip a few steps from our condo, so she was always accessible. We regularly sailed the bay on weekends, occasionally taking longer trips to the Delta and Drakes Bay. It was also a great way for me to entertain clients who were not restrained by the fear of becoming seasick. After Sagitaire we bought a 32' Challenger which I named Septimus, since it was my seventh boat.

One morning, I received a telephone call at my office from Mrs. Olsen, a woman in Phoenix, Arizona who wanted to see me about a ship load of KD houses going to Saudi Arabia for housing foreign workers who were going to build a new port. She asked me to come to Phoenix as soon as possible so she could fill me in on all the details. The morning I arrived, she came to my hotel and told me she was the contact for the importer's agent in Saudi Arabia. I told her that the first thing I needed to know in order to secure shipping space was accurate information regarding the weight and the cubic measurement of the proposed shipment. If the cargo was to be transported in containers, the measurement would be easy to estimate, but if it was to be loaded loose we had to have a detailed description. Mrs. Olsen. didn't look or talk like a business person, and she brought her little grandchild with her to our meeting. She said her husband was in Detroit buying a new car.

When I returned to San Francisco I thought I wouldn't hear from her again. Instead, I made two more trips to Phoenix. When all the material was listed, they decided to have it manufactured near Houston, Texas and ship it from that port, so I secured space on a Canadian flag ship. When the ship was at the dock ready to load, the supplier of the windows for the houses said he couldn't meet the scheduled deadline. I suggested that they load the ship and when the windows were ready, they could ship on a cargo plane.

The woman thought it was ridiculous that the ship couldn't wait idle at the dock for a week, until I explained to her how much the charterers were paying per day for the use of the vessel. I went to the New York bank where the letter of credit had been opened with the "on board" bills of lading. I was supposed to pick up a certified check to cover the whole deal, but one of the bank officials had found an odd provision in the instructions. The provision prohibited the bank from issuing a check until the contractor provided an affidavit guaranteeing that the transportation provider, both by air and water, had no member of their board of directors or company officers who were Jewish. Fortunately, both the operators of the ship and the cargo airline had head offices in New York.

I knew the shipping company was run by Scandinavians, so after getting their statement, I went to the cargo airline. They weren't so easy. The local manager said he didn't know whether he should sign or not, so I had a tough selling job before I headed back to the bank with the required documents. When the draft was issued, I called Mrs. Olsen in Phoenix and made arrangements for her son to meet me at the airport in Phoenix with a check for my $15,000 commission, in exchange for the bank draft.

I thought it was the last I would hear of the deal, but I was wrong. When the ship arrived at the port in Saudi Arabia, the receiver of the cargo was nowhere to be found. The operators of the ship unloaded the cargo, building materials, furniture, and rugs, on an open dock. Apparently the Saudi Arabian who ordered the stuff and opened the letter of credit to pay for it couldn't be found. It was rumored that he was visiting his girlfriend in Beirut, Lebanon.

My home phone rang at about 2 A.M., and when I answered, it was Mrs. Olsen calling long distance from Saudi Arabia, trying to get things straightened out. She called me every night for seven nights in a row at about 2 A.M., and before it was over I knew I had earned every penny of my $15,000. commission.

Chapter Six ⚓

A Leisurely Cruise to Panama

When my son graduated from college he wanted to be a naval architect so I gave him a desk and a phone in my office, and some part time work. He had worked for a naval architect in Newport Beach during the previous summer, and before long had a permanent job in San Francisco, and stayed there for eight years.

I began thinking more about Robinson's trip around the world, and wondered how long it would take me to financially prepare to undertake a long cruise on my own sailboat. Sandy also thought it would be fun and said that she would take a leave of absence from work to go with me when I was ready. The first step was to sell my business. Unfortunately finding a buyer for a business like mine wasn't easy. In the course of business, I mentioned to several people that I was ready to sell my business. About six months later I met a man named Mr. W., who had been president of a large freight forwarding company with offices on both the East and West Coasts. He had apparently been in some kind of trouble, lost his job, divorced and was remarried. His new wife wanted him to get back to work and was willing to finance the cost of buying or starting a business similar to the one he had been in. I could sell any of or all of my business, but I could only sell my foreign freight forwarder license to someone bondable, with substantial experience in the business. Obviously Mr. W. had the experience but I thought that there might be something in his history that could prevent him from being bonded.

While I continued looking for a buyer I kept Mr. W. in mind, and when I hadn't seen him for a while inquired about him. The person who had introduced me to him was a freight solicitor for a Philippine steamship line who I frequently saw around town. Eventually, Mr. W. and I met to go over all aspects of the deal in detail. The foreign freight forwarding portion of my business was expanding, contributing a progressively larger portion to my total income, which made my business more appealing to Mr. W. He sent his lawyer over to discuss terms and investigate my claims of income.

I read a story about cruising in the Greek islands known as the Cyclades, and discussed it with Betty, who had spent some time there while traveling with her husband. She thought it was the most wonderful place in the world to visit. When Sandy and I discussed our proposed sailing trip, I said I would like to sail around the world, but she objected to such a long trip. She did agree to sailing from San Francisco down the coast past Central America, through the Panama Canal and spending some time going down the chain of islands that stretch all the way to Grenada. We had already chartered boats in the Bahamas, Virgins and Grenadines sailing from St. Vincent to Grenada, so we didn't want to go that route again. We decided to go up to the Chesapeake and spend some time there on our own boat.

The deal to sell my business had not yet been closed, so I suggested chartering a boat in Athens, Greece and sailing around the Greek Islands as training for our upcoming years on our own boat. She agreed suggesting that we ask my old friend Paul and his wife to go with us. They said they'd love to go, so long as we wouldn't be gone longer than ten days. We made a deal with a yacht broker in San Francisco who represented a Greek broker in Athens. Landing in Athens, we went to our hotel, and Paul found out that there were some people from Vallejo, where he lived, who were also going along with us. Our boat was a 33' Carter sloop and after we were shown how everything worked, we headed for the island of Kea.

In order to convince Sandy and Paul's wife, Marion, that we would be there before dark I had to stretch the truth a little, and as it turned out, we didn't arrive until almost midnight. When they complained, I told them, "A sailor cannot always predict the strength of the wind in the future."

We found out that Kea had a taverna on the dock, and the action didn't really get started before 11 P.M. As we entered the port, we heard the music and people singing in Greek. The natives helped us tie up and we walked across the dock to the taverna. All of the tables were full, so the owner and a waiter ran down to the next taverna, picked up a vacant table and brought it back to where we were standing. We asked if they had anything to eat, and they ushered us into the kitchen where we could look everything over, smell it and, if we wished, taste it. We gave our orders to the cook and the waiter brought it to us.

We relaxed, ate our food, drank our retsina wine, watched the dancing and listened to the singing until about 2 A.M. When we asked for a check, the waiter asked us what we ate and drank, and from the information we gave him he made out the check. We added a generous tip, and paid him. We managed to get back to our boat and sleep soundly for the rest of the night and into the following day.

We slept late, then after breakfast took a walk around the island. When we returned to the port we wanted to take on fuel and water but were told that it was after noon and no one would be working until about 3 P.M. When traveling it is necessary to compromise with the natives so we took another walk up the hill where the houses, all whitewashed, gleamed in the sun. As soon as we were able we filled up with fuel and water, then later, enjoyed our last evening of dancing and singing at the taverna. While we were there we noticed that some of the people who lived on the hill apparently didn't have cooking facilities because they brought pans of prepared food to the taverna to have it cooked.

The second morning we got an early start for the Island of Serifos about fifty miles away. It was similar to Kea with a couple of tavernas on the dock and a village of white houses on the hill. From Serifos we sailed due east to Paros and tied up at the quay. We were back in civilization, there were tourists around giving the place a completely different atmosphere. There were restaurants, hotels and a variety of modern shops. We were told that a local retsina and a red wine were produced on this island, and a car ferry from Piraeus called daily, connecting with Naxos.

My sister told us we must see Santorini no matter what we had to miss, so we sailed from Paros at sunup.

Santorini is an extinct volcano that erupted out of the ocean in ancient times, and there has been much historical speculation written about the eruption. The original island sunk below the ocean but the round crater, broken in several places, has become a circle of islands on which the standard whitewashed villages stand. The principal village is Thira where we tied the bow to a mooring buoy and the stern to the dock. The only way to get up to the village, besides walking, was by riding donkeys. The road zig zags up the face of a cliff and from the top I looked straight down to the deck of our boat several hundred feet below. They said the animals we rode were sure-footed, but on the trip down the donkey decided to nibble a little grass from the side of the road, and I could see over his head all the way to the bottom. It was a bit hair raising. Sandy refused to go down by donkey, she walked down instead. The town was very interesting, but we were unfortunately running out of time and could stay only a couple of days.

It was almost dark when we dropped our anchor in a well-protected bay at the island of Amorgos, backed into the dock and made fast. Amorgos is a Greek island without tourists, but there was a small restaurant, and fuel and water for boats. The next morning before we left, we took a walk up the hill to the old monastery. It was closed but from the outside, the building looked ancient and interesting. On the way back to the dock a farmer came to the fence between the properties, holding out some cucumbers and a couple of tomatoes to us. I thought he wanted to sell them and asked, "How much?"

He was insulted and said, "No, no I give for you."

We thanked him profusely. We had been spoiled by the tourist islands, but could once more appreciate an island where the small population made a bare living by farming the rocky soil.

We set sail for the island of Naxos, approximately 45 nautical miles away. We anchored and tied to the dock just before dark. Naxos is the largest of the Cyclades, lots of people and water craft crowded the harbor. There was a lot of activity along the waterfront too, restaurants and tavernas, steamers coming and going, and caiques loading and unloading. We were tired from our day's sail, so we went ashore for an excellent dinner, then returned to Lilly, our chartered boat, for the night. Above the port a few interesting remains of the old Venetian town are scattered across the side of the hill.

The next morning we hired a taxi so we could see as much of the island as possible in the one day we had available. A number of monasteries dating from the 15th century, and the Frankish castle behind the town had been taken over by a convent school. The population of the island was approximately 20,000 people. The white marble used by sculptors is one of the Naxian exports today. The Venetians captured the island from the Byzantine

Empire early in the 13th century, and ruled until 1566, when they were overwhelmed by the Turks.

We didn't have time to visit the colossal Apollo. 34 ft. tall, cut in solid marble about 2,000 years ago at the northern end of the island southeast of Cape Stavros, it was originally intended for export to Delos. At the last moment, they decided that the quality of the marble was inferior so Apollo was abandoned without ever being detached from his bed.

Mikonos and Delos were our last island stops before heading for the mainland. Mikonos is strictly a tourist port where all the cruise ships stop and the streets are crowded until early in the morning. There are many fancy hotels and restaurants where everything costs more than double what it does elsewhere. Delos, on the other hand, is unusual and very interesting. We were told that we could not take our boat over to Delos because the landing area was allocated to the boats that made a business of taking tourists from Mikonos to Delos. Since the tourist boats didn't run between 11:30 A.M. and 2:30 P.M. we arrived there at 11:30 A.M. and remained until the first load of tourists arrived at about 3:00 P.M. Our plan worked except there was no one to take our line so Paul, in his swimming trunks, jumped in the water and took our line ashore. The operator of the last tourist boat said we couldn't do what we were doing but made no effort to stop us.

In ancient times, Delos was a banking center, with vaults full of gold and jewels. There were rows of larger than life size statues of lions, meant to guard the vaults of gold and precious stones. One of the guards told us about the ruins and how the island looked in ancient times. There were no tourists on the island while we were there so we had it all to ourselves.

We returned to Mikonos for the night and sailed early the next morning for Merika Bay on the Island of Kithnos. From there we went to Cape Sounion to see the temple of Poseidon for our last evening on the boat. The next day we were on our way up the coast to Piraeus, arriving late in the day, and returned to our hotel to enjoy some of the comforts of living on land. I flew from Piraeus to Alameda via New York and Sandy went to Washington, D.C. to visit her parents.

Everything was in order at my office, apparently my business ran pretty well without me. Mr. W. had left calls for me every day for three days before I returned. He was anxious to proceed with the sale and set up a meeting with me and his attorney for the next day. We soon had an agreement but his wife insisted that I pay for the bond. I refused, but agreed to finance the sales price over a period of several years at a high interest rate. The deal was made. That was in 1978, and according to the phone book he was still doing business in 1993.

After the sale was completed I started preparing for my cruise, beginning with looking for a larger sailboat. I traded in Septimus, my 32' boat, for a 38' Morgan that I named Belo Horizonte, after the Philippine flag cargo ship I had chartered to the War Shipping Administration for a cargo of army supplies to Vietnam at U.S. flag rates.

Sandy and I both took refresher courses in celestial navigation at a local school to prepare for our cruise. When our new boat arrived from the factory on the East Coast I had to outfit it with equipment for an extended ocean cruise. We installed an Alpha Marine automatic pilot, two anchors (a Danforth and a CQR), 300 feet of anchor chain, an inflatable dinghy with a small Johnson outboard, a set of sails made by Sobstad, a ship to shore radio, and a new, made in Japan sextant. I installed a kerosene cooking stove because I knew natural gas wouldn't always be available in the ports we were going to visit. When we got to St. Augustine, Florida, I added loran which was good going up the East Coast when we were under way at night.

When fully loaded with cruising gear we drew $6\frac{1}{2}$ feet. The designed draft was 6 feet but I had some after thoughts about going up the Intracoastal Waterway with 6½ feet. As it turned out, we did hit the bottom a few times and once stopped in the middle of the channel and got off only by hoisting sails which heeled the boat over, reducing the draft until we came off the bottom. The boat was factory equipped with a 110 jib and a mainsail with two rows of reef points. To this we added a light 150 jib and added a row of reef points on our 110 jib. The only time we reefed the jib was crossing the Gulf of Tehuantepec during a blow when, without any other sails up, we averaged 7.5 knots for 250 miles.

In my youth I had read everything I could get my hands on about long distance cruising in small sailboats. I thought about William Albert Robinson sailing around the world. I was on the verge of fulfilling a life-long dream of long distance cruising in a sailboat with one other person.

We had to sell our condo at Ballena Bay before we could leave but when we couldn't get a decent offer, we rented it furnished to the daughter of a friend. On the 25th of February, 1979, we departed from Ballena Bay Marina early in the morning, with my old friend Paul Barney who was going with us as far as San Diego. Our water and fuel tanks were full and our three cylinder Yanmar engine purred. We soon had our new sails up and were going at a modest pace towards the Golden Gate Bridge. Our friends, Rod and Char, had a plane and were going to fly in circles above us for a few moments to say farewell. I couldn't believe that after all those years of hoping and wishing, at the age of 68 my dream was coming true.

Just as we went under the bridge I spotted the plane. Rod and Char proceeded to fly around in circles then dip their wing and turn back towards the Concord airport. Our first stop was at Half Moon Bay where we anchored for the night. While we were getting warmed up in the cabin from the trip down the coast, I heard a rattle outside and went out to investigate. A man stood in his dinghy alongside us, trying to get our outboard loose from the stern rail. I yelled at him, and he quickly dropped into his dinghy, saying that he came out to warn us that we were not anchored in good holding ground.

I told him that if I caught him near the boat again, I would call the harbor police on my radio. He rowed away cussing under his breath.

The weather report the next morning said the wind was blowing at 32 knots. Looking at the sea outside the breakwater I believed it. The direction was from the northwest which is normal for that time of year. I steered for several hours then turned the wheel over to Paul so I could take a rest. About half an hour later I heard a crash and the boat heeled over. I went to the cockpit and Paul quickly disappeared below. The main sheet tackle was all tangled up and there was a mark on the boom where it had hit the shrouds. Apparently, Paul had gybed in a 32 knot following wind and since the rigging had not come down we didn't ever have to worry about it again.

We were outside Monterey at about 10:00 that night and as we rose to the top of each swell I looked for lights marking the entrance channel. We found our way in and looked for an empty slip where we could tie up. The only one we could find was in the commercial fishing boat section and no sooner had we tied up than a harbor master came along to tell us to move. The slip we were in belonged to a fishing boat that might show up during the night. It took some convincing on our part, but he agreed to let us stay if we promised to get out if the other boat showed up. We promised and he left. We were all in the cabin getting warmed up when Sandy announced that if we were going to have dinner I had to plug in the shore electric cord. I put on my sheep skin coat and in my wet, cold, exhausted condition, decided I could jump over to the dock. I didn't quite make it and landed in the water. The cold water and the freezing wind were bad enough, but the worst part was, I couldn't climb out without calling for help.

We spent the next night in Morro Bay, then we went around Point Conception sailing all night in a pouring rain storm with howling winds to an anchorage in the lee of Santa Cruz Island. We dried out when the sun came up and Paul corrected the steering trouble we were having. Our next stop was at the isthmus of Catalina where we got a good night's sleep before heading for San Diego. We got a slip at the San Diego Yacht Club for a week and Sandy's parents spent a week there with us. It was our last stop in civilization so we took our time getting everything we needed and moved the boat to the Coronado Yacht Club where they let us stay for about three weeks. While we were there I got my income tax return filed and bought spare parts for Belo Horizonte. The time came when we had no more excuses for staying so early one morning we said good-bye and sailed from San Diego heading for Guadalupe Island. As we departed from our last U.S. port early in the morning, I thought of the going away parties that Rod and Char, Annie and Nancy and Ken in San Diego had given us, and wondered when we would see them again.

We sailed all that day and the following night. At daylight the next morning we started looking for Guadalupe. There was a cloud bank on the horizon, so we could not see the island. At around noon the cloud bank lifted and there was Guadalupe. This was the second time I had done any celestial navigation since World War II, so I was relieved when the cloud disappeared and the island came in sight. We anchored in a deep bay at the south end of the island, the first and last time I ever had all of my 300 feet of anchor chain out except for the time in St. Augustine when I took it to Jacksonville to have it regalvanized.

There was a Mexican fishing boat nearby, and soon after we had anchored, they came alongside in their dinghy asking if we had any liquor. We had half a bottle of Tequila, and they offered us some abalone for it. They brought us a dishpan full of delicious abalone that took us about three days to eat. The wind blew us around the anchorage all night long, but my 300 feet of chain and CQR anchor held. Late the next afternoon I heaved up the chain with my ratchet windlass and we headed for the Mexican mainland.

We found the Mexican mainland where it was supposed to be, but sailed right by the entrance to Turtle Bay. Rather than turn back I decided to keep going to Santa Maria Bay where we arrived two days later. Santa Maria Bay is just north of Magdalena Bay where most boats stop on their way to Cabo San Lucas. We stayed in Santa Maria Bay overnight, then headed for Cabo San Lucas. The first day in Cabo, we were occupied with the usual hassle of going through customs, immigration and filling out endless papers. We also located a laundress who took care of all our dirty clothes at a bargain price.

Early the next morning I heard someone with a foreign accent calling, "Belo Horizonte, Belo Horizonte." I stuck my head out the companion way hatch and there was Paul Barney approaching on a native shore boat. A friend had mentioned that he was flying his private plane to Cabo San Lucas so Paul got a ride down to visit us. When we told him our next port was Puerto Vallarta he decided to go along for the ride. The last night at Cabo San Lucas we listened to some wonderful mariachi music at the new Finisterre Hotel high on the end of the cape. We also revisited the Cabo San Lucas Hotel where Sandy and I had spent a couple of short vacations. Paul had a room at the Hacienda Hotel and we borrowed his bathroom to take showers.

After filling our fuel and water tanks we headed for Isla Isabel. We had been told that the island had interesting wild life and except for a couple of fishing camps it was uninhabited.

The next morning we passed the Islas Marias on our starboard side and went on to Isla Isabel. After looking the island over we decided to keep on going to Banderas Bay and Puerto Vallarta where we arrived April 20th. We spent the first few days at an anchorage and then moved to a dock with electricity and water hook-ups. Paul moved to the Hotel Playa de Oro where they had a Fiesta Mexicana which we enjoyed along with the shower in his room. There were many other "yachties" at the dock where we were tied up, some on their way north or south, and some had decided to stay where they were indefinitely. Next to the dock where the yachts were tied up, there were commercial fishing boat docks. In the middle of the night one of the fishing boats suddenly burst into flames. Every one was up and ready to move their boat if the fire should spread. Fortunately the fire was extinguished, but only after three fishing boats were destroyed.

Paul departed for the civilized world. Brad, who had worked in my office in San Francisco for several years, joined us for a few days of vacation. Sandy had been to Puerto Vallarta several years before and wanted to show us a spectacular waterfall at Yelapa on the south coast of Bandera Bay. We anchored off a beach and went ashore in our dinghy. The walk to the supposed waterfall was long and uphill, when we got there it was only a small trickle of water. A nearby resident told us it was the wrong time of year to see the falls.

Back on Belo Horizonte we headed for Las Hadas but anchored at Tenacatita before we got there. The next morning we went on to Las Hadas, a beautiful resort hotel. We lived at the huge pool with waterfalls, a bridge, a partially submerged bar that we could swim to and beautiful music playing all the time. We left Las Hadas in the evening, sailing for two nights and a day to reach Zihuatanejo, an old Mexican village. Zihuatanejo was the opposite of Las Hadas, it was a charming little native Mexican village with lots of friendly people who gladly helped anyone in trouble. We felt like we were in a story book town from long ago. Brad left us here and flew back to his job in San Francisco.

Our next stop was Acapulco, where we anchored in front of the Club de Pesca Hotel, close to the Club de Yates. The Club de

Pesca Hotel was unable to compete with all the new hotels that had been built since I was there in 1953, 26 years before, but it was still there. It brought back memories, so we had dinner there one night.

A cruising catamaran anchored close to us was owned and built by a man who was following Sir Frances Drake's route around the world. He came aboard one night and we spent a pleasant time with him.

The stores in Acapulco carried practically everything available in the U.S. so we went on a shopping spree, loading up with everything we thought we would need for the trip to Panama. My son, Jim, was going to meet us at the Club de Yates and go with us to Puntarenas, Costa Rico, so we wanted to stock up.

The next evening at happy hour we heard someone calling to us from shore. We looked out and there was Jim. We picked him up with the dinghy and had dinner later at the Club de Pesca Hotel. At about noon the next day we sailed for Hualteco, the last port before crossing the Gulf of Tehuantepec, notorious for bad weather caused by winds from Texas, northers coming over the narrow isthmus of Mexico and crossing its waters. I had been across the Gulf before in 1953 with Guiberson's Sea Rider. The Mexican crew had said it was dangerous to cross, instead we should follow the coast line close ashore.

We left Hualteco just before sundown and got some strong puffs of wind right away. Before dark I had the main down and we were charging along with only the 110 jib. The next day the wind increased, so we put a reef in the 110 jib. It poured rain for several hours during which we filled our fresh water tanks and all took showers on deck in the rain. The seas were building but fortunately we were going with them. I took several sights during the day when the sun came out from behind the clouds and felt that I had a good position. The next morning the weather moderated and late in the afternoon we sighted land ahead. Our course took us close to the channel entrance leading into the anchorage of Puerto Madeira just north of the Guatemalan border. There were two cruising power yachts tied up in the basin that was being dredged for a harbor.

When they saw us, the skippers of the two power boats came aboard. One of the boats was about 65 feet and the other about 50 feet, both heading north. Both skippers were very concerned about the weather crossing the Gulf of Tehuantepec. The 65 foot boat was returning from a three-year trip around the Caribbean and the 50 foot was on a delivery trip from the U.S. East Coast to San Francisco. The temperature was over 100 degrees so we appreciated the invitation to use the shower on one of the power cruisers. We had dinner with them in the cockpit of our boat. The three of us pitched in to get an ice truck to deliver enough ice for all three of us before we sailed. As we were leaving the entrance channel we passed an incoming boat whose skipper we had talked to in Acapulco. We told them we would see them in Costa Rica. We were headed for the Gulf of Fonseca and the port of La Union in El Salvador.

We intended to stop in El Salvador and stock up with supplies so we wouldn't have to go into a port in Nicaragua or even go close to the coast. We had read about several American boats being taken into Nicaraguan ports against their will and in some cases their boats had been confiscated. Before we went in, we were not aware that El Salvador was in a state of revolution. When we did go ashore, all public buildings were surrounded by walls of sand bags to conceal armed soldiers. Just before sunset, a howling windstorm rose up. As night fell, we entered the Gulf of Fonseca, then went through a narrow passage behind an island. When we came to some anchored ships we checked the depth, decided that was as far as we would go that night and dropped our anchor.

The next morning we went along the coast looking for the town of La Union, then anchored off a dock near the town. A port official came out in a boat to give us documents for entry into the port. In the port director's office we were told that there was a revolution, so we must quickly get what we needed and leave. In order to get supplies we had to change our American money to Salvadoran money, then return at 1 P.M. when a port official would take us in a truck to buy whatever we needed. We changed our money and brought a supply list, the soldier and a truck were waiting for us when we returned.

While we were in a grocery store I saw some beer so I suggested we get it there, but the driver, who knew the best place to buy each item, said there was a better place to get it. The better place turned out to be the barber shop. At the ice plant I was offered a huge piece of ice that I couldn't handle on the boat. When I asked him to cut it into smaller pieces, he refused, but the soldier made him change his mind and he cut it as I requested.

It took two loads in the dinghy to get our supplies aboard. As soon as we were loaded, the soldier said, "You are to leave this port immediately."

It was late in the day and I remembered the narrow passage on the way in, so I asked if he would allow us to leave at daybreak. He agreed to daybreak, but only if we would stay on the boat during the night, not come ashore and be out of the port by 8:00 the next morning. We shook on it then went aboard.

When we left El Salvador, we felt good, our fuel and water tanks were full and we had more ice than we could use before it melted. We were headed well offshore to avoid being forced into a port along the coast of Nicaragua which was very unfriendly to U.S. citizens at the time. It was about two days and two nights to the Gulf of Nicoya through several rainstorms and lots of lightning. We had heard of a place called the Hacienda on a nearby island, and we anchored there the first night.

The people at the Hacienda told us that we had to anchor in the river behind the town of Puntarenas in order to enter through customs and immigration. When we went there, several other yachts were anchored along the river so we dropped our anchor to stay clear of the others. The next morning we started the process of entering and went ashore. We were told that an unattended dinghy would be quickly stolen, so we left ours at the ice house where there was someone to look after it.

When we bought our boat we equipped it with an inflatable dinghy powered by a Johnson outboard. The second night we were anchored in the river I had left the dinghy with the outboard still attached, tied to the stern of Belo. At about 4 A.M. I awakened suddenly, and walked out to the cockpit. Looking over the stern I couldn't see my dinghy so I ran forward and scanned the river. There was nothing visible. At first I couldn't figure out why I woke up, but when I saw that the dinghy had disappeared, I realized that the thief had made a noise.

So we had a new problem, we had to find a new dinghy and a new outboard. We yelled to the boat anchored closest to us and eventually got their attention. We told them our dinghy had been stolen and we needed transportation ashore so we could get another. At about 10 A.M. we got ashore and reported the theft to the police department. They were uninterested in our plight, so we then went in search of a new dinghy. We found a used wooden one at a shipyard up the river and they said they would deliver it to our boat. The only outboard we could find was a new one at the Seagull outboard showroom.

We went to the police office again to ask if they had any clues as to who stole our dinghy. They said they knew who did it and when possible they watched his house but the house was a long way from town. They were allotted such a small amount of gasoline, they couldn't make more than one trip a month to that area. They said that if we gave them money for gas, they would catch the culprit and return our outboard to us. We gave them the money, but they never caught the thief.

Soon after the unpleasant incident we moved our boat back to the Hacienda and relaxed with the other cruising boats that were anchored there. One of the boats had a parrot on board and the owners wanted to ride the narrow gauge railroad up to visit San Jose for a couple of days, but didn't have anyone to take care of the parrot. We volunteered to feed the bird while they were away, and they left on the train the following day. When they returned, it was our turn to go while they watched our boat, dinghy and outboard. The train ride alone was worth the time, but the city of San Jose was worth it too, old and interesting, with a lot of American retired people. We stayed in a small hotel where everyone spoke English, including the waiters and desk clerks.

One night while still anchored at the Hacienda, we had a lightning and thunder storm, the worse one I had ever experienced. At one point, we heard a terrific explosion and I ran to the cockpit to see what had happened. I saw other people in their cockpits and yelled, "Who got hit?"

Several yelled back at the same time, "You did."

One of our neighbors in the anchorage had feared we were both dead and jumped into his dinghy to row over to our boat. Our antenna, attached to the top of the mast was now reduced to small pieces about three inches in length scattered all over our deck. The man in his dinghy rowing toward us had once seen a man killed by lightning and was really shook up. I was glad that my son Jim was already on his way back to California.

As a result of the lightning strike all of our electronic gear was ruined. This included our ship-to-shore radio, depth recorder and automatic pilot. We decided we had better get to a civilized place where we could get replacements as soon as possible. Heading towards Panama we decided to stop at Golfito. Captain Tom ran a place in Golfito that catered to cruising yachts and the crews of freighters that regularly stopped there to load bananas. Captain Tom had only one leg and, according to rumors, had once been a smuggler with his 85 foot converted Coast Guard cutter. At his establishment he had a good supply of all the pleasures that seamen traditionally looked forward to after a long trip at sea. When we returned to our dinghy after a trip to town, we learned that one of our dinghy oars had been used as a club in a fight between the person who ran the dinghy dock and one of his customers. I was now obliged to paddle my dinghy with one oar, which made me anxious to get to Panama and civilization where I could get things fixed.

Between Golfito and the Gulf of Panama we didn't see any other yachts.

We anchored every night and slept, rather than sail all night without electronics. The first night we anchored in a protective cove and before long were joined by several boat loads of native fishermen whose boats were loaded with fish. They gave us fish which we had no way of keeping fresh because we had no ice, and we tried to politely refuse, but they kept on handing us fish because we didn't speak the same language. They were all happy and friendly, but we had to get some sleep, so we went among them saying "Buenos Noche" and "Mucho Gracias" until they finally got the message and left.

Because our radio wasn't working we had some difficulty getting admittance to the Canal Zone. We anchored at the entrance and at about midnight a Canal boat came alongside and wanted to board. We were relieved that we could finally talk to someone and gain admittance to the Canal.

After breakfast the next morning I started pulling up the anchor chain in preparation for going in to the yacht club where a Canal officer would meet us. An official Canal boat came up alongside of us and asked me what I was doing. I told him in an offhand way that we were going in and continued to heave up the anchor. He got very excited and yelled, "You are not going in. Drop your anchor immediately and I mean NOW!"

I stopped heaving in the anchor and looked at him for a moment wondering what was going on and he yelled again, "I said drop your anchor now!"

By this time it looked like he was reaching for his gun so I let go the anchor, period. There was another officer in the wheel house who had been calling headquarters on the radio. He stuck his head out and told the officer on deck that headquarters said we had been cleared for entrance. Meanwhile, I had 200 feet of chain to haul up again.

When we went into the yacht club anchorage, a boat was waiting to take us ashore and showed us the buoy where we were supposed to tie up. The Canal official in the club house was very friendly. After we found out that his name was Simmons, the same as some of Sandy's relatives in Texas, he decided he was related to Sandy and bent over backwards to help us. I had made a reservation by mail to have Belo Horizonte hauled out in Panama and the bottom painted. We also had to have our radio, auto pilot and depth recorder repaired from the lightning strike. The office said we had to deal with the operators of the haul-out facilities regarding the date they would be able to handle our boat, but there was a limit of two weeks that a transiting boat could stay at the yacht club.

The day finally arrived for our haul out and, believing that the operators of the carriage would have looked at the plan I gave them, I headed into the carriage in the water. When a boat was being hauled the members of the club lined the porch and shouted instructions to the helmsman. This was confusing because some of the members were influenced by the drinks they had consumed, not by logic. My boat had a fin keel which extended six and a half feet below the water line and obviously some provision had to be made to support the bow. In spite of the members' yelling, I put the boat into the carriage, but when they started hauling the carriage up, the boat fell forward. I shouted at the man running the engine to release us back into the water. He quickly did so, and there was no damage done because the water supported us as we dropped back.

It was a good show for the onlookers and they all cheered when we backed out of the carriage. For me it was the cause of a few more white hairs. Now we had to wait another two weeks before we could be hauled, exceeding the time allowed to us at the yacht club by a month. The club office was sympathetic, so to prevent the other members from objecting, they told us to go to the anchorage at the entrance of the Canal for two days, then return to the club.

The Canal entrance was alongside a man-made jetty that had a paved road and a large parking lot adjacent to the Canal building at the end. During our time at that anchorage, there were riots all over Panama. The Panamanians yelled, "Down with the Americans! Panama for the Panamanians!" One man stirred up a riot at the parking lot alongside of us. We ignored it for a while, but as it got larger and louder I decided to pull down our American flag. Some of the rioters were pointing at us and yelling but they finally quieted down and went away.

Before we were hauled out the second time, I spent an afternoon arranging braces and a marker on the carriage to show the brace for the bow, so it could be seen before the carriage came out of the water. I showed the man who ran the hoist a complete plan and gave him a copy of it to look at during the haul out. The onlookers hadn't had as much to drink the second time around, and everything went well. When we were in place a loud cheer went up from the audience. The ways were at a sharp angle to the ground, in our final position the bow was ten feet higher than the stern. This was all right for painting the bottom but a little uncomfortable for sleeping in a bunk.

While we were in Panama, Sandy met an American school teacher who continuously told her how dangerous it was for a woman to shop alone in Panama. To make her feel safe Sandy and I volunteered to go shopping with her one day. As she looked for a coin in her purse, she held it up so she could see inside, and a man grabbed it and started running. She screamed and I chased the thief. He didn't get far before he saw me and another man chasing him, so he threw down the purse. Sandy picked it up and returned it to our friend. I kept on running after the robber. At the time I didn't know that one of the others who was running along with me was a plain clothes cop. When we got the man cornered the cop was glad for some help to handcuff the thief.

The evening before we were scheduled to transit the Canal we remembered that the pilot would require us to have help handling lines while we were going through the locks. We asked for volunteers in the club bar, offering to pay railroad fare back to Cristobal, and got more volunteers than we could use. We settled on several members of a large family who were going through in their own boat later.

Sandy's college roommate, Inge, arrived from California with our repaired auto pilot, and we were ready to transit the Canal. It was not something new for me because I had been through the Canal in 1953 with the Sea Rider. In 1953 we had a regular Panama Canal pilot but in 1979 we had an advisor, a native Panamanian familiar with the Canal and an experienced boat operator. Our advisor was in radio communication with the Canal operations department. On one occasion he asked me if I could increase speed to arrive at the next lock in time to go through with a tugboat. I told him I could and we made it just in time. The size of the freighters and tankers going through the Canal had increased since 1953, and tugs were required to get them around some sharp curves in the Canal.

When I went through this time, we weren't tied to the side of the lock, we were tied to a small boat that was tied to the dock, so we did not have to adjust all lines constantly as the lock filled or discharged water.

We arrived in Colon at about 6.00 P.M., and discharged our line handlers on the boat that came to pick up our advisor. The next day we installed the repaired auto pilot Inge had brought with her. We finally had our depth recorder fixed in Panama but our radio was still able only to send or receive at very short distances.

We left Colon, heading for Portobelo, an ancient town where the Spaniards warehoused and reloaded their plunder after bringing it across the Isthmus of Panama on the backs of mules. The remains of the fort that guarded the harbor and a warehouse that held gold and coins on the other side of the bay, were still there. The bay has shoaled to the extent that Belo Horizonte drawing $6\frac{1}{2}$ feet could only get half way in. We continued up the coast anchoring at an island or a village each night until we came to El Porvenir in the San Blas Islands. We bought molas from the Indians. The Cuna Indian women make colorful clothing by using reverse applique. These molas are in great demand because of their unique design.

There were no accurate depth charts available, so we spent a day running aground and getting back off. After that we only explored the larger channels. At our last anchorage in the islands some natives came out in their canoe to sell us molas. We told them we already had molas, but would be glad to buy a lobster for dinner if they could get one. About two hours later they came back with a huge lobster that we called Big Red. Finding a pot to cook him in was a problem but we finally shortened him a little and managed to squeeze him into a bucket. We stopped at only one deep water port in the San Blas Islands where small freighters docked. It was a bustling port, loading copra and discharging general cargo from Columbia from small shallow draft freighters.

We left the San Blas Islands heading for San Andreas. The island of San Andreas is owned by Columbia but the native islanders apparently don't like Colombians very well, they identify themselves as Islanders, not Colombians. San Andreas has a large but shallow, protected harbor. Looking at the harbor chart I was relieved when a small boat came alongside, and the skipper identified himself as a harbor pilot. I paid his fee and relaxed while he took us through the shoals to an anchorage with plenty of water for our $6\frac{1}{2}$ foot draft.

We anchored near a stone dock used by yacht owners as a dinghy dock. We were awakened the next morning by a shout from the dock calling "Belo Horizonte" in a voice with a distinct Colombian accent. A man on shore in a white uniform with a lot of gold braid waved a letter in his hand. I jumped into our dinghy and rowed to the dock. It was a letter from my sister, delivered by what looked like an admiral of the Colombian Navy. Later I learned that he was the port captain.

We departed from San Andreas without a pilot and sailed overnight to the island of Providencia. Because of our draft we had to approach the harbor by a circuitous route but made it without even scratching the paint on our keel. This island, like San Andreas, was owned by Columbia. While we were walking around sightseeing we were approached by two men who looked Colombian. They demanded we show them our passports immediately. We said we didn't have passports and tried to walk away. They blocked our path, and again demanded that we show our passports immediately.

I told the men that the port director had our passports and wouldn't return them to us until we departed from the island. At this point one of the Colombians put his face about two inches from mine and started yelling something I didn't understand. A native in a nearby parked car jumped out and told the Colombians that we were telling the truth and if they wanted to see our passports they had go to the port director's office. The Colombians backed off, we thanked the man who stood up for us, and we continued our walk.

Our next stop was a reef with shallow water a day's run from Providencia where we anchored for the night.

Before we got to Roatan Island we stopped on several other islands overnight. On one of the islands, we met a hermit who was very friendly. He needed coffee which we had plenty of, and were glad to give him.

When we were anchored close to another island, a shrimp boat was anchored near us and at our invitation, the captain came aboard. We enjoyed a drink together, and told sea stories. We were low on ice so he brought us a sack full, then asked us if we would like some shrimp. We said, "Sure," and he asked us for a sack in which to put them. The only sack we could find was the one our outboard motor came in. We assumed he would put a couple of servings in it, but he returned with the sack full of shrimp. We were about three days away from Roatan so we enjoyed shrimp at every meal along the way. When we thought we were close to Roatan we sighted land, but the island we were looking at turned out to be Guanaja. It was pouring rain and we had been out for several days so we went in and anchored.

First a man with two kids came alongside saying they were hungry, so we gave them the last of the shrimp. We had eaten so much shrimp we were tired of it, but they were very appreciative. Later that day a man came by in an outboard and introduced himself. He was a retired engineer from America who had bought property with a house on the island and was living there. He invited us to come with him to the other side of the island the next day. We accepted his invitation and enjoyed the tour and his company. After the trip he took us to his house where we had dinner and met his wife. He also showed us a house that was for sale and for a moment we considered what it would be like to live on the island. The next day we heaved up our anchor and headed for Roatan.

Roatan was owned by Honduras but many of the people living there were descendants of British pirates and spoke English. We had to go to Coxen Hole near the west end of the island to enter through customs and immigration. When we got there two other American yachts had just come in. We were finally cleared, all three of us headed for French Harbour and the adjacent anchorage.

Belo Horizonte was there for about four months, but Sandy and I went to California, then to her parents home in Silver Spring, Maryland for Christmas. We weren't in Roatan very long before Sandy developed chills and a fever. I tried to find a doctor but only managed to find a native nurse attending a woman on another cruising yacht in the anchorage. I brought the nurse to Belo to take Sandy's temperature. The temperature was so high the nurse told me I must go ashore to the pharmacist's house and get a drug to reduce Sandy's fever. It was pitch dark outside, there were no street lights in French Harbour let alone lights to mark the channel to the town.

I jumped in my dinghy, started the outboard and headed for French Harbour. After a couple of wrong turns I found the town, tied up the dinghy and wandered down the dark street looking for the druggist's house. A couple of times I had to stop people on the street to ask for directions. Finally a man pointed out the house and although there were no lights on, I rang the front doorbell. I heard a low growl and a huge dog came out from under the porch swing. I retreated to the street. A light went on in the house and the door opened. As I started to walk back up to the porch, another growl came from under the swing. I told the person at the door what I wanted, she told me that the druggist was in church but she would look to see if she could find the pills I had been told to get. After hushing the dog, she invited me in to wait while she looked for the pills. She couldn't find the medicine and suggested I go to the church to talk to the druggist.

It took me awhile, but I located the church. When I walked in, the preacher was giving his sermon to an attentive congregation. I walked right down the center aisle up to the pulpit and interrupted the preacher telling him it was an emergency, that I needed to talk to the druggist. The preacher asked the druggist to come to the pulpit. I explained why I was there and apologized for interrupting the service. The druggist told me to come back to her house with her. She searched for the pills but couldn't find them, and gave me something "just as good." I must give one to my wife every half hour until the fever went down. I paid her, thanked her, found my dinghy and motored back to Belo where Sandy, sick and scared, wondered what had happened to me.

Throughout the night I alternated covering her with blankets, taking them back off and forcing her to take a pill every half hour. By dawn her fever was only down a little below the danger point, and I was about ready to give up. At daylight we went ashore and took the bus to a native hospital at Coxen Hole. Just being in the hospital was enough to make me sick. After an examination, the doctor still didn't know what was wrong with Sandy. I had heard someone mention that there was a retired American doctor on the island and I found out where he lived. I went by dinghy to his dock and walked up the stairs to his house. He sat alone on the porch with a glass of rum.

I told him who I was and why I was calling on him. He asked where our boat was anchored, then offered to come to our boat to examine Sandy. "I took her to the hospital in Coxen Hole and the doctor said he didn't know what was wrong with her," I said.

"That's understandable," he said, placing a glass on the table with the bottle of rum. "I'll just go shave, then we can go to your boat."

"Please," I said, "just come the way you are."

It took him about five minutes to determine that she had malaria. "Take chloroquin regularly, and keep your temperature down. That's about all you can do." To me he said, "It would be a good idea for you to take it also, it's a preventive as well as a cure. You can buy it at any store that has drugs."

Sandy was relieved that at least she knew what was wrong with her and seemed to feel better right away. In a few days she was well again, but we both continued to take chloroquin.

Paul Barney sent me a letter while I was at Roatan, he and his wife were coming to a resort there and wanted to see us. We met them as they got off the plane on the dirt runway that was Roatan's "airport." When they told us where they were staying, we let them know that the hotel where they were supposed to stay was hard to get to in the winter, charged too much and was deserted this time of year. They quickly changed to a hotel on the coast that had outboard boats to rent, making it easy for us to visit each other.

Thanksgiving wasn't far off and there were quite a few American yachts in port. We discussed getting together for a Thanksgiving dinner and they appointed me to see Dr. Wes, who had treated Sandy, to ask if he would rent one of his condos to us for the day.

When I asked the doctor, he said, "You can use my house and my servants will cook the dinner. I'll send one of my men to La Ceiba on the Honduras mainland to buy the food and we'll split the cost."

Everyone agreed to this arrangement. The doctor also imported liquor for the CSY yacht charter operation on Roatan and had a good supply in the liquor warehouse located in his basement.

We had our Thanksgiving celebration on the doctor's porch which extended across the front of the house, overlooking the beautiful Roatan coastline. The doctor's servants cooked and served the meal and drinks, and everyone fully enjoyed the pleasant surroundings and friendly group. The party didn't break up until dark when the doctor lead us all back to the anchorage where the yachts were waiting. We got lost in the dark but finally found the anchorage, all of us singing at the top of our voices, having a great time.

By Thanksgiving Sandy had recovered from her attack of malaria and I was taking my chloroquin regularly. Shortly after Paul and his wife flew back to California, we decided to spend Christmas in Silver Spring with Sandy's parents. We also decided to move from French Harbour with Spindrft to a well-protected, land-locked anchorage with a good dinghy dock at Little French Harbour. A German named Carl M. Heinz Welbach, who owned a large house overlooking the bay was rebuilding a place that had been a bar and restaurant that he intended to reopen when it was rebuilt. We and Spindrift with Clair and Dorothy on board, had decided to stay there until spring when we would continue to the islands to the north.

Our decision to stay was partly due to a storm that had hit Roatan one night between Thanksgiving and Christmas. The rain poured down and I woke up concerned that my dinghy would fill up with water and sink. I put on my foul weather gear and stumbled out to the cockpit. The wind howled and the rain poured down. The dinghy looked about ready to sink so I pulled it close to the stern ladder and climbed down with a bailer. I started to bail but it looked like I wasn't keeping up with the rain water that was slowly filling the dinghy in spite of my furious bailing. I stopped to rest, the dinghy slipped below the surface and began to sink. I barely made it back to Belo because my clothes and foul weather dragged me down as I tried to swim. Our anchor had dragged and the stern of our boat was touching some marine growth above the water. After a struggle I got the bow of the dinghy up out of the water and lashed to the stern rail, then went below and turned in.

A couple of days later we moved to Little French Harbour. We had no chart for the entrance, but with the help of some fishermen and the information that Clair and his friend, Dorothy, of Spindrift had told me, we made it into the anchorage. The people on Spindrift agreed to watch Belo Horizonte while we were in the U.S. over Christmas. Sandy went directly to Silver Spring but I had to go to San Francisco to take care of some final details in connection with the sale of my business. I planned to join Sandy in Silver Spring when I was finished. The day before I left San Francisco my skin itched all over and by morning my hands were swollen. I knew something was wrong but couldn't figure out what it was. When I arrived at the airport, I was glad that Sandy's father was there to meet me, because my hands were so swollen I couldn't pick up my luggage.

It was Sunday, so I went straight to bed when I got to Sandy's parent's house. Sandy's father called a doctor friend of his at home and told him about my symptoms. The doctor, who worked for the National Institute of Health, said, "When the football game is over bring him down to my office."

He gave me a lot of tests, then told us he would call on Monday to let us know what was causing the trouble. That night I itched so badly I had to take a hot shower several times during the night. The next day the doctor said my condition was unusual and if I wanted them to treat me I had to let their student doctors examine me for a day. By this time I was covered with scales and scabs from my scalp to my feet, but I couldn't turn down the free treatment. All day I sat naked on a table while doctors examined me and took samples of my scales by scratching off my skin. They examined me with magnifying glasses, poked and prodded all day long. I didn't mind until four women doctors came in and looked me over from head to feet.

To show their appreciation they supplied various ointments, powders and pills, which gradually improved my condition at no cost to me. My malady was a reaction to the chloroquin I had been taking to protect me from malaria. If I had my choice I would prefer malaria. By the time I was back on Belo Horizonte I was as good as new and the bout with psoriasis, caused by the drugs that were supposed to protect me from malaria, was over.

When I got back to Roatan I went to see the doctor who had prescribed the chloroquin. I asked him if he knew what effect chloroquin could have on some people. He had not practiced medicine for some time and was very curious. I showed him a copy of a picture the N.I.H. had taken of me at my worst and he was amazed. He asked me for the picture and I gave it to him. He looked at the picture, then at me, as I sat in front of him in my dinghy with no shirt, and normal skin, he couldn't believe what he saw in the picture.

As spring came to Roatan all the yacht owners who had spent the winter there planned where they were going next. It was a nice place to spend a couple of months. When I was tired of sitting on my boat and wanted to take a walk, I went down the road to Coxen Hole. Every car that passed stopped to ask me if I wanted a ride. The scenery around the island was magnificent, the coast was dotted with little bays and harbors. As the weather improved we walked across the island on trails that had been there since the days of the pirates. We found out that we could get food that had been flown in from the U.S. at the CSY charter boat base at very low prices.

Paul Barney's son, Paul Jr., wanted to sail with us to Ft. Myers, Florida and we were glad to have some help. We waited for good weather, made a false start and were forced to turn around and return to our anchorage after we rounded the west end of the island and were slammed by huge waves. After several days of good weather we decided to leave the next day. With our tanks full of water and diesel fuel and our ice box full of ice and food, we heaved up our anchor and pulled out of the French Harbour anchorage. When we got to the west end of the island and turned north, the weather remained nice with a northwest wind of sufficient force to keep us moving at about 6 to 7 knots. As we sailed north, the wind slowly died down, we lowered the sails and started the engine. A jib sheet was on deck, partly in the water, and when the engine started it got tangled up in the propeller. I tried to pull it up, but it was too late.

We were hit with a gust from the north, the boat heeled and we knew we were in for some rough weather. Unable to use our engine any more because of the sheet wrapped around the propeller shaft, we put two reefs in the main, took down the jib and lay with the wind on our port bow. The wind increased to 40 knots from the north, and we knew that a norther out of Texas was blowing down on us. The sky was overcast and the sea became very uncomfortable. We were practically hove to but a strong north setting current against the wind combined to build up huge waves.

A small container ship became visible heading toward us and although we had never been able to get our radio repaired we knew we could be heard over a short distance. I was worried about the shoal water off the coast of Yucatan so I called the freighter and asked for a position. They could hear me but could not understand, and finally gave me a position for which I thanked them. They asked if we needed help and I told them we didn't. The position showed me we were clear of shoal water, moving north with the strong current.

Just before dawn the night after the freighter passed us, we saw a beacon light in the sky, that we knew could only be from the airport on Cozumel. Our position indicated that we had passed the south end of the island and were almost abeam of the north end. The wind had been steadily decreasing and we had added sail, so when the sun came up, we had already rounded the north end of

Cozumel and turned south into the strong current under full sail. Our next problem was getting into the marina and docking with no engine. We dropped our sails at the marina entrance and when a fishing boat came along we asked for help to get in. He tied up to our stern, took us in, and we tied up to a commercial boat. We cleared the jib sheet from the propeller but the rubber shaft bearing was completely gone.

After we were docked I looked around for the fishing boat that had taken us into the marina. It was tied up in a section of the marina that was reserved for commercial fishing boats. I told the owner I had been looking for him because I wanted to give him something for helping us get into the marina without our engine. He promptly said "No, seamen must help each other. You owe me nothing! I am glad I could do something to help you." He was a hard-working Mexican fisherman who had not yet been spoiled by tourists.

There was a sport fishing tournament in Cozumel while we were there and the yacht harbor was full of fancy fishing machines that had been brought down from Texas and Louisiana for the tournament. Some of the owners brought their families with them.

We complained to the skipper of the boat next to us about the loud music blaring from his loud speaker in the middle of the night, but he didn't care. The next thing we knew the harbor master came down to our boat to tell us to move to another dock because the one we were tied to was reserved for tournament boats. I told the harbor master that I was sorry but I couldn't use my engine because the shaft bearing was burned out. It was obvious that the harbor master had been paid to tell us to get out, but he had the money and didn't care whether or not we left. We stayed there until we departed for Florida.

Cozumel was an interesting place. I had passed by it with the Sea Rider on the way to Corpus Christi and wished then that I could stop and look around. We hired a car and drove all over the island, visiting the tourist hotels and Indian ruins still visible in the middle of the island. We looked for a place to haul Belo out of the water and replace the rubber shaft bearing, but the only available place was where the fishing boats were hauled out and it couldn't accommodate our $6\frac{1}{2}$ foot draft.

While walking along the dock, I met a fellow from Panama, a delivery skipper who worked on the boats that belonged to the yacht club members. He was in the process of delivering a new boat from Florida to Panama. When I told him about my broken rubber shaft bearing, he told me he could scuba dive under the boat and replace the rubber shaft bearing with flax packing. We knew it wouldn't last very long, but it would allow us to get out of the harbor under our own power and maybe even enter the harbor at Ft. Myers. After the packing job I went over his planned route back to Panama with him, so he would know the places to bypass, the good places to stop, and a few of the hazards to avoid.

The skipper on an old wooden schooner across the bay from us said he was leaving for Texas the next morning and would like to have some company if we were about ready to leave. We told him we were, and because his schooner was faster, we left half an hour ahead of him.

The sky was overcast and the wind blew about 32 knots from the northeast. We put two reefs in the main and used our 110 jib. Before we were past the end of Cozumel our speed was up to 7 knots. The schooner that started behind us caught up and passed us with the wind and the strong north setting current. Suddenly the wind increased and the sky got black, the schooner ahead of us came about and headed back towards us. As he passed he talked to us on the radio, recommending that we turn around, too. He said that in his experience, when the day started out the way that one did, it quickly got worse. We were reluctant to turn around but watching the weather for half an hour convinced us.

Because of the strong current setting north it took us all night to get back to Cozumel.

We made our final departure from Cozumel a week later, on March 15, 1980. Again, the weather was rough and windy from the northeast. This time we hoisted the storm jib along with the double reefed main. We were heading for Ft. Myers, Florida, a port we had never entered before. The weather gradually improved until noon of the fourth day with the 150 and the full main we were making about 1 knot. An hour later we drifted with no headway. We saw a Coast Guard plane in the sky and a bale of marijuana floating in the sea, and wondered if there was any connection between the two. Finally the wind switched around to southwest, and we felt a little puff so we immediately hoisted our main and 150 jib. We made some headway but a thick fog was setting in. When we got into a depth of 15 feet and could hear land noises through the fog, we dropped our anchor.

We tried to call the Coast Guard on our limited range radio, and although they answered, they could not read us. The fog dissipated to reveal nearby fishing boats, and we decided to send up a flare to get their attention. We had a kit of several flares, so I held one while Sandy lit it. Nothing happened. The second one went up about ten feet, then fizzled out and dropped into the sea. The third one just got over the rail before it fizzled out. It was enough to attract the attention of a fishing boat, and they came by to ask if we needed help.

They called the Coast Guard on their radio and told us a boat would be out soon to tow us to a marina at Ft. Myers Beach. When we were finally tied up at the marina, I had the best hot shower of my entire life.

The next day Belo Horizonte was towed to a boat yard and hauled out. We left a long list of repairs and new equipment at the boat yard, then caught a plane to California and spent a month there selling our condominium.

Chapter Seven ⚓

Adventures at Sea

On May 20th we flew from Ft. Myers Beach to Silver Spring to visit Sandy's parents. We returned to Florida on June 1, after stopping in Williamsburg and Newport News to visit a couple we had met in Costa Rica. We arrived back in Ft. Myers Beach to find out that Belo, while at our dock in the marina, had been hit by lightning again. We had to replace or repair all our electronic gear for the second time. There were a lot of shrimpers working out of Ft. Myers Beach, so the suppliers of shrimper equipment were in abundance. One electronics firm told us they had developed a system to protect boats and their electronics from lightning damage. They said that no boat fitted with their safety equipment had ever been damaged by lightning. A radio antenna that could be folded down during a lightning storm was attached to the mast, then a ground wire with a zinc plate was installed between the back stay and the water.

With this new protection we bought a new ship to shore radio. Our auto pilot was sent back to the manufacturer in California for repair and our depth recorder was replaced with a new model protected by a fuse. When we arrived in Ft. Myers we had been on Belo for about a year, so the idea of a home ashore would be a comforting thought when at sea in a storm. We found a furnished condominium overlooking the Caloosahatchee River with a dock, cooking utensils, dishes, vacuum sweeper, washing machine, bed clothes, pictures on the walls and a beautiful view of the river for $50,000. We bought it and returned to it during the next six years whenever we got tired of the boat and needed a place ashore. We rented it during January, February and March for $1,000.00 per month to people from the north who wanted to get warmed up.

We found several other boat owners in Ft. Myers that we had seen along the way from California, and we all agreed that we would leave Ft. Myers together on Sunday October 26th. for the Caribbean.

The wind blew all night before our departure date, lowering the water in the channel so much that we ran aground in the middle of the channel. Several boats tried to tow us off but no one could move us. When the tide was up a little in the middle of the night we moved a short distance but soon were aground again. Early the next morning, with aid of a fishing boat, we finally got into the Caloosahatchee River. The day we left we were supposed to have lunch with friends on a house boat at Ft. Myers Beach, but instead we asked a passing boat to tell the people on Low Bid that we were aground and would be a day late. When we arrived they had received the message and lunch was ready. We were in the Moss Marina, where the Coast Guard had towed us when we first arrived.

Two boats went with us to Naples, Florida; Surrender who we met in Costa Rica, a Down East 38, and an Irwin 37 named Snow Drift whose owners, Jay and Joan we met in Ft. Myers. We anchored overnight in Naples, then headed for Marathon Island in the Florida Keys. We sailed and motored all night because there was very little wind, by daybreak we were approaching the highway bridge underpass to Marathon Island. We spent the night at Boot Key Marina and sailed to Rodriguez Cay to anchor the next night. We woke up the next morning to find out that during the night we had dragged anchor about a quarter of a mile. The next morning we, accompanied by Surrender, headed across the Florida Straits and arrived at Great Isaac Light at about sunset the second day. The last three or four hours of the run we were beating into head seas, throwing spray all over the boat and making very slow progress, but we were first to arrive and get anchored. Until I got enough scope out, I thought we were going to pull the anchor windlass out of the deck by the roots. Surrender came in about two hours later, her owners looking wet, cold, and tired.

The next morning we got our anchor up and headed east to the Northeast Providence Channel and then south to Nassau. I had been to Nassau before but under slightly different conditions. As national marketing manager for Western Gear Corp. I had been making some calls in Florida when I realized it was Friday, 1 had more work to do in Florida, and would have to stay a weekend, so I flew to Nassau. The hotel was luxurious, and I was on the beach most of the weekend, looking at the pretty women, just relaxing.

After the nine-day trip from Ft. Myers, I was tired and hardly looked at the women on the beach. All I wanted was a dock where we could tie up, remain for a few days and replenish our supplies for the next leg of our trip. We spent the first night at a beautiful marina, but it was a little too rich for our blood. When we found out how much it was costing us, we moved to another marina that had everything we needed, closer to town and not so expensive. Surrender was with us but Snow Drift didn't arrive for several days. They found us and tied up in Yacht Haven with us. Our arrival in Nassau was on November 5, 1980. The only inexpensive item in Nassau was rum. Dee and Nardine also joined us in Nassau on their boat, "Heck Fire."

One of the things I remember about Nassau is the 60 foot power boat that was tied up on the other side of the dock alongside of us. Everything aboard was shipshape and clean with two husky crew men to do all the work. The boat was named Lois Jane. Every evening a good looking young woman in a fancy dress relaxed in a large chair facing the dock. She greeted many of the men who came down the dock, by 10 P.M. she was usually below where music played.

The day before we sailed a skipper came aboard the Lois Jane, and they were suddenly all business getting ready to sail. After they left there were a lot of stories being told about them but I don't think anyone really knew what they were talking about.

We departed from Nassau at 8:30 A.M. November 17th and went out the back entrance through a shallow pass that we would only attempt at high tide. We got out without hitting the bottom and headed for Allan's Cay in the Exumas where we arrived at about 4.30 P.M. The harbor was full of yachts from all over the world, but there was nothing ashore except one abandoned stone house on the beach, and a family of iguanas that will eat any offered food out of your hand. They are sometimes a little careless and will bite a hand in their hurry to get food. We gathered a big pile of conchs on the beach, took out the meat, cleaned it, then divided it up between the people on the three boats with us. We had a conch stew cook-off, using our best cooking and seasoning skills. We all relished all the stews, but Ilene on Surrender won the contest.

We continued on down the Exuma chain, stopping at Hawksbill on Staniel Key where we met Wayne and Kristina Carpenter. They had set out from the U.S. West Coast in a 27 foot Nor'sea sailboat with their two daughters and Wayne's mother-in-law. They were down to one daughter and themselves which, I imagine, is better than five in a 27 foot boat.

Our next port was Galliot where we anchored for the night. As we started through a pass to the outside of the Exuma chain I suddenly lost engine control of the boat and assumed that the propeller came off. We got a jib up faster than we ever had before, made a U-turn in the pass and sailed back to the anchorage. Surrender was fast behind us to help, and Heck Fire hadn't left yet, so all three of us were back where we started that morning.

The key in the slot on the propeller and engine shaft, had come out and fallen into the bilge under the engine. With John's help we got it put back together and were ready to start again the next morning. We had 30 knot winds, so John and I started but Dee said it was too rough and turned back. John and I arrived at Georgetown at 3:45 in the afternoon and spent several days doing laundry and re-supplying. John caught two barracuda that he shared with us and Dee, who arrived at Georgetown one day later. On December 12 the three of us left Georgetown for Cape Santa Maria at the north end of Long Island. There was nothing but an anchorage where we spent the night and prepared for the long trip down Long Island to Clarence Town on the East Coast.

We departed Cape Santa Maria on December 13 at 8:45 A.M., arriving at Clarence Town at 2:55 that afternoon. We spent a couple of days there talking to the natives who were clean, healthy and hard working. We watched the inter-island freighter loading and discharging with the natives' help. We left Clarence Town early in the morning and arrived at Pittstown on Crooked Island that afternoon. We decided the anchorage was too rough and unprotected, so we continued to Hogsty Reef where we arrived the next morning. There John on Surrender helped me make a new key for the key way on the propeller shaft out of a screwdriver, and re-connect the shaft to the engine. On the trip from Clarence Town the key had fallen out of the shaft and I had to go down into the bilge, find the key and reinsert it into the key way while the boat rolled in the sea. With the new key the problem was temporarily cured.

John and I were below working on the propeller shaft for some time, when we came up we found out that the anchor had been dragging and we were close to the wreckage of a Liberty ship which had gone on the reef soon after World War II. The wind was up to 40 knots, John was back on Surrender and we decided to get out of the shallow water over the rocky reef. Heck Fire had dragged and re-anchored and did not want to move, so we left Hogsty Reef, heading for the sea. We sailed toward Great Inagua in a southeasterly direction with a 40 knot wind from the west which gradually diminished until we could use the auto pilot again. We had no charts for the entrance to Matthew Town, so I discussed the situation with John on the radio. We decided to go to the south side of Great Inaugua to find a comfortable anchorage. We anchored in about 30 feet of water with large swells. The wind had decreased. Dee called to say they were following and we explained to him where we were anchored. He arrived at our anchorage at sunset. By 2 A.M. we were rolling and pitching, and the wind howled again.

Early in the morning of December 19th John sang Happy Birthday to me on the radio and soon afterward Dee came in with his version. It was too rough to paddle a dinghy, so John and his wife put their son in their dinghy and, since they were upwind from us, slacked off the painter until I could throw a line to their son and pull him in to Belo Horizonte. He had a fancy birthday cake which John's wife had made. We cut off a few slices for John and Ilene, then they hauled their son back aboard. That afternoon all heaved up our anchors and headed for Cape Haitian, one of the ports I visited in 1930 as an ordinary seaman on the S.S. Martinique. We arrived the next day and tied up to the very same wharf where the Martinique had been tied up when I was aboard.

Cape Haitian looked very much the same as it did in 1930 except then the U.S. Marines occupied the town. It was a little dirtier the second time, and more crowded. The day after we arrived we were ordered to leave the dock and anchor out in the harbor because a cruise ship was expected, and it would take up all of the dock. At 6:30 the next morning the M.S. Skyward of the Norwegian Caribbean Line docked there. Where we were anchored, the passengers could see us and many yelled to us, asking where we had come from. One female passenger on the ship asked if she could change places with one of us, to which Ilene shouted back a resounding yes. We all went aboard the Skyward and had a free lunch because the stewards thought we were passengers. When we saw the huge Christmas tree on board, we all got in the Christmas spirit.

When I first visited Haiti as an ordinary seaman on the Martinique I learned about Emperor Christophe. When I visited Haiti the second time, we hired some horses and followed the trail to Christophe's Citadel. For a person like Christophe with no education, only basic tools and mules to haul building materials, it is a marvel of determination.

Christmas was only two days away and we all wanted to celebrate Christmas at a civilized place with a good dinner at a beautiful location on the water. Dee and I were given the job of finding a place. We located a French hotel with the dining area beside a huge pool on the side of a hill overlooking the ocean. The place was decorated for Christmas, and the people serving us spoke enough English to take care of our requirements. It was nice to get away from the dirt, noise and confusion of the town where peddlers followed us down sidewalks crowded with people and animals.

The day after Christmas at 7:00 A.M., we pulled out from the harbor at Cape Haitian and headed for Manzanillo, our first port in the Dominican Republic. After clearing customs and immigration we sailed at about noon and headed for Puerto Plata. It was an all-night sail in pouring rain with up to 50 knots of wind. We tied our stern up to a concrete dock, and the first wave that came along pushed our stern against the dock bending our transom ladder. To go ashore we had to put our dinghy in the water alongside, then get in and pull it back to the dock. After we were ashore we had to pull it back alongside to keep uninvited guests from going aboard. Puerto Plata was a pretty civilized place compared to Haiti, there were hardware stores with marine supplies. Prices were very reasonable on everything and meals ashore were so good we didn't want to eat aboard very often. A hotel owned and operated by an American, offered hot showers and good dinners at a reasonable price.

For New Year's Eve we decided to have dinner at the American owned hotel. The dinner was excellent, but before we were finished, the owner came to our table and told us the building next door was on fire, and we had to leave because the building we were in might catch fire any minute. We tried to find out how much we owed so we could pay him but he just told us to get out as quickly as possible. We told him where our boat was docked and wished him luck. The next morning a man from the hotel came to the dock with our bill. He told us that the building next door had burned to the ground but the hotel was undamaged.

On January 1st at 9:00 A.M., we left Puerto Plata, sailing all day with light wind from the north, arriving at Samana Bay before daybreak. I hove to until daylight but the others went on in to the bay. As soon as the sun came up we went on in and caught up with the others before they were at the dock. Dee chose to anchor but John and I tied up to the dock. We had a water hose on the dock for fresh water and good places to eat ashore at reasonable prices. The town was being developed as a recreation area with hotels and restaurants, everything was clean and neat and the people were very helpful. We bought supplies at bargain prices and washed clothes. I even got a good haircut at a barber shop next door to what appeared to be a house of assignation. Those waiting for a haircut sat on the front porch of the barber shop and greeted the girls as they went to work for the night. To top it off, the port officials made entering and clearing as easy as possible.

On January 6th we departed from Samana at 8:15 A.M. and headed for the north coast of Puerto Rico. There were frequent rain squalls, the wind circled around the compass, then as the squall abated, went back to southeast. We sailed all day and all night and on the next day picked up the coast of Puerto Rico. Heck Fire was a little ahead of us most of the time but Surrender went north of us and we didn't see them until the next afternoon. Dee called us on the radio to tell us they were going into Arecibo, so we continued close behind them. We were told that Arecibo was well-protected except during north winds. Dee went in close to the beach where the surf was so high we lost sight of them momentarily. We stayed out of the surf and tied up to a buoy after a native swimmer took our line and made it fast.

We sent Dee and Nardine a line from our bow which kept us both from moving with the wind. Dee and Nardine had to move to let a tug boat out before we were settled for the night.

About an hour later Surrender came by the entrance and called us on the radio to ask if there was room for another boat at our anchorage. We both told him that the surf was dangerously high and there was no place for another boat. The next morning we headed for San Juan. We arrived at 1:30 and found a place to anchor between Club Nautico and the San Juan Marina. Surrender and Heck Fire were anchored nearby. I found a place to get my outboard motor repaired and a sailmaker to stitch up my jib and perform a minor repair on the mainsail. Sandy, Ilene and Nardine found interesting grocery stores where they could buy all the things we had got along without for a while. Tony and Sabel, a young Puerto Rican couple who were interested in buying a Morgan 38, came by to talk with us. They took us on a tour of Old Town, introduced us to their parents and entertained us at a private club. In return we invited them to come with us on Belo Horizonte to Isleta Marina near Fajardo where we were going to get hauled out for a bottom job.

We met up with Joaquin, who was delivering a new boat to Puerto Rico. He offered to drive us to Fajardo, where we planned to go when we left San Juan. We were going to get hauled out there, because their equipment was adequate and their prices were reasonable. We decided to sail instead of driving with Joaquin, so on January 24 we left San Juan and sailed with Tony and Sabel to Fajardo, on the northeast coast. Dee and Nardine came in the next morning, John and Ilene followed the next day. The three of us made a deal with the marina for a flat price of $80.00 for two weeks. Isleta Marina is a small island with frequent free ferry service to the mainland. About half of the island is built up with high-rise condos, and half is covered with docks for pleasure boats and a boat yard for repair and upkeep.

It was time to clean and paint the bottom of Belo, something that hadn't been done since we were in Ft. Myers. The bottom was covered with marine growth, considerably reducing our cruising speed. We had experienced a lot of trouble with the connection between the engine and the propeller shaft. The key way on the shaft was so rounded that the key was coming out at frequent intervals. The cure was to install a new shaft made out of better stainless steel, but to do this, we had to drop the rudder. John and Dee agreed to help me, so I bought lunch and drinks while we worked.

We went to work at 6:00 A.M. the day after the boat had been hauled and blocked. We cleaned and painted the bottom, removed the rudder and the old propeller shaft and installed the new shaft. At the end of the second day everything was finished and the boat was back in the water. Belo was towed back to her slip because I wanted to be sure everything was properly lined up before I ran the engine. With help from a former General Motors mechanic, we aligned the engine with the propeller shaft. It had to be done right, so we kept at it until 8:00 P.M., when we were both satisfied every thing was perfectly in line. I had no more trouble with the keys coming out of the key way of the shaft, and vibration was reduced to a minimum.

To celebrate we all went down to the navy base at Roosevelt Roads for lunch and dinner. Three days later, Dee had Heck Fire hauled and I returned the favor which he had done for me. The job of cleaning and painting the bottom of Heck Fire was simple compared to what we had done to Belo Horizonte.

We became acquainted with a resident of a condo on the island, and she took us for a tour of the condos. Most of them had dramatic views and were well arranged. I thought of retiring in one of the condos with my boat at my front door and a view of the world from every room, but Sandy, who wanted to return to teaching, had different ideas.

Paul and his wife Marion told us they wanted to spend a week or so on the boat with us, so since we planned our next sail down to St. Croix, we invited them along. Some years before, the four of us had been on a chartered sailboat that we sailed from Norman Island to St. Croix on Christmas day with the Christmas winds blowing about 40 knots.

We sailed from Fajardo at 8:00 A.M., February 20th, for Culebra where we arrived at about 3:30 in the afternoon after an eight hour beat to windward. From Culebra we had a beautiful sail to Christmas Cove close to St. Thomas, then we powered all the way from Christmas Cove to St. Croix. At the yacht club in St. Croix we met people on other boats with whom we had shared anchorages before. We were welcomed by Bill and Clare on their 50 foot Challenger, and Gloria and Jerry who had lost their boat in Belize and bought a house in St. Croix near the yacht club. We were anchored in front of the St. Croix Yacht Club where we could get food, drinks, and hot showers.

Bill and Clare who had been in St. Croix for some time, took us on a sight-seeing tour with Dee, Nardine, John and Ilene. The tour included a restored Great House from a plantation dating back to when the Danes owned St. Croix and black slaves worked on the sugar plantations. We visited Fountain Valley Country Club and Comanche restaurant where Paul, Marion, Sandy and I had Christmas dinner when we sailed to St. Croix from Norman Island in the Virgins on a chartered sailboat.

There was a large colony of Americans in St. Croix who didn't see people from the U.S. very often. Many of them worked for American companies and were required to sign agreements to work for several years in order to get a job. They were so starved for conversation, they invited to dinner any and all Americans who stopped there. We reciprocated by hosting dinners at the yacht club for those who had entertained us.

We made big plans for the Around St. Croix sailboat race on Belo, we borrowed a light sail from Dee, and John and his son Rod were my crew. There were ten boats signed up for the race and Belo was first across the starting line after the gun went off. We hadn't even got down to the end of the island when the wind completely deserted us and the race was called.

On March 28 we left Belo anchored in front of the St. Croix Yacht Club and boarded a plane for Ft. Myers with Dee and John's promise to look after her. We enjoyed getting off the boat for a while and had some neglected business to take care of. Our condo had been rented during January, February and March but was well-stocked and in good condition. We returned to St. Croix on April 12th. The wind was blowing hard, we were told that it had been blowing up to 48 knots for nine days. One night while we were gone, Dee heard a bang on Belo and investigated. The anchor chain had pulled the anchor windlass right out of the deck where it was bolted. Belo would have been set adrift, except the anchor windlass caught in some line I lashed the bag holding the folded up jib, still attached to the head stay.

I had to remount the anchor windlass on a new piece of deck and attach it with six large stainless steel bolts, but that was simple compared to getting a new boat.

In spite of all the friends we had made in St. Croix, it was time to move on to other places and people. On April 2, 1980, we sailed to Great Cruz Bay on the end of St. John. Dee was there with Heck Fire. Dee's friend from California who had Sisu, a sister ship of Heck Fire, heard Dee talking on the radio and came over to see him.

Our next stop was Trellis Bay on Beef Island, close to an airport, where I received an air shipment of a 35 pound Danforth anchor to replace my CQR anchor. Then we sailed to Virgin Gorda and anchored off Bitter End with Surrender and Heck Fire. We averaged 6.5 knots with only our 110 jib. We, Paul and Marion, had chartered in the Virgins seven years before, so that part of our trip wasn't new to Sandy and me. We stopped at Spanish Town, and after we were anchored Surrender and Heck Fire came in. We were on Virgin Gorda, and would be on our way to St. Martin the next day.

After sailing all night, we stopped at Philipsburg, the capitol of the Dutch half of St. Martin. While anchoring we were well documented by a shore boat load of passengers from a cruise ship. Our home port of San Francisco attracted their attention, they all got out their cameras and took pictures of us. We went to town and checked-out all the duty free items, and ended up by buying Dutch cheese and chocolate.

We entered the harbor of Saint Barts early in the morning on May 7th and were surprised to see an island with no black people. Owned by France, the island was a smuggling rendezvous in the fairly recent past. We walked around town looking for the place to enter and report our arrival. I hadn't practiced my French in quite a while, so I had a little trouble asking where to go. We were told to go up a hill. It was very hot, so we decided to stop half-way up for a drink in a small French hotel. It was off-season, so the manager, a beautiful French woman, said she would make us a martini if I told her how. We were joined at the bar by a couple from France who were staying in the hotel. I don't remember everything that happened, but it seemed like only a few minutes passed before the manager looked at her watch and announced that the office where we were supposed to report was closed.

The next day we replenished our supply of beer and looked the town over. It was unique and very interesting, the kind of place where I would like to have a winter home and a private dock with a 50 foot sailboat tied up to it. The next morning we were awakened by the whistle of a ship. I looked out the porthole and saw that a ship was turning around in the crowded harbor, clearing us by about three inches. We pulled up our anchor and headed for the island of Antigua. We arrived in Falmouth Harbor the next morning, just after Antigua Race Week had finished and many of the contestants were still there. It was interesting to me that most of them were from European countries. The boat anchored next to us was from San Diego, California, its occupants had apparently gone native because they were running around naked.

The son and the two daughters looked all right but the father and mother looked awful. We got in the dinghy and headed for shore. I looked around but didn't see a dock or any place where we could leave our dinghy while we went ashore. I saw a boat anchored nearby, so I thought I would ask them where we could land. I slowed down the engine and glided up to the stern of the boat. When I looked up I saw there was a naked woman in the cockpit taking a bath out of a bucket of water. She didn't seem alarmed that I stopped to ask directions. When I looked at her I thought of how much better she looked than the mother on the boat from San Diego.

We went to the office of the port captain in English Harbor and told him we wanted to enter. He asked where our boat was and we told him it was in Falmouth Harbor adjacent to English Harbor. He said we had to bring our boat to English Harbor before he would enter us, so we didn't enter. Nelson's Dock Yard was located at English Harbor. There were old buildings and a lot of the equipment that was used over a hundred years ago for the British fleet, still in good condition. There was also a museum with a lot of very interesting displays. We took a bus to St. Johns, a town with a commercial port. While we were standing on the dock a dinghy with an outboard went by with an all naked crew.

Back in Falmouth Harbor we saw another Morgan 38 just like Belo and the owner came over to talk to us. He liked his boat as well as we did ours, and asked casually if we had an extra anchor we would sell him because he planned to spend the winter in Falmouth Harbor. I told him I had a CQR I would sell him for $100 and he bought it. I had seen a wooden sailboat with several natives working on it near our anchorage. It looked like it might be Don Street's boat and the fellow with the Morgan 38 confirmed that it was. Don Street wrote several books about long-distance cruising and sailed between the West Indies and England several times. His books were how-to text books for cruising, that is, before the advent of fiberglass hulls and electronic navigation. He usually employed West Indian crews.

On May 17th we departed Falmouth Harbor for Deep Bay on the northeast corner of Antigua Island. A large sailboat had been sunk in the middle of the entrance to the harbor and was visible to boats that came and went. It was a beautiful harbor with no signs of civilization and nothing ashore. We spent a night there swimming, relaxing and inspecting the wreck. We left the next morning at 3:45 A.M. so we would arrive at St. Barts before dark.

Our plans worked out, we arrived in Gustavia before dark. The racing fleet that had been there the first time we visited the port, was gone. We filled up with fuel and water and went shopping for food. We were running a little late but managed to get the last two loaves of bread from the bakery. The boat anchored next to us was a 28 foot sloop from West Germany that had been cruising for three years and had already gone around the world once.

Our next stop was Marigot, St. Martin on the French side of the island. We anchored and went ashore in our dinghy to look the place over. We were walking down a street that ended at the beach, so we kept walking down the beach. Out of the corner of my eye I noticed that the occupant of the beach chair nearest us was a bare breasted girl. At first I wasn't sure whether or not I should look. After walking about half a mile (with my wife) I got used to it, and one of the bare breasted beauties even smiled at me. That evening we had a fancy French dinner in a tourist restaurant at a higher price than it would have cost in San Francisco.

After spending all our money in Marigot we decided to go to Anguilla for a couple of days of laying on the beach. We anchored off of a white sand beach on the south side of the island and although we could see for miles there wasn't another person visible on the beach. Sandy had such a good time hunting for shells that I couldn't get her to leave. The next day we pulled up our anchor and headed for St. Croix. In the middle of the night a cruise ship came up behind us, heading right for us. We called the ship on the radio several times and finally received a response in a foreign language which I didn't understand. Eventually someone who could speak English came on the radio to tell me they were changing course to the right to avoid me.

At daybreak we went into the anchorage behind the reef. It was pouring rain and visibility was about two feet. We went right up to the stern of Heck Fire and gave them a toot on our whistle.

Dee come out into the cockpit in his pajamas, and I said, "I told you we would be back on the 27th."

Dee gave us our mail and we backed off to our previous anchorage. We went to the yacht club and everyone welcomed us back with a drink. We had dinner with John, Ilene, Dee and Nardine on Surrender.

We sailed to Isleta Marina where we had been before just off the northeast coast of Puerto Rico. There we made final preparations, including installing new steering cables, for sailing north to the island of San Salvador where Columbus is said to have landed on his first trip to America.

Dee left with Heck Fire early on June 11th. When I moved the boat to fill up with diesel I discovered that I had installed the cables backwards and when I turned the wheel to the left the boat went to the right. I called Dee on the radio to tell him we would be getting started a day late as a result. Sisu was leaving from St. John, also heading for San Salvador.

The first two days we had plenty of wind and made good speed. The wind blew at the same velocity night and day. For the first 24 hours we averaged 6 knots according to our noon position. I used my sextant to take two sights, one just before and one just after the sun crossed our meridian. The third day the wind calmed down but was sufficient to keep us sailing night and day.

On the fourth day we talked by radio to Rod on Sisu, giving him our position, and in return, he gave us his and Dee's positions. We were all converging on San Salvador. On the afternoon of the 16th we had to start the engine because we were down to 2.5 knots sailing. Early in the morning while it was still dark we spotted the light on the east coast of San Salvador and changed course to go around the south end of the island, then up to Cockburn Town on the lee side.

The engine heated up and I assumed that the impeller on the water pump needed changing, because it occurred approximately once every third month if we frequently ran under power. At the time I didn't have a spare impeller, but I knew that Dee had an electric pump with a by-pass hose that I could use after we caught up with him. For the time being I had to sail as much as possible, then run the engine until it heated up. As the sun came up we saw Dee ahead of us rounding the southern end of the island. When we talked to him on the radio, he said Sisu was already up near Cockburn Town. We arrived at about 10 A.M.

We started to walk from the anchorage to Riding Rock Inn, then a bus came along and the driver invited us to ride. He showed us part of the island and took us to our destination at no charge. We had a couple of drinks on the porch overlooking clear, blue water, the landscape looked like a travel poster. We had completed the longest non-stop leg since we departed from San Francisco, a distance of about 600 miles. Everyone was tired and sleepy, we all needed baths, so we returned to our boats, took a swim and turned in.

The next day eight of us took a tour of the island with Nat Walker. We were shown the three monuments, each one supposedly marking the spot where Columbus first set foot on the New World. We were also shown Watlings Castle, and the hand operated light house we had seen from a distance the night before as we approached the island.

We had drinks at Driftwood, then went down to the Lazy Tree. We sat out under the tree with some locals, drank beer and ate hamburgers. When we got back to our boats, Rod and Yvonne, and Dee and Nardine swam over. We drank rum and told sea stories all afternoon. With diesel fuel and the stores we needed, Heck Fire and Belo left at 6:30 P.M. It was a beautiful night of sailing with our 150, full main, and a full moon to keep us company. We were abeam of Cat Island Lighthouse at 5:07 A.M., and at 11:55 A.M. we anchored in New Bight. It was just a beautiful sand beach. Dee came in two hours later on Heck Fire and the four of us had dinner together on Belo. Our next stop was in Cape Eleuthera where we rafted up to Sisu and later joined Dee and Nardine at the Mauna restaurant.

Because my engine heated up periodically, Rod volunteered to help me hook up Dee's emergency rig for worn out impellers on the water circulating system. His rig was an electric motor that ran on DC current with a section of hose into and out of the motor. We attached the hoses to the engine, then ran wires from the DC batteries to the motor and we were off and running. On our way to Governors Harbor, we had to go through an area of shoals and reefs for which there were no available charts. Robin, Rod's daughter, sat on the mast spreaders pointing to shallow spots and reefs, we moved slowly. When we finally got through the bad stuff we hoisted sail and passed Sisu with only our 150 jib up. Heck Fire was ahead and took a picture of Belo going along at 6 knots with only a 150 jib up, one of the best pictures I have of the boat. We arrived at Governors Harbor late in the afternoon, anchored, and waited for the others.

The people at Governors Harbor do everything possible to help cruising yachtsmen and strangers who happen into their midst. When we arrived I had already made up my mind to get a new impeller for the salt water pump in my engine cooling system. I knew they were available in Nassau and an air delivery service ran between Governors Harbor and Nasaau. I looked at the Nassau phone directories at the telephone office, and armed with a list of marine supply store phone numbers, I started calling. I found what I was looking for, but I couldn't get anyone to ship to me in Governors Harbor. I was disgusted and started to walk out, but one of the operators came running out with her headset still on and asked if she could help.

As it turned out, there was an auto parts store in Governors Harbor, and the son of the man who owned it worked in a marine supply store in Nassau. The kindly operator gave me his name, then connected me with the store where he worked. He had the part I needed, but I wasn't sure if he could deliver the part to me in Governors Harbor before we left. He suggested that I talk with his father, who ran the auto parts store in Governors Harbor. He had parts coming in from Nassau almost every day, and might be able to arrange for his son to include my impeller in one of the shipments. I told him I needed the impeller the next day.

"My daughter is dating a pilot who flies every day between Nassau and here," he said. "Meet me under the tree on the shore at 3:00 P.M. tomorrow, and I will bring your impeller."

I could not believe that it would work, but I had no other choice. I was under the tree at 2:30 and at by 3:00 P.M., a pickup truck drove up and the driver asked me if I was Richard Abbott. When I said that I was, the man gave me my new impeller.

"What do I owe you?" I asked.

"$13.75," he said.

"What about the taxi to deliver it to the airport and the air freight to bring it here from Nassau?" I asked.

"My daughter's friend picked it up at the store in Nassau and brought it here in his pocket," he said.

I tried to give him a bottle of rum but he wouldn't take it until I asked him to give it to his daughter, which he agreed to do.

We departed from Governors Harbor at 5:00 A.M. on June 28th with no wind, and after about twenty minutes the engine started to heat up. I stopped and went over the side with a screwdriver, to clean out a lot of small shells from the through hull fitting. That did the trick and cured the heating up problem for the rest of the trip. As soon as we went through Flemming Cut the wind came up and we sailed with our 150 only until 8:00 P.M. when we switched to our 110 only, registering 7 knots on the knot meter. There were many other boats around us all night. Sisu got ahead of us so waited behind Settlement Point for us to catch up. Heck

Fire came back into sight, then headed more to the west. We passed Settlement Point about 4:20 P.M. and Sisu came out from behind the point to maintain visual contact. In the Gulf Stream we took a pounding from huge waves caused by the wind blowing against the Gulf Stream current.

At 4:00 A.M. Dee called on the radio to tell us that he had hit a tanker and was going into Ft. Pierce to survey the damage. By daybreak the wind was going down, we hoisted the 150 but soon were only doing 3 knots, so we put up the main. We finally had to start the engine because we weren't making headway. We arrived off St. Augustine on July 1st, and followed Sisu into an anchorage outside of the marina. The channel into the marina was only navigable for us around high tide. Rod and I went to the customs office by dinghy and made our official entry. At 6:30 P.M., Sisu went into the marina without trouble and I followed.

Dee and Nardine came up the inland waterway from Ft. Pierce to St. Augustine a week after we arrived. When they hit the tanker one side of the hull was pushed in, destroying some of the interior paneling and breaking the fiberglass on deck. The headstay was pulled loose from the deck, but Dee reattached it with cable he had on board, which prevented the mast from coming down but couldn't be used to sail. They were under power only, all the way back to St. Augustine. After the collision, Dee and Nardine were so tired of their boat they rented a motel as soon as they set foot in St. Augustine. He repaired the damage little by little over a couple of years and finally sold it to a navy officer. They bought a house in St. Augustine and lived there until 1993, when they moved to Texas, a long way from any water.

The Morgan Yacht Company from whom we bought Belo Horizonte, told us they wanted to inspect our boat. They had found some defects in a couple of their hulls that were built at the same approximate time. They said they would pay to have the boat hauled and repair any defects they found. What more could a boat owner ask for?

We had been aground several times and had once hit a rock coming out of Providencia. When they arrived, we had the boat out of the water. They took apart everything inside the cabin so they could inspect the inside of the hull. They found the hole inside the keel where I had hit a rock and as a result, the keel was partially filled with water. They bored additional holes to drain out all the water, then filled them in when the inside of the keel was dry. They asked if there was anything else we would like fixed while they were there, and we mentioned a couple of minor things which they promptly and efficiently repaired.

Before leaving St. Augustine we took our self-inflating life raft to Jacksonville to have it tested for self inflation and replace the food and water contents. I insisted on pulling the cord myself to see if the rubber raft would actually break the metal straps and inflate. It passed my test with flying colors so we had the food and water replaced. I substituted beer for some of the water, and put in a new battery for the automatic distress signal sender.

Our main anchor was a 35 pound Danforth with 300 feet of $\frac{5}{16}$ chain, so after inspection we took it along with Sisu's to Jacksonville, to have them regalvanized. We revarnished the rails and polished the fiberglass so that Belo would be in good condition when we started our next trip. With the owners of Sisu living on their boat close to Belo and Dee nearby working on his boat almost every day, we felt that Belo would be safe while we took time off to check on our condo in Ft. Myers.

As it turned out we spent two months in Ft. Myers, and during that time we drove up to St. Petersburg to visit the factory where Belo was built. While we were there we bought spare parts and got some maintenance information.

In January and February, we rented our condo to my brother, Charles, and his wife. They lived in a suburb of Boston and liked to get away from the cold weather during the coldest months. Sandy and I drove back to St. Augustine and lived on Belo during that time. There was never a dull moment. The owners of Sisu were looking for a place to buy in the St. Augustine area, living on their boat until they found the right place. The Clam Shell, a restaurant at the marina, was very popular and served excellent food and drinks.

While we were there, we bought and installed our first loran set. It was hard for me to get used to pressing a few buttons and turning a couple of dials to get an accurate position in the middle of the night. We were preparing for our next voyage up the East Coast to the Chesapeake Bay, but we couldn't persuade any of the boats we had cruised with to join us, so we were going alone. Just before we departed we visited Sandy's parents in Silver Spring, Maryland.

On April 12, 1981 at 8:20 A.M. we departed the dock in Saint Augustine, heading out the channel to the ocean. Soon after we had cleared the sea buoy we received a radio call from Dee who was using his ship to shore radio at his apartment. We laid down a course to the Charleston, South Carolina entrance channel and arrived there at 2:30 the next afternoon. We had light winds and had to turn on the engine a couple of times during the trip. We arrived at the municipal marina at 5:00 P.M., and tied up to pilings that rose five feet above our deck. The transit consumed 32 hours and covered 202 nautical miles. We spent a day repairing our masthead light and walking around the city. We had dinner ashore at a restaurant in the marina, the chef there was once employed by Onassis on his yacht. After the meal we knew why, the food was terrific.

We departed the Charleston sea buoy at 12:52, after about two hours in the entrance channel and got to Cape Fear outer buoy at 11:40 April 17. We anchored in Dutch Man's Creek just south of Southport. The area looked a lot like the delta up the river from San Francisco.

We departed at 8:57 the next morning, took a short cut through Frying Pan Shoals and sailed until midnight. Five navy ships crossed our bow ignoring the Rules of the Road, forcing us to change course or get run over. We arrived in Beaufort, North Carolina at 10:40 A.M. on April 20th, logging 127 nautical miles.

We went ashore the next day and looked the town over. Our tour included the post office, the museum and a restaurant where we had a an excellent lunch. The next day a cold front came in with a cold north wind and rain all day long, so we stayed in the boat with the heating stove going and read.

When the temperature increased a little we went ashore again and took a tour through two old houses, an old courthouse and an old jail. We bought some charts for the waterway and took showers. On April 4th at 6:30 A.M., we departed in freezing cold weather. We went under three bridges on the waterway and stopped for the night at Bellhaven, a distance of 68 nautical miles. We dragged the bottom on Adams Creek between markers 11 and 12, learning that $6\frac{1}{2}$ feet is too much draft for the waterway. We hoisted the mainsail for a lift through the Neuse, Pamlico and Pungo rivers. River Forest Marina showed up at 4:00 P.M. We took on only 15 gallons of diesel because we wanted to be careful about our draft. After hot showers available to yacht crews, we had dinner in the Manor House. The dinner was a delicious smorgasbord for $10.95, that included oysters, shrimp, and crab.

We departed at 7:30 the next morning with three sailboats right ahead of us through the long, narrow Pungo Canal. We put the main up in the Alligator River to give us a lift and got our speed up to 6.5 and 7 knots. The bridge tender left the bridge open for us at the Pungo Alligator River Canal because we were so close behind the three other boats. At the mouth of the Alligator River we sailed up dangerously close to the bridge and the tender opened it at the last minute to let us through. We continued across Albermarle Sound with a favorable south wind and headed into the North River. We anchored in Broad Creek at mile 61 at 6:15 P.M.. The days run was 70 nautical miles averaging over 6 knots. The next day we ran hard aground in a rain storm, put the 150 jib up and waited. In about ten minutes we came off and continued on to Coinjack Bridge. We were cold and wet, so we called it a day and tied up at the Coinjack Marina at 10:15, making the total distance for the day's run 11 miles.

The next day we plowed straight into a fierce northeast wind, taking spray over constantly with the wind at 20 to 30 knots. We went through a narrow channel but there were plenty of markers so we knew where we were all the time. There were three bridges along the stretch, all three only open on the hour or the half hour, so we lost a lot of time waiting. We arrived at Great Bridge, Virginia at 3:00 P.M., and tied up at Atlantic Yacht Basin. We had covered 38 miles in seven hours.

We took on fuel and water at Atlantic Yacht Basin and departed on April 29th at 9:00 A.M. We went through a bridge that opens only on the hour, then into a canal with locks that required tending lines adjusted according to the depth of the water.

During the early part of the day's run we were in warm sunshine with beautiful scenery but the view became less attractive when we got into an industrial area. We went through eight bridges that day, arriving at Willougby Bay at 2:00 P.M. We made good a distance of 25 miles.

On April 30th we departed at 7:05 A.M., and ran aground in the marked channel at about 7:30. Low tide wasn't until 9:57 A.M., so we decided to pump out some of the fresh water in our tanks to see if that would allow us to float. We didn't get off the bottom until 12:05. We continued on to Put In Creek up the East River from Mobjack Bay. We powered for a while, then put up sails and went along at four knots. There were many crab pot markers we had to avoid to prevent them from getting wrapped up in our propeller. We anchored for the night and the temperature was so warm we were able to have drinks in the cockpit for the first time for about a month. We made 31 miles that day.

On May 1st, we heaved up the anchor and sailed all day dodging fish stakes and crab pot buoys. We anchored at Sandy Point on the Great Wicamico River at 7:20 P.M. A 40-mile run became a 58-mile run because of tacking under sail. On May second we departed at 8:00 A.M., and sailed all morning but had to turn on the engine in the afternoon. After dodging crab pots again all afternoon we were at Solomon's Island and anchored in Mill Creek at 5:15 P.M. There was only one other boat in the anchorage and the shore was lined with nice homes.

We heaved up the anchor the next morning and started looking for a place were we could tie up to a dock so we could get ashore. We saw an unoccupied dock alongside a restaurant so we tied up. The people running the restaurant said we could stay as long as we wanted if we ate all our meals there. The name of the restaurant was Pier 1. Our home port of San Francisco under the name of the boat on the stern caused the usual plethora of comments. During the day we explored the town, visited the Maritime Museum, the marina and some houses that were over 100 years old. We stayed on our boat at the restaurant that night and had dinner and breakfast there. We didn't have much privacy, because everyone who visited the restaurant came out to look at Belo. The next morning we heard an unusual noise outside, a white goose was in the water near the stern of our boat, urging her newly hatched goslings to jump off the dock for their first swimming lesson. After some hesitation, they jumped into the water, one-by-one.

The next day we continued on up the bay towards Annapolis. We arrived at Pier 7 Marina on South River about 5.00 P.M., about 45 miles from Solomon's Island.

We were fairly close to Silver Spring, Maryland, so we cleaned up the boat and called Sandy's parents to pick us up so we could spend a few days with them. I asked the marina manager if I could leave the boat there for a few days, and he said the price was $10.00 per day. I countered at $50.00 per week and he grabbed my money. I moved Belo to a well-protected berth and Sandy called her parents who said they would be down to pick us up the next day. We had been on the boat continuously since we left St. Augustine, and it seemed to get smaller all the time.

We spent a relaxing week with Sandy's parents and visited Annapolis where we saw a couple we had known in Ft. Myers. They were on their way from Ft. Myers to the Great Lakes on their power boat. They had gone across Florida on the river, were on their way up the coast to the Hudson River and beyond. They had left Ft. Myers about the same time we had sailed from St. Augustine.

Getting back to Belo, we decided to sail to St. Michael's on the eastern shore, once a commercial port in the days when sailing ships were running between England and ports on the Chesapeake. The marinas charged such high prices for places to dock, we anchored instead, and took the dinghy to shore. We had steamed crab for lunch at the Crab Claw and later paid $2.00 each to take a shower at the marina. We spent some time looking around the interesting Maritime Museum. From St. Michael's we headed to the Chester River in order to go up to Chestertown, also a former port for seagoing sailing ships. We anchored along the way in the Corsica River which runs into the Chester River. We were near a huge building owned by the Russian Embassy, used to entertain Russian and foreign diplomats. From our anchorage, we heard music, singing and shouted words in a foreign language, which, we assumed was Russian.

Going up the Chester River, we had to be very careful to stay in the channel or we would be aground. As the river narrowed we resorted to the engine to be sure we made every turn within the marked channel. At the town we tied up at Kibbler's Marina and had crab cakes at the Wharf Inn. The town looked like it had been built circa 1750. The customs house was still there, and we looked at manifests of sailing ships that unloaded there over 100 years ago.

In preparation for our May 19th departure, we filled our water tanks and cleaned up the boat. We took icy, cold showers at the marina, because they had not yet connected their hot water heater. We were ready to leave at 7:00 A.M., but were enveloped in dense fog. We found the first three channel markers but couldn't find the fourth, the water became increasingly shallow, so we anchored out of the channel. Half an hour passed and we were in daylight again. We continued down the Chester to the Magothy River and anchored there. Because we were in the vicinity of Baltimore, we saw lots of homes along the shore. The next day after sailing forty-one miles, we anchored at Ordinary Point on the Sassafrass River. We left at 10:00 the next morning and sailed about five miles up the river to Georgetown. The scenery is beautiful up there, we were surrounded by lush green hills and lots of trees. We tied up at the Granary Marina, formerly used for grain storage for cargo brought in by ships.

The next day we had good sailing all day long and dropped anchor off Gibson Island on the Magothy River. As soon as we were secure it began to pour rain. The next day we sailed all the way up to the bridge on the Severn. We roared into the entrance of the Severn at Annapolis doing seven knots under sail. In spite of the ugly day, there were lots of pleasure boats out. The Severn is very beautiful with high bluffs on each side, and we were reluctant to leave our beautiful anchorage, because we had it all to ourselves, and it was a rainy cloudy day. We departed at noon and had to wait for the bridge to open, then detoured around some yellow buoys that the Naval Academy had put out. We anchored at 1:50 P.M. in the anchorage at Annapolis. The Blue Angels were supposed to give an airshow, but it was canceled because of the weather.

The town of Annapolis was crowded with people, partly because of the graduation at the Naval Academy, and partly because of the large number of yachts docked and anchored around town. Sandy did our laundry at the yacht basin, ran into several people we had met on boats in other places, and received an invitation for cocktails from one couple. Annapolis is an interesting place to spend an afternoon looking at the old houses and narrow streets lined with shops and restaurants. Some of the buildings looked like they had survived since the 18th century. We also visited the local Morgan Yacht dealer. In the late afternoon a sailboat race finished at the yacht club close to our anchorage, and some of the racers cut through the anchored boats narrowly avoiding collisions.

On May 28th we departed from Annapolis at 7:15 A.M. in pouring rain for Oxford, Maryland, where we arrived at 2:30 P.M., a distance of 38 miles. It was peaceful sitting in the cockpit after our arrival, watching the boats sailing up the river. In the early evening we had another short rainstorm, but it abated by the next morning, so we rowed ashore and walked all over the neat little town. We went into the tiny customs house, a replica of the original, with some of the original furnishings.

The lady in the old customs house told us that prior to the revolution, Oxford was a thriving port. Many of the original residents there had once been indentured servants who, after a designated number of years, were given land grants. The showers at the marina were locked but we persuaded one of the people who worked there to unlock them so we could take showers. Back at the boat we witnessed a steady stream of boats going up the river towards Easton. According to the Waterway Guide the seven miles between Oxford and Easton is the most cruised waterway on the Eastern Shore. Live music from the yacht club added to the gaiety.

At about 8:30 P.M., the sky suddenly became black and we heard thunder in the distance. By the time the storm hit, it was as dark as the middle of the night. A gust of wind, probably about 60 knots, hit the anchorage, then we were hit by an electrical storm worse than anything I had ever experienced. It was even worse than the time we got struck by lightning in Costa Rica. Boats were dragging anchor all over the place; one boat's anchor line parted, another lost their dinghy when the painter parted, yet another was hit by lightning and lost two feet off the top of his mast. The boat that was struck called for help on his radio and the fire department sent four fire engines to the waterfront with their red lights flashing. It was a beautiful display but of no help to the boat in the anchorage. We turned in at about midnight but were awakened at 1:00 A.M., when a boat dragged its anchor and drifted into us. The next day everyone was leaving, the weather was fine so we had crab cakes for lunch ashore at the Morris Inn, built in 1710.

We departed at 7:15 the next morning after some difficulty breaking our anchor out of the clay bottom. We had reserved a dock at Zahnizers Marina on Solomons Island where we arrived early in the afternoon. The next day while taking sails off the rigging to be repaired, I lost my wallet over the side. It contained several credit cards and $150.00 cash. I hired a diver to try to find it but he came up with nothing. Sandy's mother and father drove down to Solomons Island and took us back to Silver Spring where we stayed for a week with them. Among other things I had to get parts for our broken water heater.

After a week in civilization we returned to the boat, departed the next morning and sailed up the Patuxent River. We had a fair wind and made 5 to 6 knots with the 150 jib only. We got as far as Benedict and decided we didn't want to stay because our depth recorder kept showing less water under the keel than the chart showed. It was tobacco country, the scenery was nice with lots of farms. We went in to Leonard's Creek and found a good anchorage in 12 feet.

We launched the dinghy with the outboard on it for the first time in a long while, and explored several small creeks off St. Leonard's. The outboard started to heat up so we had to row back to Belo Horizonte. I cleaned out the water pump and took off again. A marina with a supposedly south sea decor was visible up ahead but then the spark plug fell out of the outboard, and we had a long row back to Belo.

The next day we took Belo over to Satterly and inspected a plantation dating back to 1717, where people still lived in the plantation house part of the year. At the dock, there was a phone that we used to call the plantation to ask someone to come and take us up there. When we got there, the hostess asked us where we were from and how we came. We told her we were from San Francisco, by boat. "Oh!" she said, "This is the first time anyone has come from San Francisco by boat to see our plantation!"

It was now the middle of June and we decided it was a good time to do a little land cruising. I wanted to revisit Andover, Brookline, and go up the East Coast to Boothbay Harbor, Maine, where I had spent some boyhood summers with my cousin. We persuaded Sandy's dad to lend us the old Volkswagen that he used to commute to the university where he maintained an office. The price was two new rear tires that I had planned to buy anyway before we took the trip. We spent about a month visiting the haunts of my youth in Boston, Brookline, Andover and stopped in Weston, Massachusetts to see Charles. He entertained us at the Harvard Club in Boston. On the way back we stopped at New London, Connecticut, where I attended Merchant Marine officers school for four months in 1944, before shipping out as third mate on the Josephine Lawrence.

While we were engaged in our land cruise Belo Horizonte was waiting patiently at Solomon's Island in Zahnhizer's Marina. While we were traveling up the coast the boat was hauled, the bottom cleaned and painted and some minor repairs completed.

Chapter Eight

The Sale of Belo Horizonte

We left the dock at 7:30 A.M. on October 1st, and as we passed the entrance to the Great Wicomico River about a dozen large fishing boats streamed in towards the menhaden plants to deliver their cargoes. Avoiding the crab floats and fish stakes for a few miles up the river, we found a peaceful anchorage. When we left the next morning, we had to quickly take two reefs in the main, because near the entrance we had a thirty knot north wind. The wind took us to the mouth of the Rappahannock River, then up the Corrotoman River where we anchored in twelve feet of water off Belles Creek. We set our alarm for an early start the next morning, anxious to be on our way to Charleston, South Carolina.

We woke up to fog so thick we couldn't even see the other boats anchored close to us. The fog finally lifted, we got away at 10:15 A.M. and motored all day into the wind. We anchored off Mobjack in the Ware River at 5:45 that evening. The next morning we had light southwesterly winds and sailed into Willoughby Bay at 2:30 P.M. Unlike our first time in the bay, on the way north, we didn't run aground because we knew from experience that only half of the marked channel was deep enough for us. We passed through the outskirts of Norfolk, out of Willoughby Bay and entered the Intracoastal Waterway. We had to go under nine bridges and through the locks before we could hoist the 150 jib, but soon we were making 6.5 knots in the Currituck Cut. We arrived at Coinjack at 5:30 P.M., making 56 miles for the day. The next morning we left at 7:00 A.M., because we thought the fog had lifted, but after about $1\frac{1}{2}$ miles through the Cut, the fog reappeared and we were unable to find the next marker. Seven other boats came tentatively through the fog, and hovered around the G-125 marker, as the fog got worse. We were unable to see the other boats, but could hear them all sounding their fog horns. When the fog eventually lifted a little, all eight boats went out slowly in single file like a wagon train. When the fog lifted completely, we got sails up and motors running in Abemarle Sound and Alligator River. We anchored at Tuckahoe Point on the Alligator River at 4:45 P.M., a distance of 51 miles.

The next day we were again in a three-hour dense fog, and had to have a bow watch at all times. The fog didn't lift until about 10:00 A.M., then we sailed and motored until 5:15 P.M., and anchored at Broad Creek off the Neuse River making 66 miles for the day. About 1:00 P.M. the next day we arrived at Beaufort, North Carolina. The anchorage was crowded and after we had our anchor set the Coast Guard put in an intermediate buoy forcing several anchored boats to move, fortunately not including us.

We had been there before, seen all the sights ashore, knew where the good restaurants were and where we could take a shower, so the next day we relaxed from our trip down the waterway and prepared for the run from Beaufort to Charleston. On October 11th we heaved up our anchor and went to the fuel dock where we took on maximum fuel and water. While we were there, the Coast Guard put down more green buoys, further limiting the space for boats in transit to anchor. We departed the fuel dock at 9:00 A.M. with a light southeast wind, and by 2:00 P.M. we went through Frying Pan Shoals which stretches out from shore with one narrow passage through to the south with a light marking it.

The wind steadily increased from the west and as we went down the coast we went further and further off shore. It was a cold, wet night and we were being blown further and further out to sea. We started the engine and powered into the wind to make good our course, but the engine started to overheat. With the boat rolling first one rail, then the other under water, I struggled with the tools that were sliding back and forth on the cabin sole and succeeded in getting the new impeller installed in the pump. I hit my head on the anchor when I was struggling to get the jib down and started to have strange hallucinations. With the impeller installed I started the engine to make sure the impeller was working, but the case didn't cool off. I attached a small line to my waist and went over the side with a screwdriver to unclog the through hull fitting.

As I stepped off the stern ladder into the water, I saw a medium sized shark laying in the shadow beneath the boat. The shark ignored me, so I ignored it and swam to the through hull to insert the screw driver into it. The boat was rolling so fast I couldn't get the screw driver into the hole. I was dizzy, cold, frustrated, hallucinating wildly, and to make matters worse, the sun was setting as the strong west wind continued to blow us away from Charleston. I went back on deck, hoisted the jib and headed eastward, then slowly turned until the jib was backwinded and the boat was hove to. The motion diminished and the boat became stable again. I locked the wheel hard over, turned on the stern light and the mast head light, and turned in for a good night's rest.

By the time the sun came up, the seas had subsided and our heading hadn't changed more than 10 degrees. Our loran position showed us at about 60 miles east of Charleston, so I started the engine and headed toward the port. The engine didn't heat up and we made it into the port at Charleston by sundown.

We went straight to the Marina Cafe for several stiff drinks and a fabulous dinner cooked by Onassis' former chef, and after a solid night's sleep tied up to the dock we were as good as new.

The first time we were in Charleston we got to know a yacht broker who used his boat as an office. At that time he loaned us one of the men who worked for him to hoist me up the mast so I could replace a bulb in my masthead light. During our second visit to Charleston he saw us at the dock and came over to talk. We told him we wanted to leave our boat in Charleston for the winter, but the marina couldn't help us because they had a long waiting list. The broker told us he needed listings and would let us tie up to the dock where his boat-office was and he would tie up alongside us. We really didn't want to sell because we planned to cruise the Chesapeake again the next year. Sandy and I discussed it, and realized that we could list the boat at a high price, and if anyone paid it we could buy another boat. We went to Charleston because many of the marinas in the Chesapeake freeze over in the winter and we didn't want to leave Belo Horizonte on land for three or four months.

The broker and I dickered, but finally made a deal, so Sandy and I planned to leave Belo in Charleston until the following spring. Before we left Charleston, we had one more delicious meal at the Marina Cafe, cooked by Onassis' former chef.

On November 14, 1982, we rented a car and loaded it with our most essential possessions from the boat, then drove to Ft. Myers, Florida. Charles called from Boston to say that he wanted to rent our condo for January and February, so we made plans to visit Sandy's parents during that time. Meantime, we had a nice Christmas at Schooner Bay, renewing our friendships with the people who lived in our condo complex.

Our condo had a balcony overlooking the Caloosahatchee River, connecting to Lake Okeechobee and a waterway that led to Florida's east coast. The river, lake and waterway were always good for watching interesting boat traffic passing by. There was also a pool room in the complex, where I spent a lot of time sharpening up my game. Sandy constantly played bridge with the Schooner Bay Bridge Club.

On December 1st, Charles and Jane arrived, and Sandy and I loaded up the car for Silver Spring. We decided to go up the East Coast as far as Charleston, then stop there to check on Belo. We arrived at Charleston late in the afternoon on a freezing cold day. The broker's boat was alongside Belo where we left her, so we climbed to his cockpit. He was, according to a note he left attached to the cabin doorway of his boat, at a boat show. We opened Belo to find out that the interior was being used for storage of parts and equipment. Sandy and I moved enough of the stuff out to the cockpit to sleep aboard, but the interior was dirty and some of the boxes and crates had soiled the upholstery.

I blew my top and sat down to write the broker a hot letter. I told him he would never sell Belo if he continued to use her for a warehouse and that I wouldn't have left her if I had known he intended to use her that way. I also told him to move his inventory out, and clean her up so I could come to collect her. My letter must have been pretty nasty because he called me in Silver Spring to tell me he would do everything I asked if I would just leave Belo in Charleston. I was satisfied with his apology, so I agreed.

March 1st, we returned to Schooner Bay stopping en route to see Dee and Nardine at their new home in St. Augustine. Heck Fire was still in the marina, Dee was still working on the repairs to make her saleable. He hadn't been able to get the engine started since they arrived in St. Augustine a year before. We got the news from Dee that Rod, owner of Sisu, had bought a lot near St. Augustine on which he put a house trailer, then built a barn with a workshop and an office.

Dee was a pilot in World War II, and since he was no longer sailing, he bought a small plane. We invited him to fly down to Ft. Myers to visit us while we were there, and he said he'd love to.

Back in Ft. Myers, we bought new furniture for the condo and fixed it up a little. I played pool every morning from 10 to 12 with all challengers. Sandy played bridge whenever she could, sometimes calling on me to make a fourth when I wasn't playing pool. When we weren't playing bridge or pool, we caught crab off the condo dock, but after we got the trap full of Blue crab a couple of times, we came to the conclusion that it was too much work preparing them for the small portions of food we got out of them.

We visited neighboring cities; St. Petersburg, Tampa and some of the smaller towns along the gulf coast. While we were attending a boat show in St. Petersburg, we went aboard a replica of Captain Bligh's Bounty. A couple of years ago, while visiting Australia and New Zealand, we boarded the same ship again in the harbor at Sydney.

We got acquainted with Allen, the owner of a condo in our complex who was sailing around with a Coronado 34. He had started his voyage, as had we, in California. He asked us to meet him in the spring at the port of Charleston, South Carolina, and travel with him up the Intracoastal Waterway to the Chesapeake. It's nice to have company when cruising because we can help each other when the inevitable emergencies occur, so we accepted his invitation.

Since we had some repairs to do on Belo we decided to go up to Charleston about May 1st so we would be ready to depart on June 1st. We drove our car up to Charleston because we knew we would have a lot of running around to do, getting parts for Belo. At Charleston we went first to the dock where the broker had his boat tied up beside ours. He didn't have much to say, he just gave us three hours to move Belo. As luck would have it, we had already rented a space in another marina adjacent to the municipal marina and took Belo over there as fast as we could. We knew the bottom would have to be cleaned before we could start on our trip north, but we didn't want to have the boat hauled out by a yard we didn't know, so the first item on our list was to hire a diver. We also had varnishing to do, the exhaust hose had to be replaced, we needed spare water pump impellers, and the markings on the anchor chain had to be re-painted so we would know how much chain was in the water.

We were compelled to visit a civil war era plantation on the outskirts of Charleston that was used to make the movie "Gone With the Wind." It was completely intact, with the old slave quarters and a dock on a small stream where the cotton was loaded. The main house of the plantation is in the traditional southern style with two-story white pillars across the front.

We finally got Belo in shape to travel, then we drove our car back to Ft. Myers and left it in our condo garage. When we returned to Charleston we found a note from Allen on our cabin door. He was waiting for us at anchor in the river.

Allen, his girlfriend Barbara, and his cat were on his boat ready to leave within a couple of days. We still had to fill up with water and fuel and do some grocery shopping, so a couple of days was fine with us.

On June 1, Allen and Barbara departed on Leonidas from the marina in Charleston at about 10:00 A.M., for Beaufort, North Carolina, expecting to meet us there. We departed from Ashley Marina at 11:55 A.M., and cleared the sea buoy about half an hour later. We hoisted the main with one reef and the 150 jib, but the wind slowly diminished as we made good headway towards our destination. By 5:30 P.M., we were down to 3 knots so we started the engine. The battery wouldn't turn over the engine, so we started the Honda generator. After half an hour, we tried to start the engine again, but nothing happened, so we turned around and headed back to Charleston. As we sailed back we passed the Galadriel going the opposite way and shouted to them to tell Allen that we were headed back to Charleston because of generator trouble. They acknowledged the message and promised to deliver it.

We were back at the Charleston sea buoy at midnight, but without the engine we hesitated to go up the entrance channel. There were cargo ships entering and exiting the narrow channel, leaving little room for a sailboat without power to maneuver. We sailed around outside the channel for the rest of the night and headed in at dawn.

The pilot on a cargo ship yelled at us when they passed us in the channel, but there was nothing we could do about it. We made headway against the river current and when we got near the marina we called the harbor master by radio to tell him we would be approaching the dock in about 15 minutes under sail only, and would appreciate having somebody on the dock to catch us as we came in. The harbor master said he would be glad to help, that most boats in our condition just dropped their anchor and asked for a tow. I had everything down except about half of the 150 and Sandy was holding that out. There were five people on the dock, so as we came close Sandy took in the last of the sail and five pairs of hands grabbed us.

We hired a mechanic to work on the generator and he found out that the belt connecting the generator to the engine was stretched too loose to turn the generator. He installed a new belt, and after a few minutes of charging the batteries, we were able to start the engine. While checking out the batteries, we noticed one of them was overage, so we replaced it. The marina gave us a free slip for the night because, as they put it "You had the guts to sail right into the marina." We departed Charleston for the second time at 1:45 the next afternoon. All went well until the middle of the night when we approached the pass through Frying Pan Shoals off Cape Fear. I had a good loran fix and knew where I was but couldn't see the lighted buoy that was supposed to mark the pass. I ducked down into the cabin and got another loran position that showed me we were right at the buoy, then I dashed up to the cockpit. We passed so close to the unlit buoy I could almost reach out and touch it.

After going through Frying Pan Shoals the weather deteriorated. A radio weather report forecasted a severe storm, so we took down the 150 and hoisted the 110 but were still making 5 knots. At about 1:00 A.M. the skies got black, rain poured and lightning flashed, so we took down the 110. At daybreak we entered Beaufort Inlet. We anchored at 7:00 A.M., making 203.90 nautical miles from Charleston. Allen was there waiting for us.

The next day we departed for Bellhaven at 6:05 A.M., and used the engine all day. We received a radio report that there had been a tornado on the Neuse River right after we left.

We anchored at Bellhaven at 4:15 P.M., and spent a quiet night. The next day we pulled up the anchor at 6:00 A.M. and motored 67 miles to Broad Creek. Allen was having trouble with his fuel hose so we didn't leave until noon and went 12 miles to Coinjack Marina. Since Coinjack Bridge only opened on the hour, we had to wait there for 45 minutes.

Allen departed from Coinjack an hour ahead of us because of his slower speed. We caught up with him at North Bridge Landing around 11:30 A.M., continued with him through bridges and locks, and arrived at Hospital Point anchorage in Norfolk at 3:45 P.M. A celebration was underway, with many tall ships in parades, and although we missed most of it, we were told there would be another parade in the evening, as well as a carnival June 11th. We went by dinghy to Portsmouth where we toured an old lightship, a nautical museum and went grocery shopping. We had dinner on Allen's boat and watched a beautiful fireworks display over the harbor.

The next day we motored most of the way to East Creek with a little bit of sailing and anchored at 3:00 P.M. The following day brought us to the Great Wicomico River, where it was so very hot, we jumped over the side and went swimming.

The middle of the summer is not the most pleasant time to cruise on the Chesapeake, because it is stifling hot with little wind and the bugs come out in clouds. That day we were attacked by what looked like mosquitoes in a cloud formation, they darkened the sky above us, and we tried to drive them off with brooms and paddles. We were only able to cover the deck with dead insects, which required cleaning up. We arrived at Solomon's Island about 5:00 P.M. and anchored off Zahnhizer's Marina.

A shower ashore in the marina felt good, and as usual, our home port of San Francisco painted on the stern attracted attention and we had visitors aboard to chat. The next day we relaxed, shopped, walked ashore, fed the ducks that had hatched before our eyes the year before, and ate soft shell crab for dinner at the Pier One Restaurant for old times' sake. We departed at 4:00 P.M. to Calvert Marina for fuel and water, then went on to Leonard's Creek off of the Patuxent River and anchored for the night. We ate dinner at the White Sands Restaurant where we were entertained by the owner, Vera, who was quite a character.

June 20th we left Solomon's and headed for Oxford, about thirty miles away. Long before we got there we could see lightning and thunder over Oxford, so we slowed down a little, hoping that it would go away before we got there. We spent a gloomy day and night in Oxford, it rained the whole time we were there. We departed at 9:00 A.M. and motored up the Tred Avon to Easton, admiring the nice houses on shore, and watching watermen getting crab.

It was a beautiful anchorage, and we enjoyed a nice breeze while swimming. We departed about 7:00 A.M., after being awakened by watermen on their crab boats. The next stop was Annapolis, Maryland, 28 miles away.

There is always plenty to do at Annapolis; regattas, boat shows, historical sites, and old houses and museums open to the public.

We returned to Solomon's Island on June 30th where we had reserved a dock at Zahnhizer's Marina and could leave the boat there for a month without worrying about it.

Our next trip, starting August 1st, was to Baltimore where the inner harbor renewal project was almost finished. The project attracted a growing number of yachtsmen who braved the commercial congestion of the approach to be rewarded with excellent restaurants, an inner harbor marina and many imaginative shore side attractions, including Harbor Place. Harbor Place serves every cuisine imaginable and offers elegant clothing and nautical supplies for sale. It's an easy run up the Patapsco to Baltimore with a light current and good markers. The first day we started at 7:40 A.M. from Solomon's Island and arrived at an anchorage on the Magothy River behind Holland Point. Allen sailed with us, but alone, because his girl friend had left him along the way. There was no wind, so we ran under power all the way. The next day we left at noon, it was a late start, but we only had a short way to go. We anchored at Rock Creek off the Patapsco between White Rock Marina and the Maryland Yacht Club, at 3:30 P.M., making a distance of 23.06 miles for the day. The next day we tied up at the Fells Point dock in Baltimore, and stayed for seven days, enjoying the local restaurants and night spots.

As we approached Solomon's Island on the way back, we ran into a terrible rain storm off Drum Point, with rain denser than any fog I had been in at sea. The rain obscured our view so much, we couldn't see anything more than six feet away. It was powerful but brief, and we continued to Solomon's Island with fair weather.

We thought we should see more of the Eastern Shore before we returned to Florida, so we went to Crisfield just north of Pokomoke Sound. We motored all the way, continually dodging crab pots. Right after we were securely anchored, we were hit by a rain and wind storm that had me praying the anchor wouldn't drag.

The next day we discovered seven or eight crab packing plants ashore, and had crab cake sandwiches for lunch at the Captain's Galley. The next morning we had a difficult time breaking our anchor out, because the storm the night before had buried it. When we finally got the anchor out, we sailed all day to arrive at Solomon's Island at 6:30 P.M.

A week later we did our last exploring on the Chesapeake. From Solomon's we went down to the Potomac, up to Jutland Creek and Smith Creek off the Potomac. We anchored off of a prosperous looking small farm that looked deserted. We were alone in the protected anchorage, and the scenery was beautiful and calm.

We sailed back to Solomon's Island the next day, then went to Annapolis to replace our water pump. On our return, we stopped to anchor in the Little Choptank, after a day-long sail during which we went from double reefed main and 110 to full main and 150. We left the next morning, and kept in a marked channel until we saw a waterman ahead using tongs to get oysters, even though the chart showed a depth of twelve feet. By the time this registered we hit bottom and ground to a halt. We had to get out of the marked channel to get around the shallow place, and arrived at Solomon's around 3:00 P.M., sailing all the way, down to one knot at the end.

On October 26, 1981, the time had come for us to leave the Chesapeake and head back to Florida. After two years cruising the area we had seen a good deal of it and thoroughly enjoyed the time we spent there. We sailed with 150 and main until we got to Smith Point. Rounding the point a blast hit us, and we shortened sail. It was biting cold, so we decided to complete our day's run at the Great Wicomico instead of at Indian Creek our original destination for the day. At 3:00 P.M. we anchored behind Sandy Point having sailed 40.26 miles, averaging over 6 knots. The next day we had northwest winds again, sailed with only reefed main and anchored at Poquoson on Chisman Creek at 5:50 P.M., having made 51 miles at an average speed of 5.8 knots.

We left our anchorage at 8:10 A.M. with 20 to 30 knots of wind, arriving at Hospital Point, Norfolk about 2:30 P.M. We had difficulty getting the anchor to hold and had to reset it several times. While trying to get the anchor to hold, I sideswiped a newly painted red buoy putting a red stripe down the port side of the boat. The weather was getting colder every day with increasing winds, and while we were in Norfolk, we had the kerosene heater going all night.

We departed Norfolk and entered the waterway at 8:00 A.M. Our timing was perfect for the opening of all the bridges on that stretch of the waterway. We started out with another Morgan 38 but left them behind when they got caught behind a freighter going under a bridge. We had a twenty minute wait at North Bridge but sailed with the 150 jib up through Currituck Sound. We arrived at Coinjack at 3:25 P.M., set our clocks back one hour, and slept like babies until daybreak. We departed at 6:20 A.M., and used our engine with our jib up for a lift most of the day.

We anchored for the night at the end of the Pungo River Canal at 5:15 P.M., then departed at 6:15 A.M. and ran all day with engine and small jib up for an extra push. At Beaufort we had to wait for the bridge, which only opens on the hour, but got through at 5:00 P.M. and entered the harbor. Of our four trips through the waterway, two northbound and two southbound, the last was our fastest, a total of three days, stopping every night. Allen was waiting for us at Beaufort, and told us that Bill and Clare on Fortress Cove had been waiting for us, but left for Florida just that morning. We had been with Bill and Clare in the Panama Canal, the San Blas Islands and at St. Croix.

Unable to find a space in which to anchor at Beaufort, we went up to the fuel dock and filled our tanks. After we had paid our bill, we asked if we could spend the night at the dock since it was evening and we were leaving early in the morning. The owner agreed, but made us promise we would leave early. It gave us a chance to buy dinner, load supplies and take showers ashore. We departed Beaufort at 8:15 A.M., and outside the harbor, met winds of 25 to 30 knots. We sailed with jib only and got to Frying Pan Shoals about midnight. By morning we were wet, cold and tired and decided to head for Winyan Bay where there was an entrance to the inland waterway.

We found the entrance buoy and survived the surf in the entrance channel but once we were inside we had no chart to show us how to get to the waterway. We stopped a small power boat and asked them how to get to the inland waterway. They pointed and said, "Just go that way."

After a few minutes of going "that way" a speed boat roared up to us, sounding a siren and waving. When we stopped, they told us the area was full of fish traps and not navigable. With their help we found the waterway and a protected anchorage near it. We got warm and dry, had a good dinner, then a comfortable nights sleep.

We had planned an early start but didn't depart until 10.00 A.M., then we motored with the main up and anchored in Dewees Creek at 4:20 P.M. We made 40.42 miles, through marsh area all day and when we anchored, we were surrounded by it. We left at 8:20 A.M., arrived at Ben Sawyer at about 9:20, and had to wait for 15 minutes for the bridge to open. The current was very strong, so we slowed down. We didn't want to enter Ashley Marina in Charleston under strong current conditions. We finally docked at Ashley Marina at 11:45. We replaced our hand water pump and fixed our pressure water. Sandy did laundry, then we planned to go out to dinner but it started to rain so we stayed on board.

Allen anchored in the river and came into the marina with a passenger he was taking to Jacksonville. The next day Sandy did another load of laundry, then we left the dock at slack tide and anchored in the river. Allen and his passenger came aboard for dinner.

We departed from Charleston at 6:25 A.M. and headed out to sea. On the way out of Charleston harbor we saw Dutch and Canadian naval vessels. We sailed with reefed main and 150 jib until 4:00 P.M., when we lowered the main because it started to rain hard. Black clouds had been visible all day, and once it started raining, it continued for two hours. We took down the jib at 8:00 P.M. and started the engine. The wind was up to 30 knots right on our stern, and huge following seas came up from astern and tried to turn us broadside. It was a cold, wet, miserable night. As we approached land the seas calmed, and we entered the St. Johns River near Jacksonville at 12.30 P.M. with sun finally shining again. We continued until Mile 765 where we anchored at 5:25 P.M., making 197.61 miles in 35 hours. We left the anchorage at 8:40 A.M. when the fog lifted, arrived at Comanche Cove at 10:35 A.M., and secured a dock in the marina for the winter at St. Augustine.

After cleaning up the boat and visiting Dee and Nardine of Heck Fire we rented a car and drove to Ft. Myers. We spent Christmas at our condo, then Charles and his wife wanted the condo for January and February so we returned to St. Augustine to spend those months on Belo.

We began to consider selling Belo. We had done our cruising thing for several years and Sandy was ready to return to her teaching career in California. We listed Belo with the yacht broker in St. Augustine but didn't even get an offer out of him, then we listed Belo with a broker in Jacksonville but again, no offers. Bill and Clare had listed Fortress Cove with a broker in Ft. Lauderdale and had found a dock nearby where they could live on board pending the sale. After spending March at our condo, we returned to Belo, took her to a dock adjacent to Fortress Cove in Ft. Lauderdale and listed her with a broker there.

On April 8 we departed Comanche Cove, St. Augustine on Belo Horizonte accompanied by Dee and Nardine on Heck Fire and Allen on Leonidas for the trip to Ft. Lauderdale. Dee and

Nardine turned back after a couple of hours but we continued on with Allen, heading directly into the wind under power only until we arrived at a deserted cement plant. We anchored in the channel next to the plant, out of the waterway for the night.

The next morning the weather was miserable, winds twenty knots in the opposite direction we were going, and hard rain. After going through four bridges we decided to turn around and go into Daytona Beach Marina. We tied up to the dock in front of the harbor master's office and went in to ask for a berth. He said he could let us have a berth but asked us to wait until the pouring rain let up a bit. That suited me fine, since I was cold and wet and wanted to get warm and dry. About an hour later the weather improved and I told him about my 6.5 foot draft before he started to lead me to a berth. As it turned out, we were dragging the bottom most of the way, while the harbor master kept telling me to go faster. I told him to look at my wake and when he saw the mud coming up in the water, he stopped urging me to go faster.

We spent the afternoon looking Daytona Beach over. At 7:00 the next morning we departed, seeing beautiful scenery all the way but ran aground three times in the channel. We got off each time without any problem and motor sailed until arrival just two miles south of Cocoa Beach, Florida, at 5:30 P.M. During the day we had made 61.83 miles. The next morning we departed at 6:15 A.M. and with perfect timing, made an 8:15 A.M. bridge opening. We saw more of the beautiful Indian River, from Wabasso to Vero Beach. We arrived at Vero Beach about 4:00 P.M., after going a distance of 58.21 miles, and anchored off the Coast Guard station.

I convinced Allen that we should go outside to the ocean instead of continuing in the waterway. According to the forecast, the wind was coming from the east, but after several hours it veered around to the southeast so we had to use the engine. I noticed right away that the engine was starting to overheat, so I assumed I had to change the water pump impeller. In order to do the job it was necessary to put the boat on a course to sail without the engine. I hoisted the main and headed for the Virgin Islands while I changed the impeller. When Allen saw us change direction, he called us on the radio to ask if we'd changed our minds and were going to the Virgins. Sandy told him that I was changing water pump impellers again and needed to keep the boat under way to maintain some stability. After getting the pump apart I found out that the last time I changed impellers I had left one blade of the impeller in the pipe between the impeller and the tank, blocking the flow of water.

We arrived at Lake Worth Inlet at 5:30 P.M., three hours after Allen, and anchored for the night in a beautiful spot at the head of Lake Worth. It rained all morning, so we didn't get under way until noon. We ran aground immediately in every direction so we had to wait until high tide. Allen's girl friend, Barbara, came over from Ft. Myers with her car so we all drove over to Ft. Lauderdale to visit Bill and Clare.

Upon our return to Lake Worth, we got caught in a rain storm while on the way to our boat in our dinghy. To keep dry we parked under a bridge until the showers abated.

On April 16 we sailed out of Lake Worth at 6:30 A.M. and ran aground immediately but got off quickly and continued on a beam wind all day with beautiful sailing. We arrived at Pier 66 Marina in Ft. Lauderdale at 5:30 P.M. We spent three days there with a yacht broker who thought she had a buyer for our boat but the deal didn't turn out. The next day we moved Belo to a rented dock on Hendrick's Isle alongside where Fortress Cove was waiting to be sold. We returned to our condo in Ft. Myers, but once every month during that summer, we drove to Ft. Lauderdale to spend a night on the boat, visiting with Bill and Clare and checking with the yacht brokers. We were thankful to have Bill and Clare alongside watching Belo.

Finally we gave up on the Ft. Lauderdale yacht brokers and de-cided to sail Belo Horizonte to Ft. Myers because the cost of the dock in Ft. Lauderdale was going up 150% for the winter season. On October 19th at 6:30 A.M., after refueling and having the bot-tom cleaned, we pulled out of the Ft. Lauderdale dock and headed for Miami. We arrived at No Name Harbor near Miami at 1:20 P.M. We went 36.63 miles that day, averaging 6 knots with the 150 jib and main. The next morning we departed at 7:10 A.M. and sailed until 5:35 P.M. with the 150 jib and reefed main averaging 6 knots.

We were anchored off an island in the Florida Keys. About midnight we were awakened by a jolt which woke both of us and we knew we had hit the bottom after an unusually large wave went under us. I let out the anchor chain about 12 to 15 feet. It solved the problem and we were not awakened again. We de-parted at 7:15 A.M. with about 15 knots of east wind which brought us to Boot Key Marina on Marathon Island at 3:35 P.M., a distance of 48.91 miles. We had stopped at Boot Key Marina when we were on our way to the Caribbean with Surrender in 1979.

We spent a day there during which I lost my glasses over the side. After diving for them myself I found Howard Eckles, a ma-rine biologist who had scuba gear and he quickly found the glasses. We had dinner that night at the Castaways. We departed Marathon at 8:28 the next morning and enjoyed the best sailing and fastest run we had ever had on Belo. We were at the entrance of Charlotte Harbor, north of Ft. Myers, at 5:45 A.M., averaging 7 knots for a 147 mile run. Between the entrance to Charlotte Har-bor and Burnt Store Marina we had to stop while I cleared an-other piece of impeller blade from the cooling system. After waiting for high tide to go in we docked at 4:17 P.M. The line han-dlers were two beautiful young ladies with Florida tans and shapely legs, in addition, they knew how to throw a line. It was our first time at Burnt Store Marina, we could only get in between high tide and half tide because of a sand bar at the entrance.

It was October 1985, and because Charles would want to rent our condo during January and February, we decided to live on Belo during the two months they were in our condo. While the boat was at Burnt Store we explored Charlotte Harbor, to our surprise it was a very shallow body of water. We also located the couple who had looked at our boat when it was in Ft. Lauderdale but had bought another boat, a Tartan, docked near us in Burnt Store. The yacht club put on races every weekend and we soon found ourselves crewing on the Tartan, the boat that they had bought instead of ours. After we came in third several times, we lost interest. We took our friends on short trips to the islands around the area but if I wasn't constantly aware of the water depth, I ended up aground.

We drove up to Clearwater, talked to the folks at Ross Marine about selling Belo and they asked us to bring the boat up there so they could show it. They had been dealers for Morgan and knew all about the boat. In the meantime I had talked to a sailmaker in Ft. Myers who told me he could improve Belo's sailing qualities by cutting down the main sail and putting a shelf in it. Although he looked like a farmer, not a sailmaker, I had told him to give it a try. It completely eliminated the weather helm and allowed the boat to sail closer to the wind. With the new main I wasn't sure I wanted to sell. We decided to take the boat up to Clearwater anyway, and give Ross an opportunity to see what they could do.

In June of 1986 Ross got us an offer and after some counter offers we made a deal. The buyer was a captain in the navy, just about ready to retire. He was stationed in Balboa, Panama, and part of the deal was that I had to deliver the boat to Panama within the time allowed by the government for military transferred there, in order to avoid paying duty on it. The buyer paid me the usual boat delivery fees and our cost of transportation back to Florida.

The navy captain who bought our boat called a lot of people in the boat delivery business but, after talking to them, didn't feel confident about trusting them with his investment. The broker suggested he call me, no one knew more about that boat than I, who had sailed it for seven years under every condition.

I looked at a chart and determined that the best route would be through the Bahamas and Crooked Island Passage to the eastern end of Cuba, then to Port Antonio, Jamaica for a short stop before undertaking the last 650 miles to Colon. The alternative would be from Marathon in the Florida Keys along the northeast coast of Cuba through the Old Bahama Channel. The latter route, although shorter, would involve beating about 650 miles against easterly winds and a current setting to the west. There was also the possibility that we might require a friendly port of refuge, not available along the coast of Cuba.

The die was cast, we would sail from Marathon across the Gulf Stream to Bimini, then across the Bahama Bank to Nassau, then depart from the back entrance of Nassau, cross Yellow Bank to the Exuma Chain and into Exuma Sound. This would bring us to the north end of Long Island which we would follow to Crooked Island and Mira Por Vos Passage to the eastern tip of Cuba.

It was almost noon before the rising tide allowed us to get out of the dock behind our condominium and down the channel to the Caloosahatchee River. We reached the Gulf at Ft. Myers Beach and had a nice overnight sail down the west coast of Florida past Naples and Marco Island reaching Marathon in the Florida Keys the next day in the early afternoon. We topped off fuel and water and laid down a course to Bimini that gave us the maximum benefit from the Gulf Stream current, and in the late afternoon, we headed out for Bimini.

Several hours later I went below and turned on the automatic bilge pump. I noted that it shut itself off after only about forty seconds which indicated a normal amount of water in the bilges.

About ten minutes later Sandy went below and found the cabin sole about two inches under water. Our crew, an experienced seaman named Bob Culbertson, manned the hand bilge pump and Sandy turned on the electric bilge pump. There is a saying that the most efficient bilge pump is a scared man bailing with a bucket and that was me.

A few minutes of frantic activity showed we were controlling the rising water so we left the work to the electric bilge pump and tried to determine what had caused the sudden flooding. I tightened up the packing gland on the propeller shaft but observed that the amount of leaking water couldn't possibly have flooded the bilges in such a short time. We turned around and headed for Marathon, running before the wind.

After a night's sleep at anchor in Marathon, at Bob's suggestion, we checked the pipe from the electric bilge pump to the overboard discharge. Where it passed through the engine room the pipe looped up to a high point under the cockpit deck, then went back down to the level of the engine mounts. At the top of the loop we found an adjustable air valve. We decided this was supposed to break the siphon effect when the boat was heeled and the discharge through hull under water. The valve was plugged up with material which had been applied to the engine room bulkhead to deaden the engine noise, so we cleaned out the valve and adjusted the opening to a larger size. When we were out in the deep water again beating towards Bimini, a test proved the problem had been solved. Heeled over with the bilge discharge under water, the siphon effect was eliminated by the air hole in the pipe from the bilge pump to the through hull.

At daylight the next morning we picked up Gun Cay. We proceeded north to Bimini, across the Bahama Bank to North West Channel Light, then on to Nassau where we arrived at about 4:00 A.M. the second morning. At first light we entered the harbor and tied up at the Yacht Haven fuel dock. When the fuel dock opened we topped off fuel and water, took showers and relaxed while we waited for customs and immigration to show up.

Customs approached us in the form of a robust female with high heeled shoes who had some difficulty climbing down to our deck while maintaining her dignity. She handed us forms to fill out, then departed to board other boats. When she returned she complained about the manner in which we had completed the forms, then asked us what time we had entered the port. She informed us that since we arrived at daylight, we had to pay overtime. We politely declined to pay overtime since she had boarded us during office hours. Having failed in that attempt she explained we had to pay her transportation costs to our boat from her home which was a long way off. The transportation charge was $20. Next came immigration who did not live so far away, he only charged us $10. for transportation.

It was almost high tide, so we departed out of the back entrance of the harbor, set a course that would take us around the end of Yellow Bank, then down to Allan's Cay where we had been with several other cruising boats in November of 1980. The iguanas that run down the beach and eat out of your hand were still there. The summer boat population, on the other hand, was about double what it had been in November. Since we intended to sail non-stop from Allan's Cay to Port Antonio, we took advantage of the protected anchorage to get a good night's sleep.

Our Sitex loran gave us good fixes along the way, but as we sailed down Exuma Sound heading for the north end of Long Island, we knew we were approaching the area where loran is no longer an accurate position indicator. However, we secured a good fix at the north end of Long Island and again as we approached Clarence Town at the south end when we changed course for Bird Rock Light on Crooked Island.

At Mira Por Vos pass we had radio contact with a Coast Guard plane and a navy frigate, and saw a Coast Guard cutter. It appeared that the concentration of military power was looking for vessels engaged in narcotics traffic or illegal alien smuggling from Haiti. We didn't know it at the time, but later found out that the new owner of Belo Horizonte, a navy captain, was in charge of fleet activities in the area, and had notified all vessels to report our passage. When the navy frigate called me I identified myself as Belo Horizonte since the boat was still documented in that name, although the name on the stern had been changed to Mufti by the new owner.

We approached the eastern end of Cuba on a hazy morning, with low visibility. My dead reckoning position indicated I should be able to see land but there was nothing visible. An acquaintance of mine, while crewing in the Miami Montego Bay race had been detained in Cuba because his boat had sailed inside the twelve mile limit. I tried loran but got a blinking signal which indicated the position was unreliable. A freighter showed up going north through the haze so I called him on VHF and asked for a position. He replied with a position that indicated I was already inside the twelve mile limit. I thanked him and changed course.

Soon the haze began to clear and the eastern tip of Cuba rose out of the sea on our starboard bow. At first we expected to see a Cuban patrol boat heading towards us, but none appeared. After a while we became braver and approached to within four miles of the coast. We could see no signs of life and no settlements ashore.

Before leaving on the trip, we searched unsuccessfully for a ship chandler or marine supply store that could supply us with a chart of Port Antonio, Jamaica. The day we sailed from Clearwater, the broker who sold our boat gave us the phone number of a place in New Orleans who might have the chart. A phone call proved the broker correct, so we arranged to have the chart sent by Federal Express to our Ft. Myers address. As we approached the island in the middle of the night, although we were no longer receiving good positions by loran, we anticipated no difficulty because the chart showed a 23 mile light at the entrance to Port Antonio.

At daylight we were still looking for the light. We hailed a fishing boat whose skipper told us we had passed the entrance about eight miles back. They only turned the light on when they were expecting a cargo vessel or the occasional cruise ship.

The harbor at Port Antonio is clean, deep and protected from all directions with one commercial dock where bananas are loaded and a berth for cruise ships. There is a yacht club on an island near the entrance and Huntress Marina at the other end of the harbor has complete facilities for cruising boats at reasonable prices.

As we dropped anchor in the clear water of the harbor, after six days and nights of continual sailing, we all had the same idea and were quickly over the side and into the water. While we were still swimming, a dinghy set out from the marina with a message for us. I was instructed to call the American Consulate immediately. I spoke with someone at the consulate who informed me that the new owner of Belo, the navy captain, had reported us overdue and possibly lost because the navy frigate at Mira Por Vos Passage had not yet notified the owner of our arrival in that area. We had slipped through the navy blockade by identifying ourselves as Belo Horizonte instead of Mufti.

Our two-day stay in Port Antonio was very enjoyable. There were boats from all over the world at the marina and the personnel were friendly and accommodating. In the evening we visited some of the older hotels in the hills that had views looking down through tropical vegetation to the water. Our first night there, we spent over an hour on the terrace of such a place, sampling exotic tropical drinks. Afterwards we had a delicious lobster dinner followed by several hours of continuous local entertainment. The total cost for the three of us was $40.00.

As we rounded the eastern end of Jamaica the wind rose steadily, before long it was blowing 32 knots, and it continued for two days. In setting the course for Colon we made ample allowance for the wind and the current set in a westerly direction. On each of the first three days we passed one or two north bound cargo vessels close aboard. We assumed they were from the Panama Canal which indicated our course was taking us towards that destination. On the fourth day our log indicated that we should be making a landfall that day so, since our loran was no longer usable, we took the only sun sight of the trip. The resulting early morning line of position ran almost north and south, we were heading for Colon. A couple of hours later we saw the high land around Portobelo, and early in the afternoon we entered the Colon breakwater.

My first time in Colon was with Sea Rider, then again with Belo Horizonte when I brought her from the Pacific to the Atlantic in 1979, but never before had I received such service as on this arrival. As we entered the harbor area a navy boat came alongside. One of the men onboard said, "Follow me to an anchorage where customs and immigration are waiting for you," and they led the way.

As soon as we got our anchor down they climbed aboard and went through the formalities in about half the usual time. We had hardly got our anchor down when we were told to haul it up and go to the yacht club. As we approached the club, there on the first dock stood the new owner of Belo Horizonte with a smile from ear to ear.

The new owner, Captain Allsopp, a navy captain in charge of one part of the Atlantic Fleet at the time, got preferred service from the local pilots, immigration and customs. He allowed us the afternoon to get rested and cleaned up and was down early the next day for inspection and my dissertation on how to sail Belo and what she liked and didn't like. We showed him where everything was stowed and what he would need for different operations.

Captain Allsopp was going to drive us to Balboa, but he had to find out from intelligence where local riots were being staged and work out a route avoiding those areas. It meant that we had

Richard and Sandra Abbott enter their condo in Ft. Myers,
Florida after delivering Belo Horizonte to her new owner.

to stay overnight. The captain and his wife occupied a beautiful
home at the navy base in Balboa but the local government had
ordered the navy to eliminate the fence around the navy base
and allow natives to wander around within the base, where ever
they wished to go. We were invited to stay at the captain's home
that evening and he and his wife prepared an elegant dinner for
us. After dinner we sat in the shade of the patio and told sea stories until early the next morning.

The three of us flew back to Ft. Myers the next day. It was difficult to adjust to not having a boat, our lives revolved around the

boat for seven years. In 1989 Sandy and I bought a town house on Bay Farm Island, Alameda, California. We have, however, continued to travel.

About five years ago we flew to Tahiti and boarded a ship there named the Aranui. For sixteen days we sailed through the Tuamotus, the Marquesas, and to Raiatea and Bora Bora where we celebrated our marriage 22 tears before. A few years later we flew to the Kingdom of Tonga, chartered a sailboat and spent two weeks sailing through the islands. Australia and New Zealand were next, and then we took a trip on a Norwegian freighter from Bergen, Norway, up the coast of Norway to Murmansk, Russia. Last year we took a river boat on the Danube from Budapest to Bratislava, Vienna, and on to Passau, Germany.

Recently we enjoyed a trip to Turkey, where we spent a few days in Fethiye and took a bus to Finike. There we chartered a 35-foot boat and sailed it along the south coast of Turkey to the city of Marmaris. The coast is lined with ruins left by ancient invaders, with some dating back to before Christ. We especially enjoyed anchoring in the harbor at Ekincik and taking a riverboat from there to the ruins of Kaunos. This ancient city was originally on the coast but is now inland about three miles and can be reached by a riverboat from Ekincik. After Kaunos, we went to Dalyan for lunch and then back to our boat at Ekincik.

Dalyan is a small, charming village where life goes on as it has for a thousand years. To live to be over 100 years is not unusual in this area. I have now reached the age of 83 but I will continue to watch the Beautiful Horizon and travel where its wonders lead me.